CONSCIOUSNESS-RAISING

Third Edition

CONSCIOUSNESS-RAISING

A Primer for Multicultural Counseling

By

WOODROW M. PARKER, PH.D.

and

MARY A. FUKUYAMA, PH.D.

CHARLES C THOMAS • PUBLISHER, LTD.
Springfield • Illinois • U.S.A.

Published and Distributed Throughout the World by

CHARLES C THOMAS • PUBLISHER, LTD.
2600 South First Street
Springfield, Illinois 62704

ISBN 0-398-07679-0 (hard)
ISBN 0-398-07680-4 (paper)

Library of Congress Catalog Card Number: 2006045556

With THOMAS BOOKS *careful attention is given to all details of manufacturing
and design. It is the Publisher's desire to present books that are satisfactory as to their
physical qualities and artistic possibilities and appropriate for their particular use.*
THOMAS BOOKS *will be true to those laws of quality that assure a good name
and good will.*

*Printed in the United States of America
SR-R-3*

Library of Congress Cataloging-in-Publication Data

Consciousness-raising : a primer for multicultural counseling / edited by Woodrow M.
  Parker, Mary A. Fukuyama. -- 3rd ed.
    p. cm.
  Includes bibliographical references and index.
  ISBN 0-398-07679-0 -- ISBN 0-398-07680-4 (pbk.)
    1. Cross-cultural counseling. 2. Minorities--Counseling of. 3. Ethnopsychology. I.
Parker, Woodrow M. II. Fukuyama, Mary A.

BF637.C6P27 2006
158'.3--dc22

                                                                            2006045556

CONTRIBUTORS

Christopher Adams is a doctoral student in the Department of Counseling, School, and Educational Psychology at the State University of New York at Buffalo. He received his master's and specialist's degrees in marriage and family counseling from the University of Florida in 2004. His research interests include family violence, mental health services for rural families, and spiritual issues in counseling and family therapy. He is a student member of the American Counseling Association, the American Association of Marital and Family Therapy, the International Association of Marriage and Family Counselors, and the Association for Spiritual, Ethical, and Religious Values in Counseling.

Mary A. Fukuyama received her Ph.D. from Washington State University and has worked at the University of Florida Counseling Center for the past 23 years as a counseling psychologist, supervisor and trainer. She is a clinical professor and teaches courses on spirituality and multicultural counseling for the Department of Counselor Education and also the Counseling Psychology Program. She co-authored with Todd Sevig, a book titled *Integrating Spirituality into Multicultural Counseling* with Sage Publications. She was recently recognized as a Fellow by Division 17 (Counseling Psychology) of the American Psychological Association. Her practice specialties include working with university students from a developmental perspective, multicultural counseling and training. She is an active member of the University of Florida's Center for Spirituality and Health and her current research interests include a qualitative study on "multicultural expressions" of spirituality. Her leisure interests include birding, kayaking, music, and art.

Marie L. Miville is an Associate Professor of Psychology and Education at Teachers College, Columbia University. Professor Miville also is the Program Coordinator and Director of Training of the Counseling Psychology programs at Teachers College. Professor Miville's research interests include exploring the interrelations of identity variables, such as race and gender. Professor Miville is the author of over 35 journal articles and book chapters dealing with multicultural issues in counseling and psychology, and serves on several editorial boards.

Andres Nazario was born in Cuba and came to the United States as a political exile in the early sixties at the age of 16. For several years he worked in menial jobs until he established his own business. After five years in business he began to attend college and obtained a BA in psychology. He sold his business and went to work in a family therapy program in Miami where he remained until he obtained his Master's in School Psychology and later came to Gainesville where he completed his doctoral degree in Counseling Psychology at the University of Florida. Dr. Nazario has been involved in family therapy education, training and practice for over twenty years. He served on the AAMFT Commission on Marriage and Family Therapy Education for six years. He is on the editorial board of the Journal of Systemic Therapies, and the Journal of Marital and Family Therapy. He is a licensed psychologist and family therapist in private practice in Gainesville at the present time.

Woodrow M. Parker is a Professor Emeritus at the University of Florida, where he served as Professor of Counselor Education for twenty-six years. He now works part time as a mental health counselor for Student Mental Health Services at the University of Florida. Most recently, he co-authored a book with Jennifer Sager titled *Multicultural Responsibility: Awareness to Action in College* with Lahaska Press. His research interests are racial identity, African American males, and guilt and shame in multicultural counseling. He holds the distinguished honor of being a past president of AMCD and the honor of having been the most prolific contributor to the *Journal of Multicultural Counseling and Development* from 1982–1987. He is an active member of the Gainesville Alumni Chapter of Kappa Alpha Psi Fraternity, Inc. and serves as the Faculty Advisor for the Zeta Phi Chapter of Kappa Alpha Psi Fraternity, Inc. at the University of Florida. His hobbies include long distance biking, playing racquetball, and power walking.

Ana Puig is assistant scholar and research director in the Office of Educational Research, College of Education at the University of Florida. She received her doctoral degree in Counselor Education from the University of Florida (UF). She also holds a Spirituality and Health certificate from the Center for Spirituality and Health at UF. She is a licensed mental health counselor in the state of Florida and a National Certified Counselor. Her research interests focus on graduate student training and supervision, spirituality and health issues in counseling and multicultural counseling competencies. She is a member of the American Counseling Association, the Association for Counselor Education and Supervision, the Association for Spiritual, Ethical and Religious Values in Counseling, and the American Educational Research Association, among others.

LeLaina Romero grew up in Queens, New York and Orlando, Florida. She is a doctoral student in Counseling Psychology at Teachers College, Columbia University. As a beginning clinician, she is interested in working in partnership with communities to define their individual and collective needs, particularly through group work. Her research interests include understanding the subjective meaning of social class and the ways in which it intersects with other aspects of identity. Her family in New York includes her partner of four years and their dog and two cats.

FOREWORD

Woodrow "Max" Parker and Mary Fukuyama have always been ahead of their time, and it was about time these two great scholars joined forces on a project. I remember vividly discovering Parker and Fukuyama's work as a masters student in counseling in the late 1980s. I was struggling to understand my life experiences as a son of Latino immigrants who wanted to work as a psychologist. After a failed flirtation with clinical psychology I was drawn to counseling psychology and found the normal developmental perspective of counseling psychology attractive.

However, what really excited me about the field was my multicultural counseling course in which we used the first edition of *Consciousness-Raising*. I found the book thought provoking and invigorating—it was my first introduction to multicultural counseling. What struck me most was Parker's notion that to truly understand a different cultural or ethnic group, one had to give up some privilege and take a subordinate role. Through making action plans I could come to begin to know another group and of course, come to know myself better. The first edition of this book put into words and strategies so many of the things that I wanted to know. Through reading Parker's words I felt that my experiences as one of very few Latinos in higher education were validated.

I also remember being inspired to go to the library to try to learn more about multicultural counseling. I was intrigued to find a journal article on using poetry in multicultural counseling. Fukuyama's willingness to be creative and try other means of expression beyond "how do you feel about that?" was intriguing (and a bit scary). Further exploration indicated that Fukuyama was a prolific writer who was willing to talk about topics (e.g., spirituality and multicultural psychology) that most others were not willing to address.

I became colleagues and friends with Parker and Fukuyama when I joined the staff of the University of Florida Counseling Center in 1997.

It was intimidating at first to meet and work with one's heroes, but both were so personally and professionally generous that they soon brought me into the fold. When I was approached to write the foreword to this book, I was somewhat nervous. The first edition of *Consciousness-Raising* is one of my favorite books (it lies next to my keyboard as I type this), how will it fare in its third edition almost twenty years later?

As I read the text I was struck by the depth in understanding of multicultural counseling, the accessibility of the writing and the veteran decisions (e.g., foregoing the focus on specific groups) of text. The book reads like the best qualities of the authors: intense, accessible, caring, intelligent, and most of all hopeful. For example, the chapter on black males achieves a great deal in both content (the information) and process (a model qualitative exercise that is only possible because of the trust that Parker has earned from participants) yet manages to attend to a critical issue with a measure of hope. I note that another quality of the authors, modesty, is also present in the book. Parker and Fukuyama say little about the significant contributions they made to the development of multicultural counseling–but perhaps that is for others (like me) to say in other venues. Another part I greatly enjoyed was all the questions that begin Chapter 2; I think those questions are an effective way for counselors to begin to understand the complexities inherent in multicultural counseling. Parker and Fukuyama are kind to lead with questions because the reader is immediately put at ease knowing that the questions they have are not unusual or uncommon. This is one of the many ways Parker and Fukuyama use their considerable clinical skills to convey potentially threatening information.

Parker (along with Fukuyama and the other contributors) has accomplished his goal of leaving a better textbook on multicultural counseling than his previous one, and this is no small accomplishment. Regardless of your level of awareness and knowledge of multicultural counseling, this book is ready to guide and challenge you.

Edward A. Delgado-Romero
University of Georgia

PREFACE

The third edition of this book is new and different from previous editions. In the first edition published in 1988, the emphasis was on counseling members of specific ethnic minority groups (African American, Hispanic American, Asian American and Native American) and ways to acquire knowledge about them. In addition, there was a major focus on counselor self-knowledge as a means of improving counselor effectiveness. The belief was that when counselors know themselves, including their weaknesses and learn how to change them, they become more effective in multicultural counseling. The first edition also emphasized a variety of experiential exercises designed to make the participant learner a culturally flexible helper.

The second edition was written ten years later in 1998 with a continuation of focus on the development of *person-as-therapist* and with chapters on counseling members of the four major ethnic minority groups. The former was given the greatest attention since it is more challenging to achieve personal growth than to acquire cultural knowledge about special populations. In addition, counselor self-awareness is one of the foundations of multicultural competency, which is also a focus of this edition.

In the second edition, racial identity development was used as a vehicle to facilitate counselors knowing themselves and their clients. Racial identity models were presented for the four major racial/cultural groups in addition to models on white racial identity. The concept of world view was also introduced as a vehicle of conscious raising for self-understanding and for understanding others. A weakness of this edition was a lack of emphasis on skill-building and on therapeutic and counseling interventions for culturally diverse individuals and groups. In this third edition, culturally relevant skills in multicultural counseling and training will be integrated into the chapters.

In this third edition, the theme of counselor self-awareness and growth is expanded in keeping up with changes in the field. I invited colleague Mary Fukuyama to join in the writing and editing of this book. We have collaborated since the 1980s in designing and teaching a multicultural counseling course and continue to work as colleagues at the University of Florida as practitioners in providing mental health services to college students. Our philosophies on multiculturalism are complementary even though Mary tends to have a more universalistic approach than my cultural specific orientation. This edition emerged through our conversations about what were the most important features for multicultural counseling and training. In addition, this book includes contributions from the intercultural communication field. Throughout this book we emphasize experiential learning and personal consciousness-raising (C-R).

One major change has been to extend the definition of multicultural populations to include sexual minorities (LGBT), individuals with disabilities, and religious diversity. In addition, we see multiculturalism as being inclusive of much more than knowledge of specific populations *per se.* Therefore, rather than include chapters on the four major ethnic groups in this edition, we chose to include one representative chapter (Chapter 7 by Andres Nazario on counseling Latino families) and have included broadly-defined culturally diverse examples throughout. This edition combines practitioner-oriented culture-general guidelines and culture-specific interventions, with new chapter contributions on counseling multiracial persons and introducing spirituality into multicultural counseling.

Didactic questions are raised for stimulation and exploration in the second chapter. Such questions and issues are expected to clear the way for exploration of deeper personal issues later in the training process. In this edition, racial identity is presented through application rather than in isolation. A new chapter on emotional preparation is added to help participants learn to reduce their anxiety about managing emotions from exposure to multicultural training experiences. Specific strategies are presented to help trainees deal with guilt and shame in Chapter 3.

In Chapter 5, I put forth a special effort to discuss the topic of understanding and counseling black males from a more positive perspective. It is my fear that continuous negative dialogue about the plight of black men worsens the condition through reinforcement. In addition, many black men say they are tired of the negativity when there is a brighter side. A special feature of this revised chapter is hearing the voices of black men themselves through a qualitative study.

Please note that whenever case examples are presented, fictitious names are used and details changed to protect confidentiality.

W. M. Parker
March 1, 2006

Author Personal Statements

W.M. Parker. I was born and reared in a small Southern Alabama town in the rural South in the early 1940s where lines between blacks and whites were clearly drawn. I grew up in a predominantly black world until southern schools integrated in 1968. Relations between blacks and whites have mainly influenced my focus on multiculturalism, but I also worked side by side with Mexican and American Indian migrant farm workers in the fields of Alabama. The recognition of other racial/cultural groups has made it possible to expand my definition of cultural diversity to include groups beyond blacks and whites. In keeping with the trends in multicultural counseling and listening to student training needs, I have come to believe that it is essential to include oppressed groups such as those stigmatized by sexual orientation or disability. Any other approach would be exclusionary.

Mary A. Fukuyama. I was born in Denver, Colorado into a racially mixed family a few years after the end of World War II. As a part of the *boomer* generation, I grew up with an acute awareness of differences. However, as a *preachers kid* I was privileged to grow up in a caring community in rural Iowa. My personal journey has taken me to diverse places both literally and spiritually, ranging from world travel to dream work. I am proud to say that I participated in women's consciousness-raising groups as part of the feminist movement in the 1970s. For me, consciousness-raising is an infinite spiral of deepening awareness and connection with self and others. It is for these reasons that I welcomed collaboration with Max Parker on the third edition of *Consciousness Raising: A Primer for Multicultural Counseling.*

ACKNOWLEDGMENTS

This third edition of *Consciousness-Raising: A Primer for Multicultural Counseling* is dedicated to the memory of my Mother, Mrs. Nellie Jane Parker. She passed away on February 7, 2004, after a brief illness. While we miss her physical presence, we are comforted and guided by the legacy of her extraordinary commitment to the well-being of her children, by her unshakable integrity, and by the incredible manner in which she practiced and modeled forgiveness.

Toward the end of my career as a university professor, I wanted to leave a better textbook on multicultural counseling than the one I had written earlier. To strengthen the book, I invited Dr. Mary Fukuyama, a dear friend and a multicultural specialist, to co-author the third edition with me. I am thankful for Mary's impeccable intellect, her unrelenting attention to details, and her calming spirit.

The chapter on understanding and counseling black men could not have been completed without the input of my brother-in-laws and their friends from Huntsville, Alabama and Austin, Texas. In addition, input was also provided by several of my friends who are community leaders from Gainesville, Florida and who are faculty and staff members from the University of Florida. Also, special appreciation is extended to the Diversity Advisors and their students from Santa Fe Community College in Gainesville, Florida. Without the input of these focus groups, the level of consciousness-raising for black men could not have been achieved.

I am also thankful for the moral support and the technical assistance that my daughter, Farha and my wife, Sylvia provided throughout the writing process. Their encouragement and emotional stimulation played a major role in the completion of the work.

W. M. Parker

I want to acknowledge my parents, T. Tom and Betty M. Adkins Fukuyama, whose lives shaped my world view and values. Their inspiration has moved me towards *hope* even in the midst of great difficulties in the world. Much appreciation and thanks goes to my partner, Jackie Davis, for editorial assistance on this project. I also appreciate the many colleagues and trainees that I have known at the University of Florida Counseling Center, which has been my professional home for over 24 years. Additionally, I want to acknowledge all of the many students who have gifted me with their stories about the human struggle to become fully human. Being a therapist and teacher has been a privilege, and I am grateful.

M. A. Fukuyama

CONTENTS

CONSCIOUSNESS-RAISING

Chapter 1

INTRODUCTION: WELCOME TO A CULTURALLY DIVERSE WORLD

Through our scientific and technological genius we have made of this world a neighborhood, and yet we have not had the ethical commitment to make of it a brotherhood. Somehow and in someway we have got to do this. We have to live together as brothers [sic]or we will certainly all perish together as fools.

The Rev. Martin Luther King, Jr.
(cited in Bennett, 1996)

Abstract

In this chapter, we review briefly the historical development of multicultural counseling competencies (MCC), provide an introduction to the basic premises of consciousness-raising and multicultural counseling, and preview the scope of the textbook. We invite personal engagement from you (the reader) in terms of self-reflection and interpersonal involvement in this challenging and rewarding work.

INTRODUCTION

The twenty-first century and *the information age* are noted for telecommunication technologies that have increased contact between nations, cultures, and religious groups (Naisbitt & Aburdene, 1990). Global consciousness is now an everyday experience for many. Concurrently, the changing demographics in the United States reflect significant shifts from a mono-cultural society toward a multicultural vision in which cultural differences are respected and social equities are being forged. All of these social forces have a profound effect on the mental health professions.

Pedersen (1991) called multiculturalism a *fourth force* in psychology following psychoanalytic, behavioral, and humanistic movements, and it has created a significant ripple effect throughout the mental health professions and counseling training. If we visualize this social shift as being like a wave of change, this book is intended to help the reader ride the wave with the skill of a surfer! In order to do so, we will describe both content and process dimensions relevant to the task of developing multicultural counseling competencies (MCC). Our purpose is to simplify complex and multilayered phenomena in order to make the process of becoming a multiculturalist both inviting and accessible.

Over the past three decades, we have taught graduate level multicultural counseling courses, supervised numerous counseling and counseling psychology students, and provided leadership in infusing multiculturalism into agencies and educational systems. Our professional careers span time from the introduction of MCC to the counseling profession to the present day, when MCC guidelines are being developed and adopted by professional associations, such as the American Counseling Association (2005) and the American Psychological Association (2003). This book highlights important theories and structures, which are foundational for MCC, and combines them with exercises and suggestions for implementation. You will find guidance for personal self-reflection, which is an essential component of consciousness-raising (C-R). The purposes of this book are to distill key MCC issues from an increasingly large body of literature, to balance cognitive and affective dimensions of MCC in training and practice, and to provide a down-to-earth approach to learning MCC skills. Our hope is that students and seasoned professionals will be inspired and encouraged by this book to be lifelong learners of MCC.

However, This Is Not a Cookbook!

Beginners in any new venture want to be shown *how*. This desire for guidance is commonly found in any new activity, such as learning to play a musical instrument, studying a second language, or traveling in a new country, but as one learns the basics, it becomes clear that proficiency no longer depends upon directives but is developed through personal practice and integration of knowledge through experiential learning. Similarly, becoming a skilled counselor or psychotherapist requires a combination of book learning, supervised practice, and continuing education and professional development. Thus, we will provide guidance and concrete suggestions to begin the process of mastering MCC. However, the true test of MCC will be realized over the long haul in professional practice. Our hope is to provide guidance that allows for incorporating MCC into one's *whole person* and professional practice, not a cookbook that is prescriptive. Thus, we hope that the reader will acquire a desire to learn more and to stay actively engaged in acquiring MCC. We also hope to stimulate your appetite for culturally diverse experiences to help you see how multicultural work is both personally and professionally enriching and rewarding.

A Brief History of Multicultural Counseling Competencies

There is a popular saying, "To know where you are going, you must know where you have been." Therefore, we will include a brief summary of the history of multicultural counseling and identify some interesting trends.

Most of the original multicultural counseling strategies and techniques focused on meeting the needs of African Americans. Some of the models included the following:

- Preparing Negro students for college, proposed by Clement Vontress (1968).
- A systemic approach for counseling disadvantaged youth, developed by Gunnings and Simpkins (1972).
- Transcendent counseling with blacks, discussed by Harper and Stone (1974).
- Action counseling for working with the oppressed, designed by Tucker (1973).
- A dramaturgical model for counseling minority youth in alternative high schools, created by Smith (1979).

Additional strategies were developed to include more ethnic minority groups. Some of these strategies and their contributors included the following:

- Transcultural counseling: An eclectic approach (McDavis, 1981).
- Counseling Japanese in America: A cross-cultural primer (Henkin, 1985).
- Counseling strategies for dealing with life stress, social support, and mental health issues of ethnic minorities (Smith, 1985).
- Cultural relevant and behavioral counseling for Chicano college students (Ruiz & Casas, 1981).
- Pluralistic therapy for Hispanics (Levine & Ruiz, 1984).
- Counseling Asian Americans (Sue, 1981a).

It is interesting to note that the multicultural counseling movement, from which the above strategies emanated, was inspired by the Civil Rights Movement of the 1950s and 1960s. Essentially, members of oppressed groups recognized that they were not really included in mainstream American life. Certain ethnic minority leaders in counseling, such as John McFadden, Samuel Johnson, Derald Wing Sue, Elsie Smith, Fred Harper, Win Stone, Gloria Smith, and many others, challenged the professional organizations to become more responsive in meeting the counseling and mental health needs of ethnic minority clients. Since the beginning of multicultural counseling in the 1950s and 1960s a great deal of progress was made; still a great deal of work remains to be done.

Much of the social consciousness within the profession was and continues to be influenced by human rights' movements in U.S. society, such as the women's movement, ethnic and racial pride movements, gay rights, disability rights, and so on. For example, "Black is beautiful" was a popular saying in the 1960s. African Americans developed pride in their black racial identity, demonstrated for their civil rights, and demanded equality in their treatment in all aspects of their lives, including their professional engagements. This social movement was reflected in the mental health professions by the formation of The Association for Non-white Concerns (ANWC) in 1972. ANWC was founded as a vehicle for including African Americans in the core structure of the American Personnel and Guidance Association (APGA), now known as the American Counseling Association (McFadden & Lipscomb, 1985).

In 1985, the Association for Non-White Concerns changed its name to the Association for Multicultural Counseling and Development (AMCD) to recognize more ethnic/racial groups beyond blacks and whites. There were many heated debates over the name change. Some felt that AMCD should focus only on African American issues since the organization started from the Civil Rights movement. Others felt that the Association should focus on all groups since the demographics were changing so dramatically. In particular, the growth and visibility of other minority groups such as Hispanic Americans, Asian Americans, and American Indians gave support to the argument that the focus must be multiethnic and not for African Americans alone (Parker & Myers, 1991).

Over the past decade, we have observed many changes in the AMCD Division of ACA. One such change was that the leadership became inclusive of more ethnic groups (Hispanics, Asians, and American Indians). A second change was a focus on integrating multiculturalism into other divisions of ACA. A third trend was to expand the multicultural movement to be inclusive of more groups, such as LGBTs, persons with disabilities, older adults, economic class, and religious minorities (D'Andrea & Daniels, 2005).

A parallel process also evolved in the American Psychological Association. Professional interest groups formed both inside the organization and independently. Within APA, the following divisions expressed interests in multicultural issues: Divisions 9 (Social Issues), 17 (Counseling Psychology), 35 (Psychology of Women), 44 (Lesbian, Gay, and Bisexual Issues), 45 (Ethnic Minority Issues), 51 (Men and Masculinity), and 52 (International Psychology). Independent from APA, the Association for Black Psychologists formed in 1968; the Asian American Psychological Association formed in 1972; and the National Association for Latino Psychologists was founded in 1979. The Society of Indian Psychologists is also accessible through the Internet (see web sites at the end of the chapter).

Over the past 30 years, since multicultural counseling was introduced into the counseling and mental health professions, several approaches were developed and used for preparing counselors to work with culturally diverse clients effectively. Some of the approaches and counseling models are described in the next section.

Models of Multicultural Counseling

The initial emphasis in the field of multicultural counseling focused on minority clients' cultural backgrounds, historical perspectives, and relevant socio-political-economic factors. In this model, which is still used in many settings, ethnic minority groups are observed figuratively through a one-way mirror. The major focus of multicultural counseling originally was on blacks and whites. One piece of evidence of this emphasis was an article titled, *The Black man's burden: The White clinician* (Wesson, 1975), demonstrating a need for white counselors to understand black clients. Other racial/ethnic minority groups were added to the curriculum, including Asian Americans, American Indians, and Hispanic Americans.

A second development in multicultural counseling was a focus on counselor self-awareness. In his article *Counselor: Know Thyself,* Hulnick (1977) suggested that counselors know their hang-ups, blocks, and anything that might get in the way of their being fully functioning individuals. Parker and McDavis (1979) developed an awareness group experience designed to help counselors become aware of their attitudes, stereotypic views, or negative perceptions toward ethnic minorities. Similarly, pioneers of multicultural counseling advocated that counselors who worked with minority clients should be aware of their biases and racist attitudes (Sue, 1981b; 2003).

A third focus in the development of multicultural counseling included the concepts of racial identity and world views, both of which are important avenues for counselor self-understanding and for understanding clients. Helms (1984) defined racial identity as the extent to which people identify with their race. She also defined it as a dynamic force that influences how people feel, think, behave, and make decisions. Embedded in one's racial identity are cultural values and societal messages about how one's group has been treated by society in general. Given this definition, it is understandable why various individuals would respond to counselors and counseling differently. Specifically, clients of color who are socialized to embrace white cultural values will probably feel more comfortable with counselors from the dominant culture. Knowledge of racial identity helps counselors to know themselves and their clientele, promotes awareness of within-group differences, indicates appropriate counseling techniques and strategies, and facilitates counselor/client preferences. Over the past decade, racial identity models representing all racial ethnic groups, including whites, have emerged as one of the most valuable advancements toward the development of multicultural counseling (Carter, 2005).

A fourth area in the development of multicultural counseling over the past 20 years was the development of multicultural counseling competencies (MCC), initiated by Sue et al. (1982) and continued with the leadership of Arredondo et al. (1996) and many others (Constantine & Sue, 2005; Harper & McFadden, 2003; Helms & Cook, 1999; Ivey, D'Andrea, Ivey, & Simek-Morgan, 2001; Pedersen, 1988; Pedersen, Draguns, Lonner, & Trimble, 2002; Roysircar, Sandhu, & Bibbins, 2003). These competencies included three domains, which are the counselor's awareness of self, counselor's knowledge of the client's world view, and the counselor's development of culturally sensitive counseling techniques and strategies. These competencies have served as a model for teaching and training mental health professionals in their preparation for working with culturally diverse clients and will be discussed further in the next section.

Currently, there are discussions in the field about who should be considered a multicultural client. Initially, diverse clients meant black, but this category was expanded to include ethnic groups recognized by the federal government that included Hispanics, African Americans, Asian Americans and American Indians. These major four groups paralleled the federal government's recognition of race categories. Recently, there was an active effort to include other disenfranchised groups, such as women, LGBTs (lesbian, gay, bisexual, transgender), persons with disabilities, the poor, and others. Race/ethnicity is no longer the defining variable for what determines multiculturalism.

Rhoda Olkin (1999), in a keynote address at the National Multicultural Summit, outlined reasons for inclusion of people with disabilities in the multicultural movement. She offered the perspective that socially-based prejudices and barriers oppress people with disabilities, similar to other forms of social oppression like racism or heterosexism. People with disabilities are more often disadvantaged by environmental barriers and access issues than by personal characteristics.

Harriet Johnson (2005) writes eloquently on living with a disability from her personal life experience in her book, *Too Late to Die Young*, see Box 1.1.

Box 1.1

Because the world sets people with conspicuous disabilities apart as different, we become objects of fascination, curiosity, and analysis. We are read as avatars of misfortune and misery, stock figures in melodramas about courage and determination. The world wants our lives to fit into a few rigid narrative templates: how I conquered disability (and others can conquer their Bad Things!), how I adjusted to disability (and a positive attitude can move mountains!), how disability made me wise (you can only marvel and hope it never happens to you!), how disability brought me to Jesus (but redemption is waiting for you if only you pray).

For me, living a real life has meant resisting those formulaic narratives. Instead of letting the world turn me into a disability object, I have insisted on being a subject in the grammatical sense: not the passive "me" who is acted upon but the active "I" who does things. I practice law and politics in Charleston. . . . I travel. I find various odd adventures. I do my bit to help the disability rights movement change the world in fundamental ways. (Johnson, 2005, pp. 2–3)

The complexity of living with a disability and being an immigrant to the United States provides additional challenges. Stone (2005) compiled international perspectives on disability, including narrative chapters on persons immigrating from Jamaica, Haiti, Mexico, Korea, Dominican Republic, and Vietnam. Some authors suggested that the disability service providers may play an important role as "cultural brokers," that is, orienting and educating immigrants about living in U.S. American culture in addition to adjusting to their disability.

The content of MCC is reflective of the political movements of the times, and the emphases within these domains will shift as the social consciousness expands on these issues. Some of these changes are moving at an exponential rate due to rapid developments in technology, radical political restructuring (e.g., the fall of the Soviet Union), and shifting immigration patterns. Recent examples include resettling immigrants from the former Soviet Union and public attention on Arab Americans and Islam due to conflict in the Middle East.

As the twenty-first century begins, attention to globalization and international relations is at an all-time high. We suggest that MCC processes are highly relevant and necessary for conflict resolution and cross-cultural understanding. Although we frame much of MCC in the context of counselor and client relationship, the understandings and insights that come from this work are applicable in many types of inter-group and intercultural relationships.

As a hint of things to come, our experience has shown us that acquiring multicultural awareness, skills, and knowledge encompasses some of the following processes:

• Letting go of the familiar and stepping into the unknown
• Having fun, being creative, and using your curiosity
• Reducing stereotypes and prejudice
• Experiencing difficult feelings, like shame, guilt, or anger
• Eliminating polarized thinking
• Thinking more complexly
• Resisting AND experiencing change and growth
• Discovering passion and compassion

Multicultural counseling educators concluded that "becoming aware of one's world view, increasing contact with members of other racial/ethnic groups, building trust in others, and increasing tolerance for others calls for a substantial amount of personal courage, risk taking, and potential awkwardness or emotional pain . . . developing multicultural competence is an active, awkward, challenging, and growth-inducing process on the part of mental health providers" (Delgado-Romero, Barfield, Fairley, & Martinez, 2005, p. 47).

In sum, the process of acquiring multicultural competencies may feel like learning how to surf, where you likely will experience exhilaration, discouragement and frustrations, and probable falls. However, we encourage you to persevere and you will develop confidence to *hang ten!*

Awareness, Skills, Knowledge (ASK!)

Most mental health professionals agree that there is a need to provide more effective counseling and mental health services for culturally diverse clients. There is general agreement that racially and culturally diverse groups underutilize counseling and mental health services. Not only are counseling services underused by ethnic minority groups, but more than half who initiate counseling do not return to complete the process (Sue, 1981a). Given this discouraging situation, several professional organizations such as the American Psychological Association and the American Counseling Association have developed multicultural counseling competencies in order for counselors to improve their level of functioning with ethnic minority clients (American Psychological Association, 2003; Sue, Arredondo, & McDavis, 1992). Fortunately, competencies have been developed to guide the interpersonal counseling interactions based on culture, ethnicity, and race. Most recently, advanced multicultural competencies have moved from theory to operationalization through direct or specific actions (Arredondo et al. 1996).

The following multicultural competencies outlined by Arredondo et al. (1996) will serve as a general guide for the overall content of this book: The first category of competencies focus on counselors' awareness of their own cultural awareness and biases. It has been our experience that the first domain presents the greatest emotional challenge to counselors and to counselors in training. In this domain, students examine their own biases, explore their true feelings about racial and cultural differences, and reflect on the personal experiences of the full range of oppressed peoples in U.S. society.

The second category of competence is counselor awareness of the client's world view or outlook on life. This competency is addressed in Chapters 5, 7, and 8 addressing culture-specific themes: understanding black males, counseling Latino families, and attending to multiracial persons' concerns. The third category of multicultural competence is culturally appropriate intervention strategies. These strategies are integrated throughout the book and can be found in case example discussions and in the suggested activities at the conclusion of each chapter. We believe that experiential learning is most valuable in learning to relate to cultural differences. It is a developmental process in which awareness of self and others plays a major role.

We have taken the liberty to reorder these three pillars of MCC to read awareness, skills, and knowledge in order to form the acronym *ASK* as a gentle reminder that becoming skilled in multicultural counseling means asking lots of questions!

A list of MCC adapted from the intercultural communication literature is provided in Table 1.1. We remind you to develop good questions (ASK!). As you review this list of competencies, we suggest that you identify areas where you feel confident and areas that require growth and development. In the knowledge area, we suggest you identify culture-specific groups that are appropriate for you to study to enhance your professional skills. Often these specific cultural groups are relevant

Table 1.1. Intercultural Competencies.

A: Awareness and Affective Variables (Attitudes and Motivation)
Motivation
Curiosity
Initiative to explore other cultures
Nonjudgmental interaction posture
Empathy and "transpection" (empathy across cultures)
Open-mindedness
Tolerance for ambiguity
Respect for others' values and beliefs
Flexibility (role and personal)
Inner strength: stability and resourcefulness
Attention to group and interpersonal harmony
Patience

S: Skills Development
Ability to gather appropriate information
Listening skills
Participant observation skills
Social adaptability
Interaction management skills
Relationship building skills
Ability to accurately perceive others
Ask open-ended questions
Anxiety management skills

K: Knowledge Base (Cognitive Variables)
Cultural and positional self-awareness
Knowledge of culture-general frameworks
Knowledge of cultural adaptation process
Knowledge of other cultures
Knowledge of impact of history
Knowledge of impact of power and unearned privilege

Adapted with permission from Martin & Sermol (2005).

to your particular community and geographic region.

Definitions

In this section we will provide definitions of key concepts related to culture, race, ethnicity, racism, and intercultural dynamics in the United States.

Culture. Culture is so pervasive and unconscious that it has been described as being like the water in a fish tank, and the fish doesn't know it's in water until it is pulled out. Culture is a multidimensional concept that may be imagined to be like an invisible web of connections that influence all aspects of human life. We offer three definitions of culture that are comprehensive in nature. Falicov (1988) defined culture as those sets of shared world views and adoptive behaviors derived from simultaneous membership in a variety of contexts, such as ecological setting (e.g., rural, urban, suburban), religious background, nationality and ethnicity, class, gender-related experiences, minority status, occupation, political leanings, migratory patterns, and stage of acculturation or values derived from belonging to the same generation, partaking of a single historical moment, or particular ideologies.

From an intercultural communication perspective, culture was defined by patterns of beliefs, behaviors, and values that are maintained by a group of interacting people (Bennett, 1996). In this definition, the focus was on interactions within visible groups, which determine cultural norms.

Finally, to illustrate the power of culture, consider this definition:

> . . . culture is within the person, develops as a result of accumulated learning from a complexity of sources, depends on interaction with others to define itself, changes to accommodate the experiences in a changing world, provides a basis for predicting future behavior of self and others, and becomes the central control point for any and all decisions. (Pedersen & Ivey, 1993, p. 2)

Intercultural communication authors described culture as being like an iceberg, with only a small portion of it being visible. The tip of the iceberg has been called *objective culture* and consists of institutions and systems like education, government, the law, religion, and artifacts like art, music, foods, customs and holidays. The hidden portion of the iceberg is called *subjective culture* and consists of language (verbal and nonverbal), meaning of time and space, values and morality, definitions of reality and perception, ways of thinking and knowing, myths and legends, death and afterlife, and universal existential human needs (Martin & Sermol, 2005).

Ironically, the greatest forces in daily life in terms of shaping behaviors and interpersonal interactions tend to be unconscious and invisible. However, awareness of these processes is raised through multicultural and intercultural contact, hence our focus on consciousness-raising (C-R) as an essential part of learning multicultural skills.

Race. A construct that was historically established in the nineteenth century to differentiate groups of people based upon real or perceived biological distinctions (such as phenotype, physical characteristics, and genetic differences) but is now recognized as a socially and culturally constructed way to create social divisions to perpetuate status differences wherein one group dominates another. Recent DNA studies through The Human Genome Project have challenged traditional assumptions about race (Marshall, 1998). In actuality, genetically speaking, people of so-called racial groups have more genetic variability within populations than between groups (Spickard, 1992), and physical features are derived from generations of adaptation to geographic regions on the planet, e.g., darker skin that has more melanin is adaptive to hotter, sunnier climates (Tatum, 1999).

Ethnicity. Ethnic identity is tied to group or communal identity based upon birth and family ancestry. It is associated with "conscious and unconscious processes that fulfill a deep psychological need for identity and historical continuity" (McGoldrick, Pearce, & Giordano, 1982, p. 4). As such, ethnicity often (but not necessarily) includes national and geographic origin, religion, and race (phenotype). It is likened to tribal affiliation and is used to create distinctions between *us* and *them*. Positive attitudes about one's ethnicity may contribute toward psychological health, but negative associations or distortions (often caused by the dominant culture) may be related to negative health outcomes.

Racism. Racism consists of systemic and institutionalized practices that advantage select groups of people over others based on race or skin color, constructed upon a hierarchical and competitive model of power and privilege. Currently and historically whites have been advantaged systemically through access to social and economic resources and decision making. Racism is not quite the same as prejudice, which is a preconceived judgment (usually a negative attitude) toward groups of people, often based upon limited information or misinformation. Can blacks be racist? No, not based on this definition, because blacks as a group do not have social power in this country. Can blacks be prejudiced? Yes, just as anyone may have negative attitudes toward others based upon stereotypes (Tatum, 1999).

Assimilation and acculturation. Assimilation and acculturation refer to two distinctive cultural adaptation processes, each with its unique nuance. Assimilation describes social forces to accommodate to a new culture but, in the process, denying or losing one's original culture and language. Acculturation, on the other hand, describes a process of learning second culture skills in order to adapt but not sacrificing ones' original culture. A growing body of ethnic literature (fiction and nonfiction) provides an insider's view of what it is like to struggle with forces of assimilation and acculturation. See Box 1.2 for an example from the writings by Pulitzer prize-winning author Jhumpa Lahiri.

Box 1.2

... When I was growing up in Rhode Island in the 1970s I felt neither Indian nor American. Like many immigrant offspring I felt intense pressure to be two things, loyal to the old world and fluent in the new, approved of on either side of the hyphen. Looking back, I see that this was generally the case. But my perception as a young girl was that I fell short at both ends, shuttling between two dimensions that had nothing to do with one another.

At home I followed the customs of my parents, speaking Bengali and eating rice and dal with my fingers. These ordinary facts seemed part of a secret, utterly alien way of life, and I took pains to hide them from my American friends. . . . I also entered a world my parents had little knowledge or control of: school, books, music, television, things that seeped in and became a fundamental aspect of who I am. . . . And yet there was evidence that I was not entirely American. . . . Many of these friends proudly called themselves Irish American or Italian American. But they were several generations removed from the frequently humiliating process of immigration, so that the ethnic roots they claimed had descended underground whereas mine were still tangled and green. . . . As a child I sought perfection and so denied myself the claim to any identity. As an adult I accept that a bicultural upbringing is a rich, but imperfect thing. (Lahiri, 2006, p. 43)

A summary of additional terms and definitions is provided at the end of the book in Appendix A.

What Is Your Cultural Baggage?

In this section we introduce the concepts of cultural baggage and world views. We offer an introductory awareness exercise on the personal influences that have shaped you into the person who you are. These influences may include but are not limited to family, ethnicity, religion, community, teachers, politics, the media, the physical environment, regional and national identities, and so on. Your *cultural baggage* is the filter through which you see the world and perceive others. The questions in Box 1.3 provide guidance for exploring your ethnicity and roots. In the next section we discuss world view from an anthropological perspective.

Box 1.3

Understanding Your Cultural Baggage

1. Identify your family origins as far back as possible by constructing a family tree or genogram indicating ethnic and national origins.
2. How did your ancestors arrive or where did they originate in this country? Imagine what conditions they experienced. Speculate if you do not know the details of your family history.
3. Your family ethnicity and racial background undoubtedly influenced how they were perceived and treated by others. What advantages might they have experienced related to such factors as religious affiliation, economic resources, language, and political involvements? What advantages or privileges do you have as a result of your family heritage?
4. Were there disadvantages associated with your ethnicity or national origins? Are there any disadvantages that continue to this day for you and your family?
5. Name your ethnic/cultural background and describe one important personal benefit that you enjoy as a consequence of this identity.
6. Are there residual relational issues between your cultural group and other cultural groups? What are they, and how do you personally experience them?

Source: Adapted from James W. Green, Cultural awareness in the human services: A multiethnic approach (3rd Ed). Copyright © 1999. Published by Allyn & Bacon, Boston, MA. Copyright © 1999 by Pearson Education. Reprinted by permission of the publisher.

Understanding World View

One key MCC concept is understanding world view. In this section we discuss a model for world view adapted from anthropology. The Kluckhohn model provides a structure for understanding values and a way to conceptualize cultural world views (Ibrahim, 2003; Kluckhohn & Strodtbeck, 1961). While *all* cultures have *all* of the values suggested by this model, each culture *emphasizes* different dimensions of these values. These values dimensions are not an *either-or* choice; they exist on a continuum. We will provide case examples to illustrate each dimension.

The five values dimensions found in the Kluckhohn model are (1) *human nature* (humans may be good, bad, mixed, and this may or not be changeable—mutable or immutable); (2) *relation of humans to nature* (humans are subjugated by, in harmony with, or have mastery over nature); (3) *activity orientation* (life is oriented around doing, being, or becoming); (4) *time orientation* (the focus is on the past, present, or future); and (5) *relational* (the emphasis is on the individual or group: collateral which means communal, or lineal which implies hierarchy).

The first dimension, *human nature,* is included in many theological belief systems. Traditional Judeo-Christian heritage has emphasized the role of sin, the human tendency to be imperfect or to fall short of moral ideals. On the other hand, the human potential movement (humanistic psychology and positive psychology) emphasized humanity's inherent goodness that becomes obscured due to social conditioning and life's hardships.

Case example: *Patricia was raised in a devoutly Irish Catholic home and had not considered her sexuality until she went away to college. During her freshman year she started to experiment sexually, but felt guilty and thought of herself as a bad person. Her counselor, Gerald was a humanistic counselor and saw her as basically good. However, Patricia had difficulty accepting her counselor's unconditional positive regard; she assumed that he would be judgmental and expected that he would guide her back on the right track.*

The second dimension, *relation of humans to nature,* provides a framework for conceptualizing beliefs in relation to both the natural and supernatural worlds. It can also be used to describe a dimension of locus of control, or empowerment. Some cultures are described as *stairstep* cultures in contrast with *roller-coaster* cultures (Martin & Sermol, 2005). The former implies that life is orderly, predictable, and under control. The latter suggests that life is out of control (subjugated to nature) with intense ups and downs.

Case example: *Juan was the oldest of five siblings in a migrant worker family from Mexico. He was sent to the counselor's office for tardiness and a "bad attitude." Juan presented with a fatalistic attitude and said that he was tired most of the time due to work demands. He complained that every time he starts to make friends, his family moves. He claimed that there was nothing he could do to improve his situation; it's out of his hands.*

The third dimension, *activity orientation,* reflects both cultural and religious values and beliefs. Calvinism (early Protestant Christian) emphasized *good works* or *doing* as an avenue to God. Americans in the U.S. seem to define themselves by what they do, and American mainstream society seems focused on keeping busy and being productive. In contrast, Mexican lifestyle focuses more on the present moment. A phrase, *sobremesa* ("over the table"), suggests that conversations after a meal may take priority over other activities. In some American Indian cultures, the process of *becoming* by walking the path of the medicine wheel emphasizes a circular and holistic paradigm of life purpose.

Case example: *Donny explained that it is a native practice to observe nature carefully and to communicate with the spirit world through noticing things like the wind and plants. He complained that the principal of the school called him lazy when all he was doing was sitting and observing nature. He felt unsafe to explain his spiritual beliefs.*

The fourth dimension, *time orientation,* reflects the potential to focus on the past, present, or future. Some cultures focus on ancestor worship and others on the present moment. U.S. Americans tend to focus on the future through such priorities as retirement savings accounts and goal-oriented five-year plans, for example. Travel in other cultures is an excellent way to learn about these cultural dimensions, see the narrative in Box 1.4.

Box 1.4

One of the authors confronted differences in time while volunteering on a humanitarian project in the Rio Dulce area of Guatemala. Here is a quote from her journal.

I am learning how to be more in the moment. Planning is not a big thing here. The usual speed is more gradual. It's like "people may get things done but we don't know when exactly. But things do happen; just don't get in a hurry over it." I'm not trying to be sarcastic, but the life here is much more circular (or organic) than linear (and direct). For example, getting people on the boat to leave for anywhere looks like this: What time does the boat leave? Oh, around 1 PM. So at 1 PM the *gringa* (that's me) shows up but no one else does. Gradually, people who are going on the trip arrive and leave and arrive again. Finally, the boat driver gets in the boat and whistles or otherwise announces that he is ready to leave (based upon the collective mass of people waiting). There are always a few stragglers who have to hurry to jump on. The bigger the group, the more elongated the process. Things here definitely do not work on clock time (except that the express buses between cities run on clock time). (Fukuyama, 2004, pp. 21–22)

The fifth dimension, which focuses on interpersonal *relationships,* may emphasize the individual over the group or may emphasize the importance of community and collective identity first. The group identity may be hierarchical (with respect to ancestry and authority) or collateral, as in communal affiliations.

Case example: *In the United States, people frequently operate on a first-name basis (individualism). In China, people introduce themselves by their family name first, which is more important to identity.*

The Kluckhohn model was developed originally by studying Anglos, Native Americans, and Hispanics in the United States' Southwest. One needs to exercise caution in generalizing these values orientations to specific cultural groups, for example, white Americans encompass much *within-group* diversity. Extrapolating white values to all Americans is an additional big leap. Nevertheless, dominant culture and subordinate cultures comprise the fabric of U.S. American culture, and this paradigm is useful in discerning individual and family values' orientations within culture as well as in the international arena.

Traditionally, counseling and psychotherapy training was developed for a predominantly white, European American, middle-class clientele, based upon Eurocentric values and psychological theories (Katz, 1985). Thus, the Western-trained counselor is likely to hold a world view that emphasizes mastery, doing, future time orientation, and individualism. It is important for the multicultural counselor to be able to understand diverse client world views.

How Is This Book Different from Other MCC Texts?

Consciousness-raising was a term used during the feminist movement of the 1970s and involved creating social change through awakening personal awareness about gender roles and inequities. Personal awareness was essential to create social change. The *personal is political* was a familiar slogan that supported individual work in the context of making systemic changes. Similarly, we address this process of social change by focusing on cultivating personal awareness related to multicultural issues. This emphasis on the *person-as-therapist* is an essential cornerstone to the development of MCC.

Social change is also reflected in cultural arts, music, and other creative expressions. We believe poetry to be one way of expressing the heart of MCC (Fukuyama & Reid, 1996), and poetry and literature will be included throughout as well. For example, early twentieth century Chinese immigrants' experiences were captured through poems scribbled on the walls of their detainment cells on Angel Island in San Francisco Bay, illustrated in Box 1.5.

Box 1.5

Immigration Blues, from Songs of Gold Mountain

The moment I hear
  we've entered the port,
I am all ready:
  My belongings wrapped in a bundle.
Who could have expected joy to become sorrow:
Detained in a dark, crude, filthy room?
What can I do?
Cruel treatment, not one restful breath of air.
Scarcity of food, severe restrictions—all
  unbearable.
Here even a proud man bows his head low. (Hom, 1991, p. 143)

Source: Copyright © 1987 by The Regents of the University of California. Poem reprinted by permission of The University of California Press.

Overview of Book Chapters

The first part of the book explores general themes found in the MCC literature in this chapter and in Chapters 2, 3, and 4: beginning with questions, preparing emotionally for C-R, and understanding racial identity development.

The very nature of multiculturalism is based in questions. Elie Weisel (1974), a Nobel Peace Prize winner, once said, "There are no answers to true questions. There are only good questions, painful sometimes, exuberant at others. Whatever I have learned in my life is questions, and whatever I have tried to share with friends is questions" (p. 276). We invite readers to explore 12 questions in Chapter 2 and dialogue on issues that contain differing and sometimes opposing perspectives.

In Chapter 3 we focus on preparing for affective/emotional experiences that typically arise while engaging in multicultural training. Our experience has shown that preparation will facilitate dealing with difficult emotions that normally occur when encountering the *-isms*, that is, various forms of social oppression. We address dealing with shame and guilt, particularly as related to racism, and conclude this chapter with a discussion of how to become an ally.

Chapter 4 provides an overview of racial identity development and implications for counseling are discussed. This discussion prepares the reader for exploring in depth the experiences of black males, as described through a focus group study in Chapter 5.

In Chapter 6, we discuss important factors to consider in the first hour of counseling in terms of developing a working alliance and applying fundamentals of intercultural communication skills in counseling.

Andres Nazario presents a comprehensive view of counseling Latina(o) families in Chapter 7 and has introduced an oppression-sensitive family therapy model that incorporates consciousness-raising in the therapy room. Latinos represent one of the fastest growing ethnic groups in the United States today, with projections that they will comprise 25 percent of the U.S. population by the year 2050. Nazario's chapter is a model for studying culture specific groups.

In Chapter 8, Marie Miville and LeLaina Romero address counseling multiracial persons by challenging myths and discussing race as a social construction influenced by social contexts. They recommend strategies for a holistic approach to multiracial identity development. In Chapter 9, Ana Puig and Chris Adams provide reflections on the relevance of spirituality to multicultural work and explore further the dimensions of cultural diversity found in expressions of religion. Learning how to navigate culturally diverse expressions of spirituality and religion is important to becoming skilled in MCC. Finally, in Chapter 10 we conclude the book with a synthesis approach to cultural complexity and provide inspiration for the reader to create his/her own multicultural legacy.

We conclude this chapter with guidelines for facilitating multicultural discussions in Box 1.6, followed by suggested activities for experiential learning.

Box 1.6

Multicultural Discussion Guidelines

1. All cultures have good points and bad points; no one culture is inherently better than another.
2. The main goal in multicultural discussions is to learn from one other, recognizing that there are both similarities and differences in life experiences related to cultural diversity and oppression.
3. Social oppressions affect everyone but in differential ways. Social oppressions include racism, anti-Semitism, sexism, ageism, heterosexism, ableism, classism, and other forms of prejudice and discrimination.
4. Individuals may experience different levels of privilege and oppression based upon gender, race, ethnicity, sexual orientation, religious affiliation, and so on, depending upon social context.
5. Misinformation and ignorance are at the root of prejudice. One of the underlying meanings of racism, for example, is that people are systematically taught misinformation about Persons of Color and Whites, such that one group is devalued and another elevated to dominant status. This dynamic is similar for the other *-isms*.
6. People cannot be blamed for the misinformation but can be held responsible for repeating misinformation or perpetuating stereotypes after learning otherwise.
7. Victims are not to be blamed for their oppression.
8. Everyone shares in the responsibility for breaking down myths and stereotypes about one's own group and other groups in order to promote communication and understanding.
9. Sharing needs to occur in an atmosphere of respect and nonjudgment; practice deep listening.
10. If you experience hurt or offense during a discussion, please let others know that you are dealing with some reactions. A simple way to do this is to say "ouch!" This gives the group a chance to process reactions that otherwise might be hidden.

Note: Adapted from *Intergroup Dialogues and Multicultural Groups Handbook,* University of Michigan, based on original work by Lynn Webber Cannon, Department of Sociology, Memphis University.

Suggested Activities

1. Journal writing: What are some of your impressions of cultural diversity and the meaning of multiculturalism based upon your experiences to date? Any preconceived notions?
2. Write your family's cultural (ethnic) autobiography (review notes from Box 1.3).
3. Scan the news media for articles with cultural diversity themes (racism, discrimination, treatment of minorities, legislation, intercultural issues, and educational programs), record your impressions, and share your observations.
4. Construct a geographic community map and identify your comfort zones (see Goldstein, 1996). Share in class and discuss implications. How can you be guides for each other in terms of creating opportunities for cross-cultural contact?

Web Sites of Interest

Association of Multicultural Counseling and Development (AMCD)
American Psychological Association (APA)
http://www.apa.org/pi/multiculturalguidelines/references.html
Asian American Psychological Association (AAPA)
http://www.aapaonline.org/
Association of Black Psychologists (ABPsi)
http://www.abpsi.org/studentcircle.htm
National Latina/o Psychological Association
http://www.nlpa.ws/
Society of Indian Psychologists
http://www.geocities.com/indianpsych/aboutsip.html

REFERENCES

American Counseling Association (2005). Available online at http://www.counseling.org/Content/NavigationMenu/RESOURCES/MULTICULTURALANDDIVERSITY ISSUES/ Competencies/Competencies.htm

American Psychological Association (2003). Guidelines on multicultural education, training, research, practice, and organizational change for psychologists. *American Psychologist, 58,* 377–402.

Arredondo, P., Toporek, R., Brown, S. P., Jones, J., Locke, D. C., Sanchez, J., et al. (1996). Operationalization of the multicultural counseling competencies. *Journal of Multicultural Counseling and Development, 24,* 42–78.

Bennett, M. (1996). *Better together than apart.* Lecture presented to the Intercultural Communication Summer Institute. [Videotape available from Intercultural Resource Corporation 78 Greylock Rd, Newtonville, MA 02160, http://www.irc-international.com or see http://www.intercultural.org/]

Carter, R. T. (2005). *Handbook of racial-cultural psychology and counseling,* Vol's. 1–2. New York: John Wiley & Sons.

Constantine, M. G., & Sue, D. W. (2005). *Strategies for building multicultural competence in mental health and educational settings.* New York: John Wiley & Sons.

D'Andrea, M., & Daniels, J. (2005, July). A socially responsible approach to counseling, mental health care. *Counseling Today, 48* (1), 36–38.

Delgado-Romero, E. A., Barfield, J., Fairley, B., & Martínez, R. S. (2005). Using the multicultural guidelines in individual and group counseling situations. In M. Constantine & D. W. Sue (Eds.), *Strategies for building multicultural competence in mental health and educational settings* (pp. 39–55.). Hoboken, NJ: John Wiley & Sons.

Falicov, C. J. (1988). Learning to think culturally. In H.A. Liddle, D. C. Breunlin, & R. C. Schwartz (Eds.), *Handbook of family therapy training and supervision* (pp. 335–357). New York: Guilford Press.

Fukuyama, M. A. (2004). El Otro Lado. In G. S. Howard & E. A. Delgado-Romero (Eds.), *When things begin to go bad: Narrative explorations of difficult issues* (pp. 19–32). Lanham, MD: Hamilton Books.

Fukuyama, M. A. & Reid, A. D. (1996). The politics and poetry of multiculturalism. *Journal of Multicultural Counseling and Development, (24),* 82–88.

Goldstein, D. L. (1996). The cooperative map exercise. In H. N. Seelye (Ed.), *Experiential activities for intercultural learning* (pp. 133–137). Yarmouth, ME: Intercultural Press, Inc.

Green, J. W. (1999). *Cultural awareness in the human services: A multiethnic approach* (3rd Ed). Upper Saddle River, NJ: Allyn & Bacon.

Gunnings, T., & Simpkins, G. (1972). A systemic approach to counseling disadvantaged youth. *Journal of Non-white Concerns in Personnel and Guidance, 1,* 4–8.

Harper, F. D., & McFadden, J. (2003). *Culture and counseling: New approaches.* Boston: Allyn & Bacon.

Harper, F., & Stone, W. (1974). Toward a theory of transcendent counseling with blacks. *Journal of Non-white Concerns in Personnel and Guidance, 2* (1), 191–196.

Helms, J. E. (1984). Toward a theoretical explanation of the effects of race on counseling: A Black and White model. *Counseling Psychologist, 12,* 153-165.

Helms, J. E., & Cook, D. A. (1999). *Using race and culture in counseling and psychotherapy: Theory and process.* Boston: Allyn & Bacon.

Henkin, W. A. (1985). Counseling the Japanese in America: A cross-cultural primer. *Journal of Counseling and Development, 63,* 500–503.

Hom, M. K. (1991). Songs of Gold Mountain. In J. P. Chan, F. Chin, L.F. Inada, & S. Wong (Eds.), *The Big Aiieeee! An anthology of Chinese American and Japanese American literature* (pp. 139–177). New York: Penguin Books.

Hulnick, R. (1977). Counselor: Know thyself. *Counselor Education and Supervision, 17,* 69–72.

Ibrahim, F. A. (2003). Existential world view counseling theory: Inception to applications. In F. D. Harper & J. McFadden (Eds.), *Culture and counseling: New approaches* (pp. 196–208). Boston: Allyn and Bacon.

Ivey, A. E., D'Andrea, M., Ivey, M. B., & Simek-Morgan, L. (2001). *Theories of counseling and psy-chotherapy: A multicultural perspective* (5th Ed). Boston: Allyn & Bacon.

Johnson, H. M. (2005). *Too late to die young: Nearly true tales from a life.* New York: Henry Holt & Company.

Katz, J. H. (1985). The sociopolitical nature of counseling. *The Counseling Psychologist, 13* (4), 615–624.

Kluckhohn, F. R., & Strodtbeck, F. L. (1961). *Variations in value orientations.* Evanston, IL: Row, Peterson & Co.

Levine, E. S., & Ruiz, R. A. (1984). Redefining the goals of pluralistic therapy from the Hispan-ic-Anglo experience. *Chicano psychology.* San Diego, CA: Academic Press.

Lahiri, J. (2006, March 6). My two lives. *Newsweek, CXLVII* (10), 43.

Marshall, E. (1998). DNA studies challenge the meaning of race. *Science, 282* (5389), pp. 654–655. (Available online at http://www.sciencemag.org/cgi/content/full/282/5389/654)

Martin, J., & Sermol, D. (2005, July 25–29). *Best practices of intercultural communication training workshop.* The Summer Institute for Intercultural Communication (SIIC), Forest Grove, OR.

McDavis, R. J. (1981). *Transcultural counseling: An eclectic approach.* A paper presented at the Sym-posium on Transcultural Psychiatry, Macau.

McFadden, J., & Lipscomb, W. D. (1985). History of Association for Non-White Concerns in Personnel and Guidance. *Journal of Counseling and Development, 63,* 444–447.

McGoldrick, M., Pearce, J. K., & Giordano, J. (1982). *Ethnicity & family therapy.* New York: The Guilford Press.

Naisbitt, J., & Aburdene, P. (1990). *Megatrends 2000.* New York: Avon Books.

Olkin, R. (1999). *What psychotherapists should know about disability.* New York: The Guilford Press.

Parker, W. M., & McDavis, R. (1979). An awareness group experience toward counseling minorities. *Counselor Education and Supervision, 18,* 312–317.

Parker, W. M., & Myers, J. E. (1991). From ANWC to AMCD: Goals, services, and impact. *Jour-nal of Multicultural Counseling and Development, 19* (2), 52–64.

Pedersen, P. (1988). *A handbook for developing multicultural awareness.* Alexandria, VA: American Association for Counseling and Development.

Pedersen, P. (1991). Multiculturalism as a fourth force in counseling [Special issue]. *Journal of Counseling and Development, 70,* 6–12.

Pedersen, P. B., Draguns, J. G., Lonner, W. J.,& Trimble, J. E. (Eds) (2002). *Counseling across cul-tures* (5th Ed). Thousand Oaks, CA: Sage.

Pedersen, P. B., & Ivey, A. (1993). *Culture-centered counseling and interviewing skills: A practical guide.* Westport, CT: Praeger.

Roysircar, G., Sandhu, D. S., & Bibbins, V. E. (2003). *Multicultural competencies: A guidebook of practices.* Alexandria, VA: Association for Multicultural Counseling and Development.

Ruiz, R. A., & Casas, J. M. (1981). Culturally relevant and behavioristic counseling for Chicano college students. In P. B. Pedersen, J. G. Draguns, W. L. Lanner, & J. E. Trimble (Eds.), *Counseling across cultures* (pp. 181–202). Honolulu: University of Hawaii Press.

Smith, E. J. (1979). Counseling minority youth in alternative high schools: The dramaturgical model. In W. M. Parker, P. G. Schauble, & 1. I. Morgan (Eds.), *Counseling blacks: Issues and strategies* (Monograph, Vol. III). Gainesville, FL: Psychological & Vocational Counseling Center.

Smith, E. J. (1985). Ethnic minorities: Life stress, social support, and mental health issues. *The Counseling Psychologist, 13* (4), 537–579.

Spickard, P. R. (1992). The illogic of American racial categories. In M. P. P. Root (Ed.), *Racial-ly mixed people in America* (pp. 12–23). Thousand Oaks, CA: Sage.

Stone, J. H. (Ed.). (2005). *Culture and disability: Providing culturally competent services.* Thousand Oaks, CA: Sage.

Sue, D. W. (1981a). Cultural and historical perspectives in counseling Asian Americans. In D. W. Sue (Ed.), *Counseling the culturally different* (pp. 113–140). New York: John Wiley & Sons.

Sue, D. W. (1981b). *Counseling the culturally different.* New York: John Wiley & Sons.

Sue, D. W. (2003). *Overcoming our racism: The journey to liberation.* New York: John Wiley & Sons.

Sue, D. W., Arredondo, P., & McDavis, R.J. (1992). Multicultural counseling competencies: A call to the profession. *Journal of Counseling and Development, 70,* 477–486.

Sue, D. W., Bernier, J. B., Durran, M., Feinberg, L., Pedersen, P., Smith, E., et al. (1982). Position paper: Cross-cultural counseling competencies. *Counseling Psychologist, 10,* 45–52.

Sue, D. W., Carter, R. T., Casas, J. M., Fouad, N. A., Ivey, A.E., Jensen, M., et al. (1998). *Multicultural counseling competencies: Individual and organizational development.* Thousand Oaks, CA: Sage.

Tatum, B. D. (1999). *Why are all the Black kids sitting together in the cafeteria? And other conversations about race.* New York: Basic Books.

Tucker, S. J. (1973). Action counseling: An accountability model for counseling the oppressed. *Journal of Non-white Concerns in Personnel and Guidance, 2* (1), 35–41.

Vontress, C. E. (1968). Counseling Negro students for college. *Journal of Negro Education, 37,* 37–44.

Wiesel, E. (1974). Whatever I have learned in my life is questions. In A. Chapman (Ed.), *Jewish-American Literature: An anthology* (pp. 276–278). New York: Mentor New American Library

Wesson, K. A. (1975). The Black Man's Burden: The White Clinician. *The Black Scholar, 6* (10), 13–18.

Chapter 2

WE BEGIN WITH QUESTIONS

"Not everything that is faced can be changed. But nothing can be changed until it is faced."
—James Baldwin (cited in Tatum, 1997, p. xix)

Abstract

This chapter is intended to encourage discussion on contemporary issues in multicultural counseling training. Due to rapid social change, multiculturalism continues to be redefined, from generation to generation. You are invited to discuss these twelve questions and to formulate some of your own answers. Throughout this chapter, we have included culture-specific case examples to illustrate particular points to provide a flavor of the cultural diversity in the United States.

INTRODUCTION

Historically speaking, questions were debated and discussed in the multicultural counseling literature, courses, and convention programs in the 1970s and 1980s. Interestingly, although many of these questions have been reframed or worded differently, they continue to be controversial in the field of multicultural counseling today. Some of the questions were:

Can white counselors effectively work with black clients? In turn, can black counselors effectively counsel white clients? Are the counseling needs of ethnic minority clients different from the needs of white clients? Should counselors be "colorblind," or should they pay attention to race/ethnicity? What knowledge about ethnic minorities is essential for counselor effectiveness? (Parker, 1998)

In this chapter, we begin with questions for several reasons. First, a discussion of sensitive topics enables effective multicultural communication. An open and honest discussion of issues will clear the way for deeper exploration later in the learning process. In particular, we want to establish norms of interpersonal respect where different opinions are expressed. Second, we hope that a discussion of these issues and questions will prompt you to examine your beliefs, thoughts and assumptions about multiculturalism. Third, we want to promote a "dialectical approach" to multicultural issues. What do we mean by dialectics? We begin with some basic assumptions about the nature of culture and intercultural communication.

Borrowing from intercultural communication experts (Martin, Nakayama, & Flores, 1997), intercultural dialectics include understanding culture as being *ever-changing* and *dynamic, relational,* and *paradoxical,* that is, holding two contradictory ideas simultaneously. As such, a *dialectical approach* requires that you transcend dichotomies and think more complexly. By doing so, we intend to move from *either/or* dualistic thinking to *both/and* inclusive thinking. Examples of intercultural dialectics include exploring concepts such as "similarities and differences, advantages and disadvantages, and the individual and group." As you explore some of the following questions, practice thinking *outside of the box* and elaborate your answers to form multiple points of view.

We have identified twelve questions for discussion, listed in Box 2.1.

Box 2.1

1. Is multicultural counseling a theory?
2. How does cultural diversity include white people?
3. Should multicultural training have a specific focus on racism and visible ethnic minority groups, or a broader focus, including marginalized groups, such as lesbian, gay, bisexual and transgender persons (LGBTs) and disabled persons?
4. What knowledge is essential for multicultural counseling?
5. Are there skills, techniques and strategies for counseling culture-specific clients?
6. What is the difference between making cultural generalizations and stereotyping?

7. Since it is believed that people are more alike than different, why focus on differences?
8. What are effective counselor and client matches considering factors such as racial identity and world view? What are noneffective combinations?
9. Why do many white people deny that racism exists while many Black people hesitate to admit that progress has been made in race relations in the United States?
10. What is the future of multicultural counseling? Will it become obsolete? Will it be fully integrated into counseling practices?
11. What are good sources of knowledge for informing the *best practices* of MCC?
12. What can you expect during this course of study in terms of developing MCC skills?

The purpose of introducing these topics is to stimulate your interest to want to learn more. Therefore, our discussion of each question will not be exhaustive. We urge you to seek information that will support a *point/counterpoint* dialogue about each question.

1. Is multicultural counseling a theory?

Multicultural counseling is counseling or therapy that is done in a multicultural context. Some counseling professionals argue that *all* of counseling is multicultural in that there are invariably differences between counselors and their clients. They believe that counseling itself should be "culture-centered" (Pedersen, 2002). We see multicultural counseling as counseling and psychotherapy which attends to cultural variables that are salient to clients' presenting concerns and includes consideration of social oppression.

Some researchers argue that MCC is not a theory *per se*. Stanley Sue (2003), a clinical psychologist and researcher on Asian American mental health issues, discussed one of the challenges in defining multicultural counseling. He described it as a "process, orientation, or approach" more than a technique. Sue (2003) states, "Cultural competency involves the client, therapist, and context, as well as the therapeutic technique, because context and culture are so important" (p. 968). In other words, multicultural counseling is more a "way of being" that encompasses pluralistic (inclusive) values.

Derald Wing Sue and colleagues (1998) elaborated further and suggested that "multiculturalism embodies social constructionism, meaning that people construct their worlds through social processes (historical, cultural, and social experiences) that contain cultural symbols and metaphors. Cultural relativism . . . implies that each culture is unique and must be understood in itself and not by reference to any other culture" (p. 4). From this perspective, counseling theories need to be adapted to clients' cultural world views. In contrast, restricting one's beliefs may prevent a counselor from being able to understand a differing perspective or client world view. In this way, the counselor is asked to move beyond an ethnocentric and/or egocentric world view and take into account multiple world views.

Fuertes & Gretchen (2001) summarized and critiqued several theories of multicultural counseling that have emerged in the past decade or so. Themes and models which were presented included utilizing a social constructivist approach (Gonzalez, Biever, & Gardner, 1994), exploring internalized culture (Ho, 1995), coping with diversity (Coleman, 1995), and developing counselor wisdom (Hanna, Bemak, & Chung, 1999) as examples. They suggested that much of this work can "supplement, rather than supplant, other counselor techniques and skills" (Fuertes & Gretchen, 2001, p. 532). On the other hand, some researchers have criticized the MCC field for lack of empirical studies that support the validity of MCC theories and models (see Sue et al., 1998, for discussion of professional resistances to MCC).

In the United States individualism is valued, and at the same time, family and group membership may be equally if not more important. Sometimes South Asian clients come to counseling seeking career guidance and present with a conflict between personal desires and meeting family expectations. In such instances, the counselor may need to engage in problem-solving strategies that honor both individual and collectivistic needs. As a clinical case example, the counselor might observe in an initial assessment that a client is a first generation female college student who presents with depression. Her parents immigrated from India, and as the first-born daughter, she feels pressure to become a medical doctor. Issues of racial/ethnic identity, career development, family relationships, and racism /sexism are potential avenues for exploration.

Reflection suggestions: *Examine the counseling literature for critiques of multicultural counseling from various theoretical perspectives; find support for multiple points of view. Alternately, review traditional counseling theories and* *trace the cultural contexts in which they were developed. What are the cultural biases of traditional counseling theories?*

2. How does cultural diversity include white people?

All too often cultural diversity is a code word referring to issues of inequity on behalf of marginalized groups. Are white people included in the multicultural mix? Do Whites have culture? Of course! Much has been written about white racial identity development (Helms, 1984; 1990; 1992) and the importance of whites becoming aware of their cultural and ethnic identities. Because we live in a white dominant culture, it is more difficult for whites to be aware of their racial identity (McIntosh, 2001; Sue, 2003). Remember the fish in the water does not see the water. Whites, because they represent the dominant culture, do not typically think of themselves in racial terms.

Sometimes it is difficult to remember ancestry and ethnic stories when families have lived in the United States for generations, yet ethnicity is a strong influence on family dynamics (McGoldrick, Giordano & Pearce, 1996). As an example, a counseling graduate white student who grew up in the south initially felt uncomfortable examining her "white" identity because of its association with white racism. After learning more about white racial identity, she was able to claim her Scotch-Irish heritage in conjunction with understanding white privilege. These issues will be explored further in Chapters 3 and 4.

In addition, what assumptions do you make in response to the question, "who is an American?" For example, Chinese Americans who have lived in this country for over five generations are still asked "where are you from?"

Reflection suggestions: Interview a family elder to learn more about your family history. Note intergenerational differences in the family lineage on issues of identity and adaptation to U.S. society. Alternately, interview a white person about what it is like being white.

3. Should MCC training have a specific focus on racism and visible ethnic minority groups, or a broader focus, including marginalized groups, such as lesbian, gay, bisexual, and transgender persons (LGBTs) and disabled persons?

We would like to think that there is a *both/and* response to this question. Issues related to culture specific groups and racism are essential, and the human rights movements that have developed subsequently to African American civil rights are also important (e.g., LGBT and disability rights). But what are the priorities for MCC counseling and training?

Some advocates for anti-racism work have expressed a concern that broadening the MCC umbrella will only dilute the effects of working on racism. On the other hand, LGBT and disability rights advocates have criticized the MCC movement for not including them. Such criticisms have been openly addressed through such forums as the National Multicultural Summit Conference sponsored by the American Psychological Association, which has broadened its programming to be more inclusive (see Heppner, 2005).

It seems that there is truth in all of these points of view. Racism as an oppression is frequently side-stepped when other "-isms" are presented. Even to this extent, the focus now on globalization and international relations may eclipse domestic conflicts.

What about persons who have multiple social identities, who are affected by several oppressions? Compartmentalizing and setting up competitions *(who is more oppressed?)* does not serve the larger purpose of making society more equitable for all. For example, black gay men and lesbians may face ostracism from conservative black churches; yet splitting an already oppressed group on these issues further victimizes its members (Monroe, 2005). Alternative perspectives on this issue will be discussed in Chapter 10.

If we broaden the definition of MCC, what groups should be included? For instance, recently economic class has become salient in terms of understanding the effects of poverty. The military as a culture is also an emerging topic for consideration (Koslow & Salett, 1989). Finally, social justice themes are receiving more attention in the counseling profession (Toporek, Gerstein, Fouad, Roysircar, & Israel, 2005).

Reflection questions: *Why is it difficult for members of various oppressed groups to acknowledge the oppression of other groups? What do people have to gain or lose by being inclusive or exclusive?*

4. What knowledge is essential for multicultural counseling?

In the early development of multicultural counseling, the prevailing question was "what should counselors know about ethnic minority clients?" Since the focus was on the client, counselors were asked to learn culture-specific knowledge about four major ethnic minority groups (African Americans, American Indians, Asian Americans, and Hispanic Americans). We recognize that it is not possible for us to include all cultural groups in a comprehensive way in one book. We elected not to present the four major ethnic groups as in previous editions for several reasons.

1. Culture-specific knowledge of ethnic populations is necessary, but not sufficient to develop MCC.
2. The four major ethnic groups have historical significance in the U.S. but are not inclusive of all groups under the broad umbrella of multiculturalism.
3. There is a vast amount of *within-group* diversity in these four major groupings, which necessitates caution to not make cultural generalizations that can lead to stereotyping.
4. It would be misleading to believe that *objective* knowledge of these four major groups will lead to MCC without considering *subjective* intercultural skills, which is the emphasis of this text.
5. We encourage readers to pursue cultural-specific information about groups relevant to your practice and community (For an overview of a multicultural history of the United States, see Takaki, 1993; for a sampling of ethnic narrative web sites, see Microtraining web site available online at http://www.emicrotraining .com/links/links_multiculturalism.html.).

Following this tradition, however, we have included a culture-specific chapter on counseling Latina(o) families in Chapter 7.

The question of knowledge acquisition and its usefulness in multicultural counseling is complicated and still unresolved for at least two reasons: First, the expectation for counselors to learn about all of the social sciences of the various racial and cultural groups is unrealistic because there is too much to learn about too many groups. In addition, within-group differences further complicates matters concerning knowledge about groups. For example, one group of Cubans differs from another depending on time of arrival in the U.S. and socioeconomic conditions.

Second, what evidence exists that proves that knowledge of various groups ensures that counseling will be effective? In fact, the results of one study suggested that counselors with knowledge about the client's culture might do worse than counselors with no knowledge (Lloyd, 1987). He suggested that such knowledge could lead to stereotyping, inappropriate diagnosis, and inappropriate treatment. If one is not careful, the use of cultural knowledge can be harmful.

Often, people want to have cultural-specific information to understand cultural differences to prepare for cross-cultural encounters. However, cultural-specific knowledge is often situation-specific, and cultural interactions are changing and dynamic. Storti (2001) recommended that a more effective way of learning intercultural behaviors is through observation and self-reflection. More intercultural communication perspectives will be discussed in Chapter 6.

Counselor self-awareness was deemed a major domain of MCC advanced by Arredondo et al. (1996) and is still one of the key guidelines for training mental health professionals today. Because counseling is an interpersonal process, counselors' self-awareness of their personal *cultural baggage,* biases, and world views are as important as understanding culturally diverse clientele. Interactions with culturally diverse persons are important and informative ways to learn effective communication skills. It is our view that knowledge can be gained across all domains through personal interactions with a wide variety of individuals and groups from diverse cultures. Although personal involvement may be the most robust way to acquire cultural knowledge, there are additional ways that are fun and less risky. For example, one can learn about the lives of culturally diverse peoples through reading novels, attending movies and lectures, and travel, in addition to personal contact. Suggested readings, web sites, and films are included throughout the text.

Reflection questions: *What do you think are essential categories of knowledge for MCC and why; what sorts of interpersonal interactions will help you to acquire this knowledge base? Who can serve as a cultural guide (cultural broker, cultural informant) for you to learn more about specific cultural groups? Alternately, how can you help inform others about your cultural group? How have you acquired the MCC knowledge that you have already?*

5. Are there skills, techniques and strategies for counseling culture-specific clients?

We suggest that the answer to this question is *yes* and *no*. A wide range of counseling interventions are effective with clients from differing backgrounds, but may need to be tailored to fit client expectations depending upon cultural backgrounds. For example, many African

American clients expect to take something from a counseling session that offers hope for improving their condition. Traditional Asian clients are likely to expect the counselor to be an expert and to provide direction in the initial counseling session. However, applying these generalizations to all African American or Asian clients without screening for appropriateness is equivalent to stereotyping.

There are culture-specific traditional therapies and modes of healing, including such practices as shamanism, folk healing, herbs, and spiritual/religious rituals (Das, 1987). Counselors are encouraged to be educated about these practices and their appropriateness with clients (Moodley & West, 2005). Yet, this recommendation is offered with caution. LaDue (1994) pointed out that Native Peoples' healing practices have been "appropriated," just as Native lands and resources have been taken, and she discourages therapists from adapting spiritual practices without proper training and tribal sanctions.

Reflection suggestions: Investigate a culture-specific theory and critique. Alternately, identify reasons why special techniques should be used (or not) with culture-specific populations.

6. What is the difference between making cultural generalizations and stereotyping?

By definition, a stereotype is applying a descriptive characteristic to all members of a particular group, e.g., "all men are unemotional, all Asians are good in math, or all teenagers are irresponsible." Usually social stereotypes are negative, although positive stereotypes still "box people in," such as the *model minority* stereotype of Asian Americans. However, sometimes grains of truth are found in stereotypes. Someone may have had a particular experience with a specific behavior, for example, observing emotional restraint with a Japanese supervisee, and concluded that Asians are *repressed,* or worse, *devious.*

Cultural generalizations are descriptors of cultural characteristics that provide distinctions about specific groups, for example, Hispanic/Latina(o)s tend to value family first, Japanese value emotional control, and Anglo-Americans value individualism and autonomy. However, these descriptions function as "working hypotheses" about social reference groups, hypotheses which need to be checked out. Whenever one works with cultural information, it is imperative to be aware that labels carry power, and to use them judiciously and with qualification. In doing so, counselors and educators play important roles in prejudice reduction (Ponterotto & Pedersen, 1993).

Reflection questions: *What function do stereotypes play in popular culture? Why do you think the media perpetuates stereotypes? Investigate how various minority groups resist stereotyping in the media. Alternatively, what are the costs and benefits of cultural generalizations and stereotypes? How do you know when you are using stereotypes?*

7. Since it is believed that people are more alike than different, why focus on differences?

As human beings, it may be said that we are more alike than different, and yet cultural differences are significant and impact interactions on a daily basis. If one chooses to minimize cultural differences, and focus on similarities, for example, consider the question, "who defines reality or decides what is normal?" In the U.S., a White-Anglo-Saxon Protestant (WASP) perspective is the assumed dominant cultural norm. This attitude has been described as being ethnocentric and construed as a defense against engaging in multiculturalism (Bennett, 2004), as described in Chapter 1. On the other hand, subscribing to universals or existential commonalities may be a valid attempt to retain connections while exploring differences (Fukuyama, 1990; Locke, 1990). Consider the reasons for focusing on sameness, could one be avoiding the difficult work of understanding one's own culture, other cultures, and subsequently making change?

Consider this scenario: In a conversation between two friends, one black and one white, the white friend said, "I really like and respect you; I don't think of you as black." What do you think the white friend meant by this comment? How do you think the black friend felt? In this instance, the White friend has overlooked the uniqueness offered from cultural difference. In an attempt to be close, he has minimized difference, and more, he has offended the black friend with the assumption that "not black" is a positive thing.

Reflection question: *It is natural to resist change. Identify a time when you have felt reluctant to engage in dealing with differences; how did you resolve your resistance?*

8. What are effective counselor and client matches considering factors such as racial identity and world view? What are some noneffective combinations?

In the previous question, we examined the perspective of no differences, in which case one might think that counselors can work with any type of client, regardless of culture or ethnic backgrounds. On the other hand, one might think that effective counseling can take place only by matching the ethnicity of counselor and client. However, it is not as simple as this might appear.

Racial identity encompasses within-group differences, and a global category does not take into account many dimensions of difference. In Chapter 4, we review the literature on racial identity development, but as a preview consider the following factors.

Helms and Cook (1999) theorized that counselors and clients both have varying degrees of racial consciousness, including attitudes of conformity to the dominant (WASP) culture, immersion into one's own racial uniqueness, and/or struggling with the demands of conflicting cultural group memberships. Effective counselor and client matches are combinations where counselor and client share similar consciousness on these issues, and/or the counselor is at least one step ahead of the client in terms of racial identity development. Ineffective matches usually occur when the client is in a more advanced status than the counselor on such matters. For example, a Chicana-identified Mexican American woman may prefer to work with a Latina therapist as part of affirming her race and gender identity versus someone who is ignorant of the history of oppression of Mexican Americans in the United States. In contrast, another Latina who is trying to assimilate into U.S. dominant culture may prefer a white therapist who represents achievement in U.S. American culture.

Reflection questions: What assumptions have you made about good counselor-client matches? Does race matter in counselor-client matching? What are other possible demographic factors to consider and why?

9. Why do many white people deny that racism exists while many black people hesitate to admit that progress has been made in race relations in the United States?

Whites and blacks have differing perceptions about the reality of racism, discrimination and prejudice. Researchers have found that when whites and blacks are asked about the presence and incidence of racial bias, whites and blacks often have opposite views, with blacks seeing it and whites not. In this post-modern age, expressions of racism often are subtle and hidden from awareness (Dovidio, Gaertner, Kawakami, & Hodson, 2002).

Unfortunately, racism is an invisible pervasive force in U.S. society, wherein access to resources and power systemically favor whites. Tatum (1997) suggested that racism is like "smog" in the air we breathe on a daily basis. It is not unusual for whites to feel defensive about racism. Some may feel personally attacked when ethnic minorities are angry. One might say something like "racism isn't my fault; I wasn't alive when there was slavery."

The reality is that blacks continue to be disadvantaged on many levels systemically. Consider the facts presented in Box 2.2:

Box 2.2

The typical African American family had 60% as much income as a typical white family in 1958, but only 58% as much in 2002. Black unemployment is more than twice the rate for whites—a greater gap than in 1972. One in nine African Americans cannot find a job. White households had an average net worth of $468,200 in 2001—more than 6 times the $75,700 average net worth of black households. At the slow rate that the black-white poverty gap has been narrowing since 1968, it would take 150 years (i.e., until the year 2152) to close the gap. (National Association for the Advancement of Colored People, 2005).

Other indicators suggest that progress has not been made. For example, even though *Brown vs. the Board of Education of Topeka, Kansas* declared that school segregation was illegal, many communities continued to practice school segregation, for example, as a result of middle-class "white flight" to the suburbs (National Public Radio, 2004).

Anti-racism work is painful, shame-inducing, and uncomfortable, yet necessary in order for there to be significant social change (Sue, 2003). Whites may not be aware of their "skin color" privilege. It is not unusual for whites to avoid engagement out of denial or feelings of guilt or shame. We believe that it is important to address these emotions, and have focused on this topic next in Chapter 3.

Reflection suggestions: *Examine local and national newspapers for articles that relate to black/white relations, economic progress, and social programs. Alternately, interview an anti-racism activist.*

10. What is the future of multicultural counseling? Will it become obsolete? Will it be fully integrated into counseling practices?

Although some progress has been made in multicultural relations in this country, much has yet to be done. New immigrants and refugees bring new languages, ways of life and unique challenges. It is not unusual to hear university administrators boast that their schools have students representing sixty or more different countries. Diversity also exists at the school levels from K–12. Unfortunately, the counseling profession has not prepared itself to deal with large and varied ethnic groups effectively even though more is known about working with culturally diverse clients than was known a few years ago.

Recently, a group of mental health professionals in a clinical case conference were discussing a Chinese International student whom they perceived as being "too dependent;" she wanted the therapist to be available to her more than once per week and wanted her to tell her what to do. While some members in the case conference questioned whether the client was acting normally within her cultural context, they also expected this Asian woman to behave as any American student facing a similar set of life circumstances. Professional mental health workers may promote the ideal of multiculturalism, but not actually put it into practice. In other words, "they can talk the talk, but can they walk the walk?" However, on a positive note, more and more resources are available on infusing MCC into the profession (Constantine & Sue, 2005; Ponterotto, Casas, Suzuki, & Alexander, 2001).

In some training programs it is debated whether or not to require courses in multicultural counseling, or to infuse MCC into the total curriculum. Having a specialized course in multiculturalism runs the risk of isolating MCC into one part of the curriculum. However, it can also function to *seed and grow* MCC consciousness for infusion into all aspects of the curriculum.

With each new emerging population there are new challenges and new issues to understand and to work through. For example, the Hmong refugees from the Vietnam War era face language and cultural barriers to acculturating into U.S. society and obtaining even the most basic services (Fadiman, 1997). New legal rulings and precedents affect social attitudes at large, such as passing legislation against hate crimes. As the world becomes a global village, there is an urgent need for international communication and understanding, and MCC is not likely to become obsolete. Trends towards globalization also are being impacted by the growth of capitalism, the Internet and computer technology. Multinational corporations now require training in intercultural communication. Rapid social change is likely to influence the meanings of multiculturalism in this twenty-first century.

Reflection questions: *What are the major influences shaping trends in MCC? What are your observations of how technology contributes to multicultural understanding (or misunderstanding) nationally and globally?*

11. What are good sources of knowledge for informing the best practices of MCC?

MCC are drawn from interdisciplinary sources (anthropology, intercultural communication, counseling and psychology, sociology, and social psychology). This book will model bridge building by drawing from multidisciplinary sources and different *ways of knowing* in constructing what it means to be truly multiculturally competent. We have drawn from three main sources of knowledge that inform *best practices:* social science, interpretive, and critical theory (Martin & Sermol, 2005). The social sciences developed in the 1950s–1970s imitated the hard sciences in terms of using the scientific method to study human behaviors. Traditionally, social science builds on existing knowledge and includes relevant literature. It entails developing research questions and consulting experts in the field. This approach uses quantitative methods and relies upon statistics to provide empirical support.

However, human and social behaviors were far too complex and did not fit easily into the linear and causal frameworks of traditional quantitative research. This was true especially in cross-cultural contexts. In addition, most social science studies were conducted on white, middle class, educated persons and did not include cultural context as a source of information. Anthropology and sociology have used qualitative approaches (e.g., ethnography). Thus, interpretive and anecdotal approaches have been added to the social science discourse. These qualitative methods were interactive and subjective, in contrast with distant observation and objective research methods, and provided rich descriptions.

Critical theory emanated from a post-colonial analysis of systems and power. It proposed questions like "what purpose is served" in this research? How is the *other* discussed/defined? Who can speak for whom? It requires the context of the research and the biases of the researcher to be fully described, e.g., "describe your location as writer" so that the research is understood in context. It implies that the researcher speaks with participants and it is a self-reflexive process (the researcher learns through *self and other* interactions in the research process).

Sometimes these three paradigms tend to conflict and compete, but all three are useful in understanding human behaviors. We believe that they are complementary in taking a holistic approach to defining MCC. See Table 2.1 for a comparative chart on these three research paradigms.

Reflection question: *What are the strengths and limitations of each of these three approaches to knowledge?*

12. What can you expect during this course of study in terms of developing MCC skills?

We see learning MCC as a process, and describe here a developmental model of intercultural sensitivity designed by Milton Bennett (1986; 2004), a noted specialist in intercultural communication. His work was derived from systematic observations of intercultural communication patterns and based in grounded theory (available online at http://www.intercultural.org/idi/idi.html). His data collection spanned a period of 10 years and was based on interviews with intercultural communication students and international business people. He took a constructivist approach researching the question "how do we know where people are developmentally in terms of intercultural awareness, in order to understand what to do next in terms of sequencing training in intercultural communication" (Bennett, 2005). A diagram of the model is in Figure 2.1.

Although it appears as a linear model, individuals may cycle in and out of the various positions. The default condition (normal) is ethnocentrism, that is, when people believe "their culture is central to reality" and they cannot see cultural differences. According to Bennett, "reality is a kaleidoscopic flux from which we organize through linguistic systems of our minds, make meaningful chunks, and construe experience" (Bennett, 2005). This perspective is another way to describe world view.

The model is composed of six positions along a continuum that moves from ethnocentrism ("my culture defines reality") toward eth-

Table 2.1 Comparing Three Research Paradigms in Studying Intercultural Communication

	Social Science (Positivism)	Interpretive	Critical Theory
Research goal	Understand & predict	Understand	Locate oppression, systemic change
Nature of reality	Single, tangible	Multiple & subjective	Multiple, subjective, shaped by socio-political factors
Relationship between Researcher/researched	Distant	Engaged and interactive	Distant and engaged, proactive
Approach to data	Reductionistic, objective	Holistic, subjective	Holistic, subjective
Relationship between culture & communication	Causal Culture–Communication	Reciprocal Culture–Communication	Contested, conflicted
Role of researcher values	Carefully controlled	Biases are explicit	Values are central to inquiry
Contribution/Emphasis	Provides Snapshots	Provides in-depth analysis, Communication in context	Provides context (economic, political) and role of power
Methods	Quantitative, experimental	Qualitative, naturalistic, interactive, discover meaning through words	Qualitative, interactive, transformation through discourse
Rhetorical style	3rd person, unemotional	1st person, participant voices, emotive prose	1st person, participant voices emotive prose
Training applications	Academic, professional audiences, business	Interventions Audience analysis	Diverse Groups

Adapted from Martin, J. & Sermol, D. (2005, July 25–29). *Best Practices of Intercultural Communication Training Workshop*, The Summer Institute for Intercultural Communication (SIIC), Forest Grove, Oregon. Reprinted with permission of authors.

Figure 2.1
Experience of Difference, Development of Intercultural Sensitivity, Milton J. Bennett (2004).

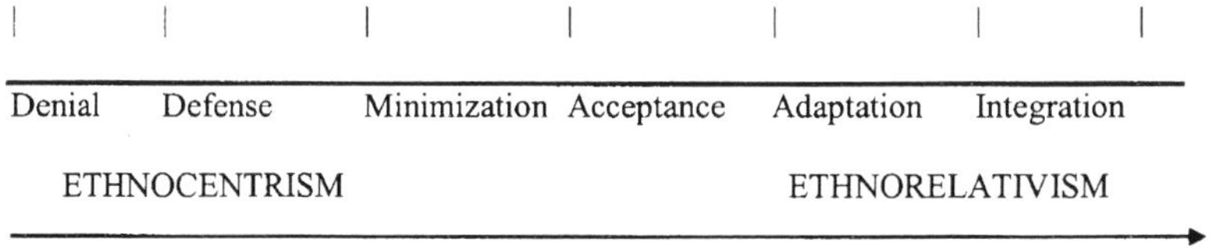

Denial	Defense	Minimization	Acceptance	Adaptation	Integration	

ETHNOCENTRISM   ETHNORELATIVISM

Note: The Developmental Model of Intercultural Sensitivity, Milton J. Bennett, Workshop presentation at SIIC, July 25, 2005. Reprinted by permission of author.

norelativism ("my culture is one of many"). Remember that all cultures have both positive and negative elements.

In general, the model describes how people perceive differences; it moves from less complex to more complex. Bennett (2005) talked about wine tasting to illustrate this point. A naïve wine taster may believe that there are three types of wine: white, blush, and red. A wine connoisseur knows that there are hundreds of types of wines, each with distinctive flavors.

The six positions are described below:

1. **Denial:** People believe that their culture is the only "real culture." They tend to live in cultural isolation and separate from others; it's like living in a bubble. They may be quite sophisticated about their own culture but clueless about other cultures. A general attitude is disinterest or avoidance of cultural differences, but people may react aggressively if their position is threatened. Those in denial need preparation to have a vocabulary and ability to make cultural perceptions. A good beginning point is to do nonverbal demonstrations, have cultural exhibits, and cultural sharing, (e.g., family heritage stories).

2. **Defense:** People see their culture as the only "good culture," and believe that their culture is superior to others. Differences are threatening and people may polarize into an *us versus them* type of conflict. People who are defensive have a general attitude of criticalness towards other cultures, whether they are hosts, guests, or cultural newcomers in their respective social situations. A reverse reaction at this stage of development is to *go native*. Sometimes due to dominant culture guilt, there may be a tendency to roman-

ticize the *other* and try to be like them. In either circumstance, there is a polarity of positive and negative traits/judgments, with the possibility of switching back and forth. Reactions like backlash may also describe some reactions. People in defense need to feel secure in themselves. Whereas it may be quite natural to derive feelings of superiority from ethnocentricity, it is not the only way to feel good about oneself. Examples of tasks at this stage include developing a positive racial/ethnic identity and learning more about one's own culture.

3. **Minimize Differences:** People tend to resist differences and see cultures in universal terms based upon their own cultural framework. An indicator of these attitudes is a desire to see people as "all the same, just human beings." The drawback to this attitude is that usually this means "all the same, just like me." Viewing cultures in universal terms tends to minimize or devalue real cultural differences. People may have an attitude of tolerance of differences (vs. affirming differences). Individuals need more cultural self-awareness at this point, to see culture as one way of organizing reality. At this point, it is helpful to use differences as a *mirror* to understand self and culture better. A beginning point may be to develop constructs for cultural comparisons, e.g., contrasting value orientations, such as understanding the difference between individualism and collectivism. It is through nonjudgmental cultural comparisons that one gets to know his/her culture better. This position may be transitional to becoming more aware of cultural complexity discussed next.

4. **Acceptance:** People accept that their culture is one of many cultural world views. They may not necessarily agree with or like cultural differences, but they are able to discern that these multiple realities exist. A general attitude is one of curiosity and respect towards cultural differences. One of the challenges is to deal with moral ambiguity, especially when there are competing value orientations.

5. **Adaptation:** According to Bennett, "adaptation to cultural difference is the state in which the experience of another culture yields perception and behavior appropriate to that culture" (Retrieved December 14, 2005 online at http://www.intercultural.org/idi/idi.html). People's world views expand to include new constructs from other cultures. With this new awareness, people may

be able to develop a repertoire of new behaviors, ways of thinking and communicating. People are able to see the world through different lenses, shift perspectives, develop transcultural empathy and work towards becoming bicultural or multicultural, i.e., acculturating, but not assimilating.

6. **Integration of Difference:** People not only are adapting to new cultures, they are negotiating the state of being between cultures. This position is not necessarily better than the previous one, but more describes what it is like to be "culturally marginal." Bennett (2005) described two features: "Encapsulated marginality" (being stuck between cultures, marked by feelings of confusion or alienation) and "constructive marginality," that is, moving between cultures in a dynamic, fluid way. This phenomenon is common among nondominant minority groups, long-term expatriates, and *global nomads*. Counseling issues may include discussing some of these questions "when does it matter or hurt to be marginal (feelings of inclusion or exclusion), and how does one become comfortable with being truly multicultural?" People may also have to resolve cross-cultural conflicts.

Bennett designed an inventory, the *Intercultural Development Inventory (IDI)* (available online at http://www.intercultural.org/idi/idi.html) that can reveal issues as "resolved, transitional or unresolved" for each stage. He notes that psychology favors "transformational experiences" whereas he believes that it's appropriate to help people move along the continuum. This model is useful in understanding the developmental tasks of becoming multiculturally competent, and can be used to plan curriculum and action plans for learning multicultural skills.

Reflection questions: Without judging yourself, where do you see yourself now in terms of experiencing and understanding cultural differences? Where do you see your "growth edges?"

CONCLUDING REMARKS

We suggest that questions are an important part of defining and co-creating the MCC field. It is through a combination of efforts by researchers, practitioners, students, educators and activists that change is happening. We invite you to write out your questions that you have about MCC as you embark on this course of study.

Suggested Activities

1. Interview a mental health professional about his/her understanding of MCC and contemporary issues.
2. Consult an elder in your family/community about perceptions of MCC.
3. Select a current "hot" issue and argue opposing points of views.
4. Attend a lecture or workshop on a current MCC issue.

Web Sites of Interest

Information about the Hmong people, refugees from Southeast Asia
http://www.learnabouthmong.org/default.asp
Multicultural Guidelines (APA)
http://www.apa.org/pi/multiculturalguidelines/formats.html
Counseling Today Online Updated Code of Ethics
http://www.counseling.org/Publications/CounselingTodayArticles.aspx?AGuid=ec8780ac-562e-4868-8530-6ef87b0b0e3d
Intercultural Communication Institute
http://www.intercultural.org/

REFERENCES

Arredondo, P., Toporek, R., Brown, S. P., Jones, J., Locke, D. C., Sanchez, J., et al. (1996). Operationalization of the multicultural counseling competencies. *Journal of Multicultural Counseling and Development, 24,* 42–78.

Bennett, M. J. (1986). A developmental approach to training for intercultural sensitivity. *International Journal of Intercultural Relations, 10* (2), 179–196.

Bennett, M. J. (2004). Becoming interculturally competent. In J. S. Wurzel (Ed.), *Toward multiculturalism: A reader in multicultural education* (2nd Ed).(pp. 62–77. Newton, MA.: Intercultural Resource Corporation.

Coleman, H. L. K. (1995). Strategies for coping with cultural diversity. *The Counseling Psychologist, 23,* 722–741.

Constantine, M. & Sue D. W. (Eds). *Strategies for Building Multicultural Competence in Mental Health and Educational Settings.* Hoboken, NJ.: John Wiley & Sons.

Das, A. K. (1987). Indigenous models of therapy in traditional Asian societies. *Journal of Multicultural Counseling and Development, 15,* 25–37.

Dovidio, J. F., Gaertner, S. L., Kawakami, K., & Hodson, G. (2002). Why can't we just get along? Interpersonal biases and interracial distrust. *Cultural Diversity & Ethnic Minority Psychology, 8,* 88–102.

Fadiman, A. (1997). *The spirit catches you and you fall down: A Hmong child, her American doctors, and the collision of two cultures.* New York: Farrar, Straus & Giroux.

Fukuyama, M. A. (1990). Taking a universal approach to multicultural counseling. *Counselor Education and Supervision, 30,* 6–17.

Fuertes, J. N. & Gretchen, D. (2001). Emerging theories of multicultural counseling. In J.G. Ponterotto, J. M. Casas, L. A. Suzuki, C. M. Alexander (Eds), *Handbook of Multicultural Counseling* (2nd Ed) (pp. 509–541). Thousand Oaks, CA.: Sage.

Gonzalez, R., Biever, J. L., & Gardner, G. T. (1994). The multicultural perspective in therapy: A social constructionist approach. *Psychotherapy, 31,* 515–524.

Hanna, F.J., Bemak, F., & Chi-Ying Chung, R. (1999). Toward a new paradigm for multicultural counseling. *Journal of Counseling and Development, 77,* 125–134.

Helms, J. E. (1984). Toward a theoretical explanation of the effects of race on counseling: A Black/White interactional model. *The Counseling Psychologist, 12,* 153–163.

Helms, J. E. (1990). *Black and White racial identity: Theory, research, and practice.* New York: Greenwood.

Helms, J. E. (1992). *A race is a nice thing to have: A guide to being a White person or understanding the White persons in your life.* Topeka, KS.: Content Communications.

Helms, J. E., & Cook, D. A. (1999). *Using race and culture in counseling and psychotherapy: Theory and process.* Boston: Allyn & Bacon.

Heppner, P. (2005, April). Stronger together: Increasing understanding through diverse perspectives. Special feature in *Division 17 Society of Counseling Psychology Newsletter, XXVI* (2), 18–25.

Ho, D. Y. F. (1995). Internalized culture, culturocentrism, and transcendence. *The Counseling Psychologist, 23,* 4–24.

Koslow, D. R. & Salett, E. P. (Eds) (1989). *Crossing cultures in mental health.* Washington, DC: Sietar International.

LaDue, R. A. (1994). Coyote returns: Twenty sweats does not an Indian expert make. *Women & Therapy, 15* (1), 93–111.

Lloyd, A. P. (1987). Multicultural counseling: Does it belong in a counselor education program? *Counselor Education and Supervision, 26,* 164–167.

Locke, D. C. (1990). A not so provincial view of multicultural counseling. *Counselor Education and Supervision, 30,* 18–25.

Martin, J. N., Nakayama, T. K. & Flores, L. A. (Eds.) (1997). *Readings in cultural contexts.* Mountain View, CA.: Mayfield Pub.

Martin, J. & Sermol, D. (2005, July 25–29). *Best Practices of Intercultural Communication Training Workshop,* The Summer Institute for Intercultural Communication (SIIC), Forest Grove, Oregon.

McGoldrick, M., Giordano, J., & Pearce, J. K. (Eds). (1996). *Ethnicity and family therapy* (2nd Ed). New York: Guilford Press.

McIntosh, P. (2001). White privilege: Unpacking the invisible knapsack. In P.S. Rothenberg (Ed.), *Race, class, and gender in the United States* (5th Ed) (pp. 163–168). New York: Worth.

Monroe, I. (2005). No marriage between Black ministers and queer community. *ChickenBones: A Journal for Literary and Artistic African American Themes.* Retrieved online on January 4, 2006 http://www.nathanielturner.com/blackministersqueercommunity.htm.

Moodley, R. & West, W. (2005). *Integrating traditional healing practices into counseling and psychotherapy.* Thousand Oaks, CA.: Sage.

National Association for the Advancement of Colored People, 2005. Retrieved August 9, 2005 online at http://www.naacp.org/programs/economy/economy_index.html Source of the data: State of the Dream: Disowned in the Ownership Society, by Betsy P. Leondar-Wright, Meizhu Lui, Gloribel Mota, Dedrick D. Muhammad, & Mara Voukydis., United for a Fair Economy web site. http://www.faireconomy.org/press/2005/Stateofthe Dream2005.pdf.

National Public Radio (2004). Retrieved online at September 22, 2005. http://www.npr.org/templates/story/story.php?storyId=1751945.

Parker, W. M. (1998). *Consciousness raising: A primer for multicultural counseling.* Springfield, IL: Charles C Thomas.

Pedersen, P. (2002). Ethics, competence, and other professional issues in culture-centered counseling. In P. B. Pedersen, J. G. Draguns, W. J. Lonner, J. E. Trimble (Eds.), *Counseling across cultures* (5th Ed) (pp. 3–27). Thousand Oaks, CA.: Sage.

Ponterotto, J. G., & Pedersen, P. B. (1993). *Preventing prejudice: A guide for counselors and educators.* Thousand Oaks, CA: Sage.

Ponterotto, J. G., Casas, J. M., Suzuki, L. A., & Alexander, C. M. (Eds). (2001). *Handbook of multicultural counseling* (2nd Ed). Thousand Oaks, CA.: Sage.

Storti, C. (2001). *The art of crossing cultures* (2nd Ed).Yarmouth, ME: Intercultural Press.

Sue, D. W., Carter, R. T., Casas, J. M., Fouad, N. A., Ivey, A. E., & Jensen, M. et al. (1998). *Multicultural counseling competencies: Individual and organizational development.* Thousand Oaks, CA.: Sage.

Sue, D. W. (2003). *Overcoming our racism: The journey to liberation.* San Francisco: Jossey-Bass.

Sue, S. (2003). In defense of cultural competency in psychotherapy and treatment. *American Psychologist, 58,* 964–970.

Takaki R. (1993). *A different mirror: A history of multicultural America.* New York: Back Bay Books.

Tatum, B. D. (1997). *Why are all the Black kids sitting together in the cafeteria? And other conversations about race.* New York: Basic Books.

Toporek, R. L., Gerstein, L., Fouad, N., Roysircar, G., Israel, T. (Eds.) (2005). *Handbook for social justice in counseling psychology: Leadership, vision, and action.* Thousand Oaks, CA.: Sage.

Chapter 3

PREPARING EMOTIONALLY FOR CONSCIOUSNESS-RAISING (C-R): THE ROAD OF COMPASSION

We have to live in a way that liberates the ancestors and future generations who are inside of us. . . . If we do not liberate our ancestors, we will be in bondage all our lives, and we will transmit that to our children and grandchildren. Now is the time to do it.

—Thich Nhat Hanh, Zen Master (1992, p. 36)

Abstract

This chapter addresses emotional responses that potentially arise when one is exposed to consciousness-raising (C-R) on issues of social oppression. In particular, we focus on white guilt and shame that accompanies awareness of the impact of racism. We discuss strategies for processing these difficult feelings, and propose that learning how to become an ally is one way of ameliorating this stress as well as healing the larger society.

INTRODUCTION

Through observation, many years of instruction, personal communication and interactions, we have noted that some participants in MCC training are open and enthusiastic about learning, growing and changing through multicultural experiences and others are closed and antagonistic toward multiculturalism. There are many reasons why participants in MCC training may become distressed, including challenges to one's reality (ethnocentrism), personal experiences as *targets* of oppression, and encouragement to go outside of one's comfort zone to learn MCC.

Unlike other courses in the counseling curriculum, multicultural counseling courses and training experiences tend to elicit strong emotions that often pose a threat to trainees' ability to become caring, sensitive and empathic multicultural counselors. Students and trainers alike may be unprepared for the emotional intensity related to course content. As a result of some of these experiences, students have reported that they felt "blind sided, baffled, stunned, shocked, immobilized and emotionally paralyzed" especially from more confrontative types of experiences. As an example, several people in an audience walked out of a presentation at a regional convention when the speaker showed a video of the history of the dehumanizing treatment of the American Indian which forced indigenous culture to be like the dominant White culture. The title of the film was *In the white man's image: In whose honor?*

Defensiveness resulting from exposure to multicultural training has been observed in trainees of all racial/cultural groups, and yet it seems to be more prevalent among white participants. As a case example, students in a MCC course were asked to form small discussion groups by race/ethnicity to talk about their experiences as white persons, persons of color, biracial persons, and so on. For some white students, this was the first time they had been asked to talk about being white and some were at a loss for words. The level of tension, confusion, and discomfort was high enough to hinder communication.

These attitudes closely resemble qualities of guilt and shame. When participants become overwhelmed by the emotions of guilt and shame, they often become resistant and defensive, to the extent that empathic understanding and the acquisition of MCC are hindered. In the training process, it is essential that the experiences of guilt and shame are recognized so that learning objectives will not become forestalled.

We suggest that learning how to recognize difficult emotions and tolerating discomfort are essential components towards reaching the goals of developing deep empathy, compassion (for self and others), understanding of the dynamics of social oppression, and developing MCC. Suffering takes many forms, and socially inflicted suffering through various forms of social oppression are particularly painful for everyone. However, we recognize that everyone is influenced through socialization to believe misinformation about self and others, and to have beliefs that are filtered through multiple social oppressions, such as sexism, racism, heterosexism, ageism, and so on. Much of these social forces is systemic and operates outside of personal awareness. After participating in consciousness-raising on these issues, it then becomes an individual and collective responsibility to be accountable for injustices and to strive towards social equity.

In this chapter we discuss (1) understanding shame and guilt and understanding the difference between the two (2) developing strategies for managing emotions, including the multicultural mentoring lab (MML), (3) understanding power and privilege, (4) motivating persons with privilege towards social action, and (5) learning how to become an ally.

Understanding Shame and Guilt in Multicultural Counselor Training

A wide variety of factors may contribute to the strong emotions that you may encounter from exposure to MCC training. It has been our observation that some of the following are reasons for these strong emotions:

1. Some students feel embarrassed that they have so little awareness of their own ethnicity as well as knowledge of culturally diverse groups.
2. Many participants feel disempowered when they become aware that the history of the United States is saturated with mistreatment of culturally diverse groups.
3. Some white trainees experience feelings of regret when they become aware of the reality of white privilege (McIntosh, 2001; Ponterotto, 1988).
4. Some ethnic minority students resent or feel burdened when they are expected to speak for their entire race or cultural group.
5. Some people who are the targets of oppression feel anger at those who have power but who are ignorant of their privileges.
6. Many successful culturally diverse individuals feel sorrowful for leaving others behind.
7. Some light skinned featured persons of color may be ashamed when they enjoy certain privileges not available to darker-skinned persons of their racial/cultural group.

Having taught multicultural counseling courses for many years, we have observed a powerful emotional process in which students shut down and struggle to open up to continue their personal growth. Some students have described the experience as being like "an invisible finger pointing at them." Others have reported that it seems that some of the multicultural authors are screaming at them from the pages of the books or journal articles. It is our belief that these students could be experiencing guilt and shame from exposure to multicultural counseling training.

Essentially, it is normal to at some point in MCC training to feel angry, sad, guilty or afraid. We encourage you to work through such feelings, and not get stuck in them. The rewards will come in terms of understanding the human condition at a deeper level, cultivating compassion, and experiencing liberation no matter what part or role you feel that you and your family legacy have played in social oppression.

Differences Between Shame and Guilt

The terms shame and guilt are often used interchangeably in the field of psychology. We will highlight the differences between shame and guilt in order for trainees to be able to recognize each, and to have a sense of mastery over them when they occur. More specifically, such awareness can serve as therapeutic tools when recognized and worked through appropriately.

Harder and Lewis (1986) explained that one way to differentiate the experience of shame and guilt is in terms of "self-transgression" (p. 89). In shame, the self is viewed as an object of scorn, disgust, ridicule, and rejection. Individuals afflicted with shame reactions feel unusually self-conscious and helpless. Shame is not associated with specific behaviors, but rather the belief that the core self is "bad" based on other people's negative perceptions. Shame is experienced as a response to one's identity rather than to one's behavior. According to Tangney (1992) the negative situation and the individual are "one and the same" (p. 670). Therefore, when one experiences shame in multicultural counselor training, he or she may find it difficult to remain open to experience the growth essential for acquiring multicultural competencies.

In contrast, those who feel guilt regard the core self and the behavior as separate and distinct. Shame is internal, and guilt is external, a way of experiencing regret for a particular act. Tangney (1990) suggested that when one experiences guilt, the self remains intact and capable of mobilizing to deal with the negative emotion, e.g., through making amends, apologizing, or taking action. In other words, guilt feelings which are connected to specific behaviors seem easier to manage or control than shame.

Box 3.1

Illustrations from real-life experiences from teaching MCC courses may help to illustrate the complexity of negotiating emotional reactions to MCC work. Consider this scenario:

Having heard a lecture by an American Indian leader about the traumatizing treatment of American Indians, Benjamin (fictitious name), a retired white male who had returned to college for personal enrichment, decided to go to a local reservation to offer free counseling for young Native American boys who were having difficulty with drugs. To his surprise, the head of the tribe did not permit him to offer counseling, explaining that guidance was provided by the elders who fully understood Indian ways. In addition, the chief was concerned about a person who presented with a "one-shot" intervention rather than making a long-term commitment of service to Indian people. He was also told that the chief did not approve of white counselors who "wanted to brainwash their boys and girls."

Discussion Questions

1. What were the counselor trainee's motivations/intentions?
2. Discuss the tribal point of view.
3. What are other ways he could have helped a local tribe?

In summary, shame is internal and global; guilt is external and related to specific behaviors. Shame involves intense and embarrassing pain identified with the self; guilt is perceived as separate from the self. Lewis (1987) believes that shame can lead to disabling anxiety and guilt can drive the individual to repair the pain-inducing situation (p. 12). According to Jannoff-Bulman (1979) shame comes from self-blame in which attributions are personal, internal, global, and uncontrollable.

In the study of white racial identity development, evidence of guilt and shame reactions emerged as participants become aware of the existence of racism. Helms (1990) reported that some whites became depressed when they learn that they have denied black people their basic human rights. Corwin and Wiggins (1989) stated that white guilt is related to the way whites have perpetuated racism. Ponterotto (1988) found shameful emotions when students acknowledged that they have fostered racism in the counseling profession. In a word, it is normal to experience some feelings of guilt and shame when engaging in anti-racism work.

It is important for MCC trainers as well as mental health profession-als to recognize the difference between guilt and shame because they have different manifestations in the training process. For example, some of the behavioral consequences of guilt include the need to be more active, gain greater control and improve the situation (Wicker, 1983, p. 36). On the other hand, emotions associated with shame are feelings of inferiority, inhibitions, and lowered self-confidence. Profes-sors and trainers should be keenly aware of shame because it is believed to be a more devastating emotion causing participants to withdraw and shut down, thus affecting their ability to be open for learning multicul-tural competencies. According to Hoffman (1984) trainers should look for signs of personal distress, self-focus and self-preoccupation.

> As a case illustration of coping with the emotional reactions in a MCC course, Barbara (fictitious name) expressed difficulty accepting the idea of "white power/privilege." Privately dealing with her own abuse histo-ry, she interpreted this phrase as meaning that she was a perpetrator of abuse, which was emotionally triggering for her. In fact, she was strug-gling to experience personal empowerment for her own healing. By dis-cussing some of her resistance to these concepts in class she was able to release feelings of shame and feel more empowered through finding her voice. In this example, one can see that the dynamics of shame and oppression are multi-layered.

Not all white trainees react with guilt or shame, however. Some trainees question the validity of social oppressions and prefer to think that the U.S. has evolved as a society where all people have a fair and equal chance to make it through their own efforts. This belief is referred to as the *myth of meritocracy,* which essentially blames those who lack power as if it were a personal defect (Black & Stone, 2005).

> **Box 3.2**
>
> As a case example, consider George (fictitious name) who came from a working class background:
>
> As a white male, he personally did not perceive that he had much privilege. His parents had achieved a high school education, and he was the first to go to college. He worked his way through undergraduate school as a waiter and wanted to become a substance abuse counselor to help out his buddies. He cannot relate to the concepts of power/privilege because he does not see this as applying to his life experience.

Discussion Questions

1. Persons who have struggled to survive economically are sensitive to power/privilege as a class issue. Even so, lighter skin color may advantage persons in the working class, although it is difficult to see this advantage. Discuss the impact of economic class as one of the dimensions of power/privilege.
2. Why should someone like George be invested in learning about racism when all his life he has struggled with economic survival?

Although the above examples centered on white students' experiences, students of color have encountered strong negative guilt and shame also. Consider the following examples (fictitious names):

- Marilyn, a Dominican student, felt shame for losing her Spanish accent in her attempt to fit in with her Anglo-friends. She had become so Americanized that her parents barely recognized her when she came home to visit. She needed support in developing her bicultural identity and skills, rather than completely forsaking her home culture in order to fit into U.S. American culture.
- Kisha, an African American who had grown up in a predominantly white community in upstate New York, was embarrassed when she did not know the name of the Negro National Anthem or heard of commonly known black historical heroes such as Fredrick Douglas, Harriet Tubman and Dr. Charles Drew. She reported she felt like a traitor for knowing so little about her own racial/cultural group. She was a prime candidate for immersing herself in learning more about her racial/ethnic identity.

• Jordan, a biracial male, was depressed and confused about his racial identity because he felt pressured to choose between black or white. Class discussions on biracial identity issues compounded his confusion. What finally drove Jordan into his shell was a personal assessment questionnaire where each participant was asked to select his/her racial group. Since biracial was not included among the choices, Jordan refused to participate and withdrew further. Materials that supported biracial identity development would have been a helpful inclusion in the course content.

When trainees withdraw emotionally, the learning process becomes counterproductive. Therefore, trainers must become keenly aware of trainees' emotional state to insure that their ability to be cross-culturally empathic is not jeopardized. Overall trainers and trainees must be willing to deal with emotions that come up from exposure to multicultural training throughout the learning process in a positive way. One more case example which illustrates dimensions of guilt and shame in training is provided next.

Box 3.3

The Case of Heather Blankenship (fictitious name)

Heather was a graduate student in a multicultural counseling course where she had been given an assignment to complete an "ethnic sharing experience."

The purpose of ethnic sharing was to demonstrate that every group has a culture, to help students learn more about their own cultural backgrounds, and to help them understand their world view or outlook on life. In the exploration of their family histories, student participants were asked to bring and present to their class a symbol that represented their cultural background. Such symbols could be a "coat of arms," jewelry, pottery, furniture, food, clothing, music, documents, books, diaries, and so on. Heather was excited that through this assignment she could learn more about her North Carolina heritage where her family had lived since the 1700s. After telling her grandparents about the assignment, they invited her to look through the family documents and historical records. In scrutinizing these materials, she found many facts about her ancestors. First, they were among the first settlers from England to homestead in North Carolina. Second, they owned large plantations of tobacco and cotton and in later years the family manufactured furniture. Third, she learned that some of her ancestors had fought and were killed in the Civil War. Finally, she found a document of property deeds showing that her ancestors owned *X* number of acres of land, *X* number of livestock (cattle, horses) and *X* number of Negro slaves. The awareness that her ancestors had owned and listed their Negro slaves with property and livestock sent her into an emotional tailspin. This awareness was contrary to everything her parents had taught her concerning respect for human dignity and social justice. She was stunned, immobilized, and visibly upset by this discovery. How could she report this discovery to her classmates who viewed her as a champion for social justice? Even though she was not responsible for the actions of her ancestors, she felt strong emotional conflicts.

Discussion Questions

1. Was Heather experiencing guilt or shame from her ancestral exploration?
2. Heather's parents had raised her to be socially conscious. How would you help Heather reconcile her commitment to social justice with her family history?

We have focused on shame and guilt due to their potential as barriers to engagement in learning. However, not all trainees will feel guilt or shame to this degree, nor should they feel that "they ought to feel guilty." That's not the point. Rather, in the spirit of the Rev. Martin Luther King Jr., "no one is free until everyone is free." Remember that to heal the wounds of the past is to liberate the past as well as the present. In the words of Thich Nhat Hanh (1992), "To liberate them means to liberate ourselves. This is the teaching of *inter-being*. As long as our ancestors in us are still suffering, we cannot really be happy. If we take one step mindfully, freely, happily touching the earth, we do it for all previous and future generations. They all arrive with us at the same moment, and all of us find peace at the same time" (pp. 36–37). In the case study of Heather, her commitment to social justice in fighting racism is one way to heal personally and systemically; it heals her ancestors, herself, and future generations.

Developing Strategies for Managing Emotions

Knowing that people have strong emotional reactions during MCC training, we believe that you can and should be prepared for the emotional experience. It is known in group work that members gain more from the group experience when they know what to expect from it. Discomfort can be reduced when roles, expected behavior, and rules, are described throughout the learning process. Yalom (1995) and Corey (1995) suggested that anxieties, fears and misconceptions are reduced and higher levels of participation are enhanced through appropriate preparation for group work.

To clarify expectations and to reduce anxiety, we recommend the following strategies:

1. Understand the purpose, nature and process of each training activity.
2. Become aware of some common/expected emotions that result from participation in specific exercises.
3. Be aware and understand that you may choose to "pass" on any exercises.
4. For instructors, it is suggested that you demonstrate through role-play any activities that may be shame-provoking before asking trainees to engage in these activities.
5. In addition, instructors should model open and supportive communication skills. When trainers take a neutral position on multicultural issues, participants have a better chance to gain new insight through self-discovery (Parker and Schwartz, 2002).

While these tips for reducing anxiety are a great beginning for both teachers and students, there are other approaches trainers can apply to prepare for the emotional challenges that may be encountered from exposure to multicultural training experiences. Developing a respectful climate for learning multicultural competencies is essential for participants to express ideas and feelings without censure or negative evaluations (Adams, Bell, & Griffin, 1997). In addition, we recommend that trainees develop anxiety management skills and develop self-care resources as highlighted at the end of this chapter.

As the training progresses, it is important for you and your teachers to recognize guilt and shame reactions. Personal journal writing can help concretize your experiences as illustrated in Box 3.4.

Box 3.4

Here is a sample journal entry submitted at the conclusion of a MCC course from a white female graduate student (Anonymous, Reprinted with Permission).

The entire idea of white privilege was new to me this semester. I'm not sure I can say that I believed it existed prior to this class, until I realized that my complacency about racial issues and my denial of the importance of racial concerns was the defining characteristic of white privilege. From that point on, I made a concerted effort to explore the role of white privilege in my life and expand my experiential knowledge base accordingly. It was painful to me when I realized that I will never be able to truly understand the experiences of my ethnic minority friends and/or clients, and it caused guilt when I realized that the same social structures that make my life so comfortable cause pain and difficulty for so many other people. These emotions have motivated me to look at issues in a different way and to take time to try to understand the experiences of people of other cultures.

Suggestions for ways to assess and deal with shame experiences:

1. Observe any changes in your mood after each multicultural experience or activity.
2. Note that feelings of discomfort or resistance are normal to the change process.
3. Practice good listening skills for self and others.
4. Both trainers and trainees can contribute to building a supportive learning climate which fosters open and honest communication, respect, and builds self-confidence.
5. Arrange to meet privately with the leader when negative emotions are getting in the way of learning.

The Multicultural Mentoring Lab (MML)

It has been our observation that an additional outlet is needed for emotional expression because there is insufficient time during the regular class time to process the range of feelings generated in the classroom. Kiselica (1998) advised that additional measures be used to help students explore intense emotions resulting from exposure to multicultural training. Other educators, recognizing that diversity training is emotionally challenging, recommended that special efforts be made to create a supportive climate where trainees can process experiences safely (Carter, 2003; Rooney, Flores, and Mercier 1998).

We have found that small group experiences are one of the best ways to provide a supportive climate for learning and growth. It has been our experience that such a small group experience is handled after class as a lab where the instructor is not present. Such experiences can be conducted by advanced students or by other professionals not directly associated with the class. This procedure maximizes opportunity for the expression of sensitive thoughts and feelings generated from a variety of activities in multicultural training (Parker et al., 2004). A more detailed description of how the MML is conducted is included in Appendix B.

Understanding Power and Privilege

In this section we will elaborate further on dimensions of power and privilege and ways to motivate persons with privilege towards social action. Power, defined by Webster's dictionary, is the "ability to do or act; force, strength, authority, and influence." Power can be attained or ascribed through work roles (job descriptions), social demographic descriptors (gender, race, and sexual orientation), educational status (degrees), economic class (wealth), seniority, and systemic factors (such as history, tradition, hierarchy). Personal power taps into such qualities as energy level, charisma, personality type, and self-esteem/self-efficacy.

Privileges are the concrete ways that power is expressed, often unconsciously. A person from a nonprivileged group can identify the privileges of the dominant group more easily than members of the privileged group. Here are some examples: heterosexual privilege—public recognition of couple relationship with spousal benefits; white privilege—positive images are prevalent in media and history books, ability privilege—access to all public buildings and restrooms; economic privilege—housing and other basic necessities are met without worry; male privilege—walk at night without fear of rape.

However, the literature on power and privilege related to social oppressions offers another view on the meaning of privilege. Black and Stone (2005) summarized the literature that defines privilege with the following characteristics: "(1) Privilege is a special advantage; it is neither common nor universal; (2) it is granted, not earned or brought into being by one's individual effort or talent; (3) privilege is a right or entitlement that is related to a preferred status or rank; (4) privilege is exercised for the benefit of the recipient and to the exclusion or detriment of others; and (5) a privileged status is often outside of the awareness of the person possessing it" (p. 244).

The authors defined social privilege as "any entitlement, sanction, power, immunity, and advantage or right granted or conferred by the dominant group to a person or group solely by birthright membership in prescribed identities" (p. 245). An example of privilege is citizenship (usually ascribed by birth, but achievable through petition). Many U.S. citizens do not realize that to have a U.S. passport grants them mobility around the globe far beyond many other countries' passports.

Although power/privilege may be granted from a variety of sources, based upon the emphases in the literature, the authors suggested that social privilege is primarily granted through various combinations of race/ethnicity, gender, sexual orientation, economic status, age, differing degrees of physical ability, and religious affixation. Usually people have varying degrees of power/privilege on these dimensions. How do you know if you have privilege? If you haven't had to think about these dimensions, you probably have it! However, rather than think of power/privilege as unidimensional, it is multidimensional, interrelated, and complex.

Peggy McIntosh (1990) has described white privilege that operates on an unconscious basis. Sometimes people feel "entitled" to privileges and are threatened if other groups desire them. Strong reactions occur in response to social justice movements and may take the form of backlash. Sometimes people fear that they will lose power or privileges when others gain them (e.g., as if it's a "zero sum game" where one person's gain is another person's loss), and so they resist these challenges to power and control. For example, a current issue is the dismantling of affirmative actions programs.

Walker (2005), in a keynote address at a conference on domestic violence, challenged women "to resist the lies, stories, and social scripts that dehumanize women and perpetuate unjust power." One way this oppression is perpetuated is through unconscious consent. She suggested that women ask questions, "Who's telling the story? Who defines the relationship and whose interests does it serve? Who gets to name it? Who speaks and who listens?" And she encourages women to be "authors and authorizers of our own stories."

In reality, there are many situations of unequal power, but power is to be used constructively. Power differentials *per se* are acceptable when there is a mutual benefit for all involved. When power becomes exploitive, people are oppressed. Having power brings with it responsibility, to be good stewards of power and to transcend the human inclination to be self-serving and greedy. More often than not people will deny that they have power because it is uncomfortable to be *called on it.* Even so, it is human nature to be unconsciously comfortable with privilege and react when privileges are threatened. This seems somewhat paradoxical. Is there any way to claim power in a positive way, not in a way that is corrupting?

Most people have varying degrees of power and privilege in many aspects of their lives, and some groups have significantly more or less power systemically. We suggest that you complete the "Oppression Sensitivity Self-Rating Exercise" located in Box 3.5.

Box 3.5

Oppression Sensitivity Self-Rating Exercise

All human relations, including counseling, occur within a sociopolitical context that influences perceptions, attitudes and behaviors. After rating yourself on the items below, consider the impact of these social constructs on the process and relationship of counseling, supervision, and your educational experiences.

Directions: Circle the number which represents your sense of privilege on each of these constructs. You may add constructs to the list below.

	Oppressed									*Privileged*
Education	1	2	3	4	5	6	7	8	9	10
Race	1	2	3	4	5	6	7	8	9	10
Ethnicity	1	2	3	4	5	6	7	8	9	10
Gender	1	2	3	4	5	6	7	8	9	10
Age	1	2	3	4	5	6	7	8	9	10
Sexual Orientation	1	2	3	4	5	6	7	8	9	10
Religion	1	2	3	4	5	6	7	8	9	10
Spirituality	1	2	3	4	5	6	7	8	9	10
Health/ Ability	1	2	3	4	5	6	7	8	9	10
Body Size	1	2	3	4	5	6	7	8	9	10

Physical Appearance	1	2	3	4	5	6	7	8	9	10
Economic Class	1	2	3	4	5	6	7	8	9	10
Computer Literacy	1	2	3	4	5	6	7	8	9	10
Linguistic Abilities	1	2	3	4	5	6	7	8	9	10
Physical Environment	1	2	3	4	5	6	7	8	9	10
Relationship Status	1	2	3	4	5	6	7	8	9	10
Birth Order	1	2	3	4	5	6	7	8	9	10
_____	1	2	3	4	5	6	7	8	9	10
_____	1	2	3	4	5	6	7	8	9	10

Source: Adapted from Continuing Education Workshop titled Race and Gender Issues in Supervision: Beyond PC by Gina Early and Herb Steier (1994).

Discussion Questions

1. In which areas of my life do I have power/privilege?
2. In which areas of my life do I feel relatively oppressed?
3. How do multiple sources of privilege/oppression interact with each other?
4. How do social contexts influence your sense of power/privilege? Explore counseling, supervision and educational types of experiences.
5. In what areas of my life do I experience any guilt or shame, and how can I constructively attend to these feelings?

Sometimes these social cultural constructs are hidden, such as in the case of some disabilities, sexual orientation, or religion. For example, Kim was a 35-year-old married man of mixed ethnic heritage. He worked as a school counselor for seven years before he felt it necessary to tell his principal that he had Multiple Sclerosis, and that his health condition was such that he may need to ask for accommodation in the workplace. His supervisor was supportive and she discussed with him how he wanted to handle disclosure of his needs to the rest of the staff.

Motivating Persons with Privilege towards Social Action

One way to respond to social inequities is to ask, "How can I use my power and privilege to better the situation for someone who does not have it?" Goodman (2001) identified three major ways to motivate people with privilege to act for social change: (1) develop empathy, (2) acknowledge moral principles and spiritual values, and (3) tap into self-interest, ranging from an individualistic *me* to a mutuality of *you and me* to an interdependent *us*. Oppression is maintained by intentional suppression of empathy, which is achieved by dehumanizing and making *the other* feel unworthy and less than deserving of full respect. Cultivating empathy and compassion is one way of reaching persons with privilege, but other means work as well. Sometimes self-interest is a good starting point. Begin with what people care about. People will take actions that involve the least amount of personal sacrifice, e.g., sign a petition versus writing a letter to the editor. However, starting with actions that are not so risky, concrete and doable may be more effective in the long run than trying to convert people to a cause.

Individuals and groups can take small or big steps towards social justice, ranging from individual acts to becoming social advocates or allies for persons with less power. Before describing the steps on how to become an ally, there are some preliminary activities that can involve people who may be interested but are not ready to make a full commitment to a particular social issue. Goodman (2006) noted that people who buy into a paradigm of hierarchy (up/down relationships) lack a vision of what it means to share resources and to have equity; they fear being dominated in return if they give up power and control. If they lack a frame of reference, it is necessary to move gently and to create an opening to begin where people are. She offered the following tips:

- Use language that makes sense to the audience (e.g., science for psychology faculty, hip-hop for youth).
- Create safety in order for participants not to shut down.
- Form a relationship and find the growth edge.
- Promote exploration and self-reflection.
- Build on all levels towards a more genuine commitment.

She explained that it is threatening to really look at oneself and to radically question one's identity and world view. When dealing with resistance, she suggested strategies including: research the problem, investigate, use curiosity, argue both sides of issues, and sometimes, find places to work out some of these feelings privately, such as in race based affinity groups (e.g., people of color, white allies).

Finding language that fits a target audience is an essential first step. Melvin Peters, a college educator, uses hip-hop to reach urban youth to raise consciousness about oppression. Hip-hop culture began in the streets in the early 1970s in New York City. Some trace rap music back to the spoken word poetry scene of the late sixties, while many go even further back to the oral tradition of African societies. Hip-hop and rap music is a popular vehicle for understanding today's youth generation, although it has been exploited through the media and marketing (Peters, 2006). For a positive sample, see Box 3.6.

Box 3.6

I Can, **from the Album,** *God's Son* **by Nas**

[B]e, be, 'fore we came to this country
We were kings and queens, never porch monkeys.
It was empires in Africa called Kush
Timbuktu, where every race came to get books
To learn from Black teachers who taught Greeks and Romans
Asian Arabs and gave them gold when
Gold was converted to money it all changed
Money then became empowerment for Europeans
The Persian military invaded
They learned about the gold, the teachings and everything sacred
Africa was almost robbed naked
Slavery was money, so they began making slave ships . . .
If the truth is told, the youth can grow
They learn to survive until they gain control
Nobody says you have to be gangstas, hoes
Read more, learn more, change the globe . . .

Source: Retrieved March 15, 2006 from http://www.ohhla.com/anonymous/nas/gods_son/i_can.nas.txt

---

Suggested Activity

1. Identify an area of privilege.
2. Identify an issue that you have worked on to help those less privileged in that domain.
3. Discuss what has motivated you. (Goodman, 2006)

How to Become an Ally

Although there are many small steps that people can take towards a more equitable society, the role of *ally* offers opportunities and support for social justice work for those who feel that they would like to make more of a commitment. Persons working against oppression see that it is in everyone's best interest to end oppression; it's not just for those who are targeted by oppression. Examples include being a heterosexual ally (to resist homophobia), white ally (to challenge racism), a feminist male (to confront sexism), and so on. Desired qualities for allies are described in Box 3.7.

Box 3.7

Wall and Evans (1999) have described important qualities for allies. They suggest the following:

- Know yourself in terms of the issue at hand, as well as understanding the specific oppression. For example, a LGBT ally needs to understand homophobia and heterosexism (both internalized and in society, at large).
- Choose the issue willingly; do not do it because it is "politically correct."
- Become an ally to meet your own self-interest. Taking on the role of ally entails commitment and personal growth.
- Celebrate small successes and accept making mistakes; this will help prevent feeling overwhelmed and burned-out.
- Have a sense of humor.
- Initiate changes towards personal, institutional, and societal justice.

In the remainder of this section, we will describe the costs of oppression, the benefits of unlearning oppression, actions that lead towards social justice, and working with oppressions issues in therapy.

Costs of Oppression

It is obvious to minorities and other targets of oppression (e.g., women) that oppression hurts, emotionally, economically, socially, and spiritually. But what is the cost for those in power? Why would whites want to do something about racism, or men want to do something about sexism, for example?

Here are some examples of the emotional costs of oppression to those in power:

1. **Fear.** People live in fear of retaliation, or of losing control of resources, even at the most basic level of "survival." This anxiety seems to operate often at the unconscious level.
2. **Shame, guilt, and denial.** Mental health professionals know how unhealthy it is for people to keep secrets around issues of betrayal, hurt and wounding. Social oppressions operate in a similar fashion. Feelings of shame effectively silence voices that need to be heard for healing (Tatum, 1997).
3. **A false sense of superiority and self-esteem.** Building oneself up at the expense of others is like building a house on sand. Just as minorities need to redefine themselves to counteract negative stereotypes, those in the "majority" will be healthier if they build a sense of self on personal qualities and not unearned privilege.
4. **Social isolation and distance from those who are different.** Some years ago, Bill Cosby made a short film called "The Bigot." He portrayed hateful attitudes towards every possible social group, and in the end, he was all alone.
5. **Sameness is boring.** Whereas it can be comforting to be with others with whom one shares commonalities, it can be stifling and unnecessarily restrictive always to be living in "sameness." There is an equally natural impulse to be attracted to differences for the sake of growth and getting beyond oneself.

Benefits of Unlearning Oppression

One of the major issues of oppression is feeling powerless, whether you are a target or not. By learning how to be an ally, you can develop a sense of personal power. An obvious benefit of being an ally is to enable change to happen on issues of social importance, and spiritually speaking, to relieve suffering. By engaging at this level, one learns the meaning of compassion. There are many rewards for persons with power to work on reducing oppression and equalizing privileges. Some of the benefits of being an ally include personal growth dimensions, such as the following:

1. Unlearning internalized oppression. For example, homophobia restricts gender role behavior; by encountering internalized rules

about what a man or woman can or cannot do, one becomes freer in terms of gender role.

2. Expanding one's sense of friends and community. By unlearning racism/prejudice, one's sense of community is enhanced, for example, to live in an integrated neighborhood, enjoy diverse music and foods, and celebrate diverse holidays.
3. Developing a positive (anti-racist) white identity is a way not to feel shame.
4. Seeing the world through different perspectives, gaining from diversity rather than being diminished by it.
5. Increasing compassion for the ways social oppression may be hurtful to self and others.

Consider this journal entry from a Chinese International student who visited a LGBT student meeting as part of a diversity homework assignment. "My personal experiences also informed me that this is a very rewarding process and definitely helps me to become a better human being. I remember the night after I attended the LGBT Assembly, I had a new but wonderful feeling of joy in my heart as being able to expand my own being, to acknowledge, respect and associate with people who in a sense differ from me significantly" (Anonymous, Reprinted by permission).

Box 3.8

Suggested activity: Here is a prejudice reduction exercise that may be useful in clarifying your experience as a target of oppression. Answer the following questions about one of your social reference groups (e.g., being a male, being white, being gay, being disabled, etc). Share this information with others in a trusting environment. Ideally, meet in similar reference groups before sharing with others.

• What I like about being a member of my group.
• What I find difficult about being a member of my group.
• What I wish I'd never hear said again about my group.

Source: Adapted from Re-Evaluation Counseling, United to End Racism, Internalized Oppression, Available online at http://www.rc.org/uer/index.html.

Actions That Lead Towards Social Justice

Having gone through a process of deciding to become an ally, the question remains, "what can I do?" Tatum (1997) suggests that people begin with their own "sphere of influence" when considering actions, that is, start with the people that you know in areas in your life where you have power and influence.

Graduate students enrolled in a multicultural course were asked this question, "What would you like from an ally?" Here are some of their responses that offer concrete suggestions.

On issues of gender oppression:

- Strive for salary equity and equal opportunity in hiring practices.
- Eliminate sexual objectification of women, reduce focus on women's bodies in the media; encourage participation of both genders in the classroom setting.
- Eliminate sexual assault/rape; a male ally can help by speaking out against sexual violence and encourage other men 1) to get consent for sex and 2) to refrain from making jokes or comments that treat women as though they are less than fully human.

On issues of homophobia, prejudice and discrimination related to sexual orientation:

- Use terms that are neutral and inclusive, such as partner instead of husband/wife.
- Add sexual orientation to anti-discrimination laws (institutional policies, community and state laws)
- Join a Friends of LGBT's program on campus.
- Interrupt anti-LGBT jokes, comments, or actions.
- Do not assume that everyone is heterosexual.

On issues related to religious intolerance:

- Understand the cultural and religious beliefs and experiences of minority religions in the U.S., such as Islam, Judaism, or Krishna's, especially those that are feared through ignorance.
- Encourage interfaith discussions and look for common ground even amidst religious differences.

On issues related to economic oppression:

- Shop from socially conscious businesses.
- Strive for equal allocation of resources.
- Volunteer for a homeless shelter.
- Support a living wage.

Concerned mental health professionals, including educators, trainers, professors, and practitioners, have collaboratively shared materials about what they are doing for social justice. Actions vary and include some of the following ideas:

- Develop web sites which advocate for social justice.
- Develop community action networks at the local level, e.g., anti-racism coalition.
- Provide pro bono work in community-based projects.
- Bring these issues to the attention of colleagues at professional conferences.
- Develop curriculum materials which incorporate social justice issues.
- Make systemic changes in institutional policies and procedures. (Pedersen, 2004)

Working with Oppression Issues in Therapy

Empowering clients is a central theme in therapy. Finding and expressing one's authentic voice is a common therapeutic goal. Resisting cultural imperatives that violate human dignity (examples, fat phobia, sexism, and other -isms) are important regardless of one's gender, race, and ethnicity. Raising these issues in a therapeutic context is consistent with narrative therapy and oppression sensitive therapy, developed by colleagues at Gainesville Family Institute (Early, Nazario, & Steier, 1994). From a Jungian perspective, clients are supported in shedding a false self for a more authentic self.

Perhaps another way to say this is to suggest that by resisting oppression personally and politically, one is strengthened psychologically and spiritually. This process is another step towards strengthening goodness in self and society. The very nature of oppression is corruptive and damaging for the oppressor as well as victims. In doing so, counselors may be co-collaborators in confronting forces that exploit and damage the human spirit. Addressing social justice issues is intrinsically spiritual empowering regardless of measured outcome. It is the very act itself that matters. In the words of Coretta Scott King, "Struggle is a never-ending process. Freedom is never really won; you earn it and win it in every generation."

Fortunately, there are many sources for spiritual replenishment, for example, socially engaged Buddhism (Retrieved February 16, 2006 from http://www.dharmanet.org/engaged.html), teachings of Thich Nhat Hanh (1992), most world religions (see Huston Smith, 2001), and transpersonal psychology for the secular humanists (Cortright, 1997).

Cultural anthropologist Angeles Arrien (1993) recommends four steps for being a spiritual warrior:

- Show up.
- Pay attention.
- Speak your truth.
- Do not be attached to outcome.

It is easy to feel discouraged in working against oppression because it is not an immediate gratification exercise. Nevertheless, it is important to maintain hope. From the words of The Rev. Martin Luther King, Jr. ". . . the arc of the moral universe is long, but it bends toward justice."

SUMMARY

It is easy to understand how the need to cover didactic course content can overshadow the importance of dealing with emotional expression. Intense emotions resulting from exposure to multicultural training still exist. It is clear that counselors must gain awareness of emotional reactions resulting from exposure to experiences in MCC training. These experiences, particularly shame may result in a loss of empathy and a disconnected stance towards multiculturalism. If these experiences are not identified and worked through using a variety of consciousness-raising activities, then trainees may run the risk of gaining limited MCC skills (Parker & Schwartz, 2002).

Multicultural specialists have recommended that special efforts be made to create a supportive atmosphere where trainees can process experiences safely (Rooney, Flores and Mercier, 1998). The use of a small group approach designed to enhance personal growth of trainees provides opportunities for expression of emotions (Parker et al., 2004). The MML invites expression of feelings without fear of being judged by instructors or by class members. It is through the MML that student trainees are able to express feelings they do not feel safe to express in a larger group.

In addition, increasing your understanding of power and privilege and becoming personally empowered on issues of social justice are constructive ways to work through negative emotions. Learning how to be an ally is an option in which many mental health professionals have engaged as a positive response to social oppression. It is normal to be imperfect and to make mistakes in unlearning oppression and learning how to become an ally. We suggest that you make forgiving yourself and others a common practice. Personal growth and change on these issues is a lifelong journey.

Finally, we recommend that social justice advocates have spiritual grounding, a way to gain perspective and to feel nurtured. Without replenishment, social advocates run the risk at minimum of burnout, and at worst they have the potential to become perpetrators also. A simple example is when peace marchers become violent out of anger and frustration.

Suggested Activities

1. Journal writing: reflect upon childhood experiences with family and community's sources of "pride and shame." Identify emotional triggers.
2. Learn calming skills, self-soothing, such as meditation and other centering activities
3. List ten things that you can do that promote self-care that are easy and accessible.
4. Reverse roles and spend a day in the shoes of a person who lives with daily oppression, e.g., straight-gay, disability, person of color, homeless.
5. Attend an event, rally, or march on a social issue, such as civil rights
6. Write a letter to the editor related to local community issues.
7. Join an organization that is a advocate for social causes.
8. Interview someone who is a known "ally" for a particular cause.
9. Read *Nickel and Dimed* by Barbara Ehrenreich

Web Sites of Interest

Heart Centered Therapies: Healing Shame—Individual and Cultural http://www.heartcenteredtherapies.org/public_documents/Healing %20Shame.html

Psychologists Acting with Conscience Together
http://www.psyact.org
National Institute for Multicultural Competence
http://www.coedu.usf.edu/zalaquett/nimc/nimc.html
Journal for Social Action in Counseling and Psychology (JSACP), an
official publication of Psychologists for Social Responsibility (PsySR)
and Counselors for Social Justice (CSJ)
www.psysr.org/social-action.htm

REFERENCES

Adams, M., Bell, L.A., & Griffin, P. (Eds). (1997). *Teaching for diversity and social justice: A source-book*. New York: Routledge.

Arrien, A. (1993). *The Four-fold way: Walking the paths of the warrior, teacher, healer, and visionary.* New York: HarperCollins.

Black, L. L. & Stone, D. (2005). Expanding the definition of privilege: The concept of social privilege. *Journal of Multicultural Counseling and Development, 33,* 243–255.

Carter, R.T. (2003). Becoming racially and culturally competent. The racial-cultural counseling laboratory. *Journal of Multicultural Counseling and Development, 31,* 20–30.

Corey, G. (1995). *Group counseling* (4th Ed.). Pacific Grove, CA: Brooks/Cole.

Cortright, B. (1997). *Psychotherapy and spirit: Theory and practice in transpersonal psychotherapy.* Albany, NY: State University of New York Press.

Corwin, S.A. & Wiggins, M.W.(1989). An antiracism training model for white professionals. *Journal of Multicultural Counseling and Development, 17,* 105–114.

Early, G., Nazario, A., & Steier, H. (1994, April). *Oppression sensitive family therapy: A health affirming model.* American Orthopsychiatric Association. Washington, DC.

Fukuyama, M. & Franklin, L. (1996). Power, privilege, and predicaments. *Student Affairs Update, 21* (3), 7.

Goodman, D. J. (2001). *Promoting diversity and social justice: Educating people from privileged groups.* Thousand Oaks, CA: Sage.

Goodman, D. J. (2006, February). *Motivating people from privileged groups to promote social justice.* Workshop presented at the 23rd Annual Teachers College Winter Roundtable on Cultural Psychology and Education. New York.

Hanh, T. N. (1992). *Peace is in every step: The path of mindfulness in everyday life.* New York: Bantam.

Harder, D.W. & Lewis, S.J. (1986). The assessment of shame and guilt. In J.N. Butcher & C.D. Spielberger (Eds.), *Advances in Personality Assessment,* Vol. 6 (pp. 89–114). Hillsdale, NJ: Erlbaum.

Helms, J.E. (1990). *Black and White Racial-Identity: Theory, Research and Practice.* New York: Greenwood.

Helms, J. E. (1995). An update of white and people of color racial identity model. In J. G. Ponterotto, J. M. Casas, L. A., Suzuki, & C. M. Alexander (Eds.), *Handbook of Multicultural Counseling* (pp. 181–198). Thousand Oaks, CA: Sage.

Hoffman, M.L. (1984). Interactions of affect and cognition in empathy. In C.E. Izard, J. Kagan & R. Zajonc (Eds), *Emotions, Cognition, and Behavior* (pp. 103–131). Cambridge University Press.

Janoff-Bulman, R. (1979). Character logical versus behavioral self-blame: Inquiries into depression and rape. *Journal of Personality and Social Psychology, 37,* 1798–1809.

Kiselica, M.S. (1998). Preparing Anglos for the challenges and joys of multiculturalism. *The Counseling Psychologist, 26,* 5–21.

Lewis, H.B. (1987). Shame and the narcissistic personality. In D.L. Nathanson (Ed.), *The Many Faces of Shame* (pp. 93–132). New York: Guilford Press.

McIntosh, P. (2001). White privilege: Unpacking the invisible knapsack. In. P.S. Rothenberg, *Race, class, and gender in the United States* (5th Ed). (pp. 163-168). New York: Worth Publishers.

Parker, W.M., & Schwartz, R.C. (2002). On the experience of shame in multicultural counseling: Implications for white counselors-in-training. *British Journal of Guidance & Counseling, 30* (3), 311–318.

Parker, W. M., Freytes, M., & Kaufman, C. J. (2004).The Mentoring Lab: A small group approach for managing emotions from multicultural counselor training. *The Journal of Specialists in Group Work, 29,* 361–375.

Pedersen, P. (Ed). (2004, Oct 12). Advocating multiculturalism and social justice: A synthesis. (email communication)

Peters, M. (2006, February). *The educating spoken word: The classroom use of poetry and hip hop.* Paper presentation at the 5th Annual Southeastern Conference on Cross-cultural Issues in Counseling and Education, Savannah, GA.

Ponterotto, J.G. (1988). Racial consciousness development among white counselor trainees: A stage model. *Journal of Multicultural Counseling and Development, 16,* 146–156.

Rooney, S.C., Flores, L.Y., & Mercier, C.A. (1998). Making multicultural education effective for everyone. *The Counseling Psychologist, 26,* 22–32.

Smith, H. (2001). *Why religion matters: The fate of the human spirit in an age of disbelief.* New York: HarperCollins.

Tangney , P. (1990). Assessing individual differences in proneness to shame and guilt: development of the self-conscious affect and attribution inventory. *Journal of Personality and Social Psychology, 59,* 102–111.

Tangney, J.P. (1992). Situational determinants of shame and guilt in young adulthood. *Personality and Social Psychology Bulletin, 18,* 199–206.

Tatum, B.D. (1999). *Why are all the Black kids sitting together in the cafeteria? And other conversations about race.* New York: Basic Books

Wall, V. A. & Evans, N. J. (Eds.) (1999). *Toward acceptance: Sexual orientation issues on campus.* Lanham, MD: University Press of America.

Walker, M. (2005, May 4). *Power and effectiveness: Envisioning an alternative paradigm.* Keynote address at the GCOSW 24th Annual Conference, Gainesville, FL.

Wicker, F.W., Payne, G.C. & Morgan, R.D. (1983). Participant descriptions of guilt and shame. *Motivation and Emotion, 7,* 25–39.

Yalom, I.D. (1995). *The theory and practice of group psychotherapy* (4th Ed). New York: Basic Books.

Chapter 4

RACIAL IDENTITY DEVELOPMENT

A race is a nice thing to have.
Janet Helms (1992)

Abstract

This chapter provides an overview of two models of racial identity development—for persons of color and white people, with discussion of applications in research, training and clinical practice. Experiential learning activities such as developing action plans are presented to underscore how understanding this construct is essential for becoming competent in MCC.

INTRODUCTION

The use of language related to race is about empowerment. Groups, which have a history of disenfranchisement and negative stereotypes, are particularly sensitive to choice of words to describe them, and African Americans are no exception. Over centuries, descendents of enslaved Africans have formed their identities in response to an oppressive society. Within the past 30 years, we have observed the following labels evolve: colored (in some circles, considered a derogatory term), Negro, black, African American, and Person of Color. In some regions of the country, some terms are favored over others. We have chosen the term *black* to refer to persons of African descent who are part of the African Diaspora. Black is a more inclusive term in our community where there are persons from the Caribbean who are visible ethnic minorities but may not identify as African American.

An important theme in MCC literature is racial, ethnic, and cultural identity development. Early models of racial identity development focused on the experiences of being black or a person of color in a white racist society (Atkinson, Morten and Sue, 1979; Cross, 1971; Helms, 1984). The early models of racial identity development were designed to help counselors in general, and white counselors in particular, to understand the different attitudes, feelings and behaviors of ethnic minority persons living in an oppressive white-dominated society. These models subsequently were revised (Helms, 1995; Sue & Sue, 1999) and new ones developed. Identity development theories were created around such cultural variables as biracial identity (Poston, 1990), sexual orientation (McCarn & Fassinger, 1996), gender (Downing & Roush, 1985), and multiple identities (Greene, 1997). Race and culture were viewed as intertwined constructs that were central for understanding psychological health (Carter, 2005). These models assisted mental health professionals in understanding within-group differences, selecting appropriate counseling interventions, and matching counselors and clients.

In this chapter, we will review the definitions and history of racial identity development, discuss implications of racial identity for counseling and research, describe two models of racial identity development: the Racial/Cultural Identity Development (R/CID) model (Sue & Sue, 1999) and the White Racial Identity Development (WRID) model (Helms, 1995), and discuss applications for counseling and training.

Definitions and History

Racial and ethnic identities are terms used in a variety of ways in multicultural counseling literature. Helms (1990) declared that the terms race and ethnicity are used incorrectly interchangeably. Racial identity was defined as the quality of an individual's identification with a specific racial group in which he or she perceives a "common heritage" (Helms, 1990, p. 3). As discussed in Chapter 1, race is a socially constructed concept, which only has meaning within a stratified society that favors one group above others. Although the biological bases for race are disputed, it remains a powerful psychosocial force. As such, race has more to do with racism (power and privilege) than ethnicity does. Race and ethnicity are overlapping constructs but in this chapter, we focus on identity formation in the context of *race* attributions. However, members of various oppressed cultural groups may go through a similar process of identity formation as persons of color, for example, LGBTs, women, and persons with disabilities.

With regards to counseling, racial identity theory was used as a model for understanding the interpersonal dynamics that occur in cross-racial relationships (Helms, 1984). Helms stated that this definition is designed for both black and white racial identity. Therefore, black racial identity attempts to explain the extent blacks identify with other blacks and/or adopt or abandon identities resulting from racial victimization (Helms, 1990). Additionally, she stated that white racial identity theories attempt to explain various ways that white people can identify or not identify with other whites in developing a nonoppressive white identity.

Racial identity is described as a developmental process in which a person moves from one level of identity to another. The stages are influenced by sociopolitical factors such as racism and prejudice (Sue and Sue, 1990). In addition, many racial identity theories propose that various kinds of resolutions can exist within racial groups. Consequently, racial awareness usually is not dichotomous, present or absent, but rather polytomous, that is, multidimensional (Helms, 1990). Helms and Piper (1994) modified the model of white racial identity development by changing stage to *status*. This change occurred to reflect the fluidity or dynamic nature of racial identity that may occur in a nonlinear fashion.

Early original contributors to racial identity development theory were black scholars such as Hall, Cross, and Freedle (1972) whose works were influenced by the social conditions of African Americans in the 1960s. They described some of the early attempts of racial identity development models as consisting of subcategories or types most often based on political views. Some models were considered conservative while others were labeled militant (i.e., challenging the status quo). Vontress (1971) developed one of the first models. He described African Americans in three designated groups based on their response to living in an oppressive and racist society. They were: (1) colored, (2) Negro, and (3) black. Individuals were placed in these types depending on the extent the black person identified with his or her racial group versus his or her identification with the white dominant culture.

These typologies were criticized for unfairly labeling a group in a fixed manner as if these characteristics were immutable personality traits rather than responses to being victimized by social and political forces within a white-dominated society. In fact, Helms (1985) pointed out several limitations of this typology: (1) it blames the individual rather than the system; (2) it becomes outdated as societal issues change; (3) it assumes that identity development follows a linear direction; and (4) it treats stages as though they were fixed and static rather than dynamic and evolving. As theories evolved, ethnic minority attitudes were seen as flexible and connected to their identity development statuses through which they may pass. The individual was no longer labeled or viewed as a fixed personality type.

One of the earlier applications of racial identity development to counseling was advanced by William Cross (1971). In this original work, he described the *Negro-to-Black Conversion Experience* as a path towards liberation. The model was later developed into the *Nigrescence Model* (Cross, 1978). Cross's four-stage model included (1) preencounter, (2) encounter, (3) immersion/emersion, and (4) internalization. In the *pre-encounter* stage, Blacks see the world from a non-black or from an anti-black perspective. In stage two, *encounter,* black individuals begin to understand the meaning of being black and begin to see themselves as black persons. In the third stage, *immersion/emersion* stage, the individuals become totally immersed in their blackness and reject non-black values, becoming totally involved in exploring their black culture. In stage four, *internalization,* black individuals become more secure in their identity as black persons and begin to rethink some of their earlier attitudes and behaviors in a positive direction. Cross (1991) added a fifth stage, *internalization-commitment,* in which the individual's commitment to civil rights, social justice and social change are identified. Such an individual's commitment goes far beyond rhetoric to taking specific actions.

Implications of Racial Identity for Counseling and Research

Identifying the client's stage or status in racial identity development may be useful in counseling for these reasons:

• Racial identity influences the degree of engagement of clients in the counseling process, the extent to which they will use counseling services, the evaluation and treatment of problems, and the assessment of outcomes.

- Racial identity for some clients determines what they view as a problem, how they respond to it, what they perceive as helpful, and what treatment strategies or interventions they prefer.
- Knowledge of racial identity facilitates the process of assessing the client, conceptualizing the problem, forming a therapeutic alliance, and selecting and executing a culturally relevant counseling intervention.
- Because a therapist's intrapsychic or interpersonal life is shaped by many factors such as race, ethnicity, gender, and sexual orientation, therapy may be ineffective if these factors are excluded from the therapeutic process.
- Racial identity provides a platform by which helping professionals can examine many of the "-isms." Being mentally healthy is facilitated by a positive sense of engagement of one's own racial/cultural group.

Finally, racial identity facilitates the counselor's ability to view the individual as unique in the context of his/her group memberships (Personal communication, Angela Ferguson, July 17, 2005).

Racial identity continues to be researched from a variety of perspectives including acculturation, clinical assessment, training, counseling competencies, and ethics (Carter, 2005). We mention a sampling of studies here. Burkard, Juarez-Huffaker, and Ajmere (2003) found a significant interaction between race of the counselor and white racial identity attitudes. Another study found that white racial identity influences working alliance formation regardless of the race of the client (Burkard, Ponterotto, Reynolds, & Alfonso, 1999). Vinson and Neimeyer (2003) found a significant relationship between trainee's racial identity development and increased multicultural competences. In particular, their study showed that both white and non-white students reported an increase in multicultural knowledge and skills and awareness over a two-year period.

Abrams and Trusty (2004) examined the relationship between racial identity development and social desirability of African American college students. They found that participants tended to select the more advanced or socially desirable racial identity statuses, i.e., internalization and internalization-commitment stages, rather than the early stages of racial identity, i.e., preencounter and encounter. Researchers should be aware that respondents often like to make favorable impressions; therefore, use caution in the interpretation of results.

Broadening perspectives at another level, Sciarra, Chang, McLean, & Wong (2005) conducted a pilot study on white racial identity and attitudes towards people with disabilities. Results showed positive correlations between higher racial/ethnic identity statuses measured by Helms & Carter's (1990) White Racial Identity Attitude Scales (WRIAS) and positive attitudes towards persons with disabilities in a sample of white counseling graduate students. They concluded, "cultural identities that are intricately linked to issues of power and privilege may be related across domains" (p. 240).

Suyemoto (2004) suggested that therapists who work with multiracial clients who present with multiracial issues should normalize their experiences of multiple identities and avoid pressuring the individual to choose only one identity. Therapists could reframe the multicultural experience by focusing on positive adaptations to being multiracial rather than emphasizing social exclusion. She suggests that therapists should develop models, measures and strategies for multiracial people that do not adhere to U.S. racial/ethnic categorization. This topic will be discussed further in Chapter 8.

We will present two models that are representative of identity development in the context of an oppressive society, in which one group is dominant and *the others* are subordinate. First, we describe the Racial/Cultural Identity Model (R/CID) that applies to people of color (Sue & Sue, 1999), and secondly, the White Racial Identity Development WRID model, as originally proposed by Janet Helms (1984) and subsequently revised (Helms, 1995).

Two Models of Racial Identity Development

Several models of racial identity were designed to understand the racial identity development of black Americans. The need to expand racial models to include ethnic groups other than blacks became apparent. To fill this void in training, research, and treatment, Atkinson, Morten, and Sue (1979) developed the Minority Identity Development Model (MID). These scholars attempted to develop a model that would include the major ethnic minority groups, including Asian Americans, Hispanic Americans, American Indians, African Americans and other ethnic groups who share a common experience of oppression as a result of living in a white-dominated racist society. Their belief was that these groups would develop attitudes, feelings, and behaviors along developmental stages similar to African Americans in the Cross (1971; 1978) model.

Sue and Sue (1990, 1999) revised the MID to become the Racial/Cultural Identity Development Model (R/CID) to include broader populations. The R/CID identifies five stages that people encounter in their attempt to understand themselves and the relationship between the minority and the dominant culture. The five stages are conformity, dissonance, resistance and immersion, introspection and integrative awareness. This model parallels Helms' (1995) Person of Color racial identity model, which will be discussed further in Chapter 8.

Each identity stage is accompanied by four sets of beliefs and attitudes: (1) how one feels about self; (2) how one feels about others in same race/ethnicity group; (3) how one feels about members of other racial/ethnic minority groups; and (4) how one feels toward whites. The interaction of these factors formulates the five-stage model briefly described below.

Racial/Cultural Identity Development (R/CID)

Stage 1: Conformity Stage. Ethnic minority persons in this stage prefer the values of the dominant white culture. They would like to be accepted by and be a part of the white society. On the other hand, they hold negative attitudes and feelings toward their own racial/ethnic group. In general, they conform to the values and wishes of the dominant culture.

Stage 2: Dissonance Stage. An ethnic minority person who might encounter a negative racial experience with a white person or a positive experience with a member of his or her ethnic group may trigger the dissonance stage. During this transition stage, the ethnic minority individual begins to question his or her earlier attitudes toward the white majority as well as previous negative attitudes toward other ethnic minorities. The individual in this transition stage is often confused and may seek counseling.

Stage 3: Resistance and Immersion Stage. In this stage, ethnic minorities totally involve themselves in their own culture, accepting their cultural values and rejecting the norms and values of the white dominant society. These persons often hold negative attitudes and feelings toward other minority persons they believe to be co-opted by the dominant white system. They may encounter serious conflicts with conformity stage persons as well as persons from the dominant culture.

Stage 4: Introspection Stage. This stage is characterized by deeper thoughts and questions about previously held ideas about their own ethnic group as well as those of the white majority. Here, individuals begin to consider individual differences as well as differences between and within ethnic minority groups. The ethnic minority person begins to make decisions about racial/ethnic identity more independently.

Stage 5: Integrative Awareness Stage. In this stage, individuals become more secure in their racial identity. They not only feel proud of their own racial/ethnic group but also are open to building coalitions with members of the dominant white culture. Their general goal is to promote interracial and intercultural understanding and to treat all culturally diverse groups in a respectful manner.

Box 4.1

The following case example illustrates how these different stages may be found in the same family.

Anthony (Tony) is a tall, handsome 17-year-old black male who is a graduating high school senior from a predominantly white high school in suburban Washington, DC. Tony's parents are middle-class professional people, one works for the federal government and the other teaches school in the public school system.

While Tony has been a model student in every way, his behavior has taken an unexpected turn, characterized by skipping classes, acting disrespectfully toward his teachers, withdrawing, and showing many signs of discontent.

Within the past few months there have been many discussions regarding plans for Tony to attend college next fall. Tony's parents believe that Tony should attend a predominantly black college similar to the ones they attended as undergraduates. They believe that by attending a historically black college/university (HBCU), he would build a strong self-concept and a healthier black racial identity.

To familiarize him with these black colleges, Tony's parents planned their vacation around visitations to black colleges in the South. In addition, Tony's father has taken him to several lectures that focused on supporting black college education. He often explained to Tony that the black college was the place where black people can best understand who they are and where they are going. Tony, on the other hand, wished that his parents would realize that the *Black Pride* movement in which they participated as undergraduates is no longer as relevant to young people today as it was when they were growing up.

Tony has lived most of his life in the presence of white individuals or groups except for occasional visits from his cousins from the south. He wonders how he would feel on a predominantly black college campus. Would black students enjoy tossing the Frisbee as with his white friends? Would black students appreciate the same music and TV shows? Thoughts of being around so many black people caused him to shudder and to feel somewhat anxious. His closest friends are white, whether his parents like it or not.

Tony's older sister is somewhat different from Tony. A year ago, she decided to attend Tuskegee, a historically black college in Alabama. She had always encouraged her parents to move to inner city D.C. which is mostly black. She made it her business to associate with the few black students in her high school and had always stayed in tune with issues related to the black community. She believes that black people are victims of an insensitive and racist society. Otherwise, the quality of life of black people would be vastly improved. She feels guilty that she lives so comfortably in suburbia while other blacks undergo so much suffering, pain and hardship.

On the other hand, Tony believes that segregation is past history and black colleges are relics of that past. Further, he believes that black people need take more responsibility for their actions and stop using race as a crutch. From Tony's perspective, skills, abilities, and economics transcend race. Frankly, he thinks that greater educational opportunities exist in white institutions with broader course offerings and greater possibilities for networking; in general, they are the places most suitable for preparing students of all races for the future.

Discussion Questions

Discuss each of the following questions as though you were making a presentation in a case conference or in an individual or a group supervision session:

1. Identify and discuss briefly the presenting problem
2. Briefly describe the history of the client's presenting problem.
3. Describe the sociocultural context from whence the client comes.

4. Briefly discuss the level of support you can either observe or hypothesize from the client's family, relatives, friends, peers and significant others.
5. What is your assessment of the client's emotional state?
6. What is your perception of the client's racial identity status? What type of conflict might the client be undergoing based on his racial identity status?
7. What culturally sensitive interventions could you employ?
8. What additional questions would you like to raise for developing your treatment plan?

White Racial Identity Development (WRID)

As a pioneer in the multicultural counseling field, Janet Helms introduced the ideas, which have founded research on white identity development (Helms, 1984; 1995; Helms & Carter, 1993). In general, many researchers who advanced the theory of white identity development in multicultural counseling believed that white counselors could not fully understand and accept the ethnic minority client unless they know themselves as racial beings. In this context, it is essential to understand how their race impacts the counseling process and interaction. Helms' model of White Racial Identity Development reflects the various attitudes and feelings white people have developed as a result of being socialized in a racist society (Helms, 1992).

Racism is one of the major barriers to the development of a positive, nonracist white identity. The goal of studying or examining white identity development is to help white counselors to develop a positive, nonracist white identity. Like other racial/cultural models of identity, the white racial identity model is based on stages, now called statuses, in which whites adopt either a racist or nonracist attitude. The goal in therapy or in training is to help the white person to move from racist levels of functioning to nonracist beliefs and attitudes. The six-status model is described below:

Stage 1: Contact. In the Contact status, the white person is naively curious about or fearful of black people and has a superficial awareness of what it means to be white. Other descriptors of an individual in this status includes: evaluates blacks according to white standards or criteria, limits interaction with blacks except for those blacks who are assimilated; and uses the assimilated black person as a source for learning about the life experiences and culture of black people. The limited contact with this narrow range of black people may result in the white person remaining in the Contact status. To the contrary, if contact persons expand their experiences with a wide variety of black people and see how they are treated differently by the white society, they may progress to a different level.

Stage 2: Disintegration. In this status, individuals are forced to decide if they are going to treat black people fairly and risk being alienated by other whites, or treat them unfairly in order to be embraced and accepted by their white racial group. Some white people believe that in order for them to be accepted as white persons, they must disrespect black people. Helms (1993) proposed three ways white persons might respond when faced with such a moral dilemma: (a) avoid further contact with blacks; (b) attempt to convince significant others that blacks are not inferior; or (c) seek information from blacks or whites to support the belief that racism is not their fault. Helms (1993) pointed out the white persons' belief system will dictate whether they will fight the white racist society or whether they will join it and become more deeply involved in the racist white culture.

Stage 3: Reintegration. The bottom line for the person in the reintegration stage is that white people are superior and that black people are inferior. They believe that the superior status they hold is their right and privilege because they have earned it. They further believe that black inferiority is due to a lack of hard work, intellectual capacity and cultural background. Their feelings about black people range from various levels of fear to anger. Many passive individuals in this stage either avoid discussing issues about race with black individuals, or they will discuss black/white issues among their white peers only. The more aggressive persons in this stage may overtly treat blacks as inferiors and in more extreme cases, may commit acts of physical violence.

An individual could remain in the reintegration status unless a dynamic experience causes him or her to reconsider. Some whites have changed their white racist identity due to a sincere and long-lasting relationship with black individuals. In addition, certain life experiences or events may cause white persons to examine their attitudes toward black people. For example, many students in our multicultural counseling courses have had positive attitude and behavior change toward culturally diverse individuals due to positive experiences with them. For example, a white student's fear of black men was reduced, after getting to know and painting a portrait of a black male classmate.

Stage 4: Pseudo-independence. The development of a positive white identity requires the individual to replace myths and stereotypes about black people with more accurate information regarding what it means to be a white person growing up in the United States. The goal of the pseudo-independent status is to help the individual rid him or herself of racism and to invite a positive white, nonracist identity into his or her life. In this stage, the individual may experience a catharsis by expressing strong pent-up feelings concerning racial issues. Many of these individuals have compared this experience to a type of religious experience where they are able to let go or leave behind many of their old negative beliefs and feelings about people of color. Some white counselors in training have been known to share these strong feelings with family members who subsequently wonder if they have had a mental breakdown! However, some students have found it both challenging and rewarding to share their new awareness with family and friends, see Box 4.2.

Box 4.2

A white woman's observation from a class journal assignment about her experiences talking with friends and family, she describes her experiences (Anonymous, Reprinted by Permission).

I also began to notice things about my family and other people close to me that lacked a multicultural awareness and at times were racist. This was almost more upsetting to me than finding out things about myself because I can work to change myself, but I don't have control over changing my family. I know that I can work to make them more aware of things, but I haven't gotten comfortable enough to do this yet. I think I am still working on things about myself. I have however, been exposing my boyfriend to a lot of the materials we go over in class, and talking to him in-depth about it. This helps me process the material more in-depth and helps him explore things he would otherwise have been unaware of. It has been really wonderful to see how he has become more aware about racism and discrimination in himself and his own family, and how he has been working to change some things.

Stage 5: Immersion/Emersion. Having undergone a major change in ways of thinking, believing, feeling and behaving toward people of color, some white people begin to focus more on their own roles, responsibilities and accountability. There is a shift from focus on others to focusing more on self on a more personally engaging level. They move from *talk* about accepting differences across cultural lines to *walk*, taking meaningful action. The individual is willing to move out of his/her comfort zone to fully understand and experience the impact of racism and racial/cultural differences. It is helpful for whites to engage with others who are going through a similar experience, for example, participating in *unlearning racism* workshops or discussion groups.

Stage 6: Autonomy. Learning to be a white person based on a new definition of whiteness is the goal of the autonomy status. Here the individual no longer has a need to oppress people of color because he or she does not fear them any longer. Having mastered the issues of race in his/her life, he or she can deal with other aspects of prejudice such as ageism, sexism, and other manifestations of oppression.

Helms (1993) cautioned that no one is perfect. People must be in a constant stage of personal growth and development toward becoming non-racist and culturally effective counseling professionals. Using the WRID model, identify some of the attitudes found in the case study of Brian in Box 4.3.

Box 4.3

A Case Study of White Racial Attitudes

Brian is a 58-year-old white male who was born and raised in Akron, Ohio. He is the fifth of six children from a highly religious family whose parents taught them all the principles of good citizenship. They were taught to be good neighbors, to be honest, to be hardworking, and to have strong religious convictions. His neighborhood, school, church and most other agencies in his community were predominately white. There was only one girl in his high school who was African American. Race was never an issue in Brian's home. His parents never discussed race and emphasized that all people must pull themselves up *by their boot-straps*. "Everyone is equal and nobody should have advantages over others" was the constant message preached by his father.

It was not until he enrolled at The Ohio State University that Brian encountered people from different races and cultures. Although he got along with people of color in general, three experiences caused him to think about his feelings about race and culture.

First, he encountered his first black professor in Political Science who blamed white folks for all of the problems that black people experience today. The professor shared further that all white people are racists, that black people cannot be racist, but are victims of racism.

Second, Brian was surprised by his feelings of anger when he noticed that some of the black male athletes dated white females. He did not know them personally, but he was uncomfortable seeing blacks and whites involved in intimate relationships.

Third, he had joined a fraternity where several of the brothers delighted in telling racist jokes or mocking black people as a favorite past time. Brian constantly felt confused because he was never sure when to laugh, remain silent, or to confront his fraternity buddies.

Now, as a university professor, Brian continues to experience questions about race. He supports higher education for ethnic groups, but he does not support affirmative action, which he views as a threat to quality education. Recently he spoke out against the trend of hiring women administrators and professors of color, suggesting that it is reverse discrimination against white men like him.

Discussion Questions

1. Identify the various statuses of white racial identity in this case study and discuss the characteristics of each status.
2. How could you respond to Brian's opinion that affirmative action is reverse discrimination?

Applications to Counseling

Smith (1985) suggested that racial identity is powerful because it represents many hidden forces that cannot be identified. The racial identity development models help trainees understand these forces as manifested in certain attitudes and behaviors of clients. These models also help counselors avoid the pitfalls of stereotypic attitudes toward minority clients that often lead to stereotypic treatment (Smith, 1977). In addition, an understanding of racial identity development provides insight into clients' preferences for counselors by race and helps counselors with diagnoses and with the selection of appropriate counseling approaches and techniques.

Counselor/Client Matching

Some counselors and their clients form a therapeutic connection easily while others struggle to build rapport. Helms and Cook (1999) suggested that the racial identity statuses of the counselor and client influence how well they connect. Four combinations were identified: parallel, progressive, regressive, and crossed, and will be described below. It has been suggested that some dyad types promote harmony (parallel or progressive), while other dyad types do not (regressive or crossed). One way to predict the quality of the counselor/client relationship is through matching racial identity statuses.

Parallel. Counselors and clients share similar racial identity attitudes and behaviors (e.g., contact, preencounter). The saliency of racial identity is similar and there may be similarity in world view with respect to racial consciousness.

Progressive. In this dyad, counselors and clients are similar to the parallel type, except that the counselor is slightly advanced and may be able to provide guidance for the racial identity development of the client. Counselors are secure in their racial identities and model good multicultural communication and interaction. This is a harmonious combination and lends itself to greater possibilities for growth.

Regressive. This type occurs when the client is more racially and culturally aware than the counselor; the client's racial identity status is beyond the counselor's. This combination is a disservice to the client and referral is warranted.

Crossed. This dyad occurs when counselor and clients' racial identity statuses are diametrically opposed to one another. For example, when one sees race as central or core to his/her life and the other does not see race as important. In such instances, the counselor and client are not in harmony and probably cannot develop an effective relationship. For example, in matching counselor and client, a counselor in the contact status may not be aware that racism exists, and a black client in the introspection status may be seeking to balance between immersion in black community and involvements in the dominant culture. A naïve counselor may miss seeing these cultural dissonances. In the crossed dyad, alliances are much more difficult to form because each member at worst, believes that the other is essentially wrong in his or her world view, or at best, they are mutually ignorant.

In applying this dyad model, we believe that clients will benefit more when matching with their counselors in either the parallel or progressive combinations. Counselors who are advanced are secure in their racial identity and are not afraid to discuss racial issues. Progressive relationships are more likely to promote positive change in areas of racial consciousness.

The principles of counselor and client matches are also applicable to supervisory matches. It is not unusual for graduate students of color who are beginning to embrace their racial identity to need a supervisor who can affirm and model positive racial attitudes, see box 4.4 for an example.

Box 4.4

An Example of Progressive Supervisory Matching

Jose was a Latino male of Colombian descent who had grown up in predominantly white neighborhoods in the U.S. As a teenager, he resented his Latin background. His first contact with other Colombian Americans his age began when he entered graduate studies at a large university. He actively sought out a Latino male supervisor who could mentor his development professionally and personally. His matching with Carlos was beneficial not only due to similarities in cultural values, but also as an enhancement to Jose's developing bicultural and bilingual counseling skills. Carlos introduced Jose to the National Latino Psychological Association, affirmed his Latino identity, invited him to co-author an article on bilingual counseling, and became a family friend after their supervision was completed, which remains consistent with Latino values (see Chapter 7).

SUMMARY

We have identified and discussed two models of racial identity development that explain various ways of responding to racism. Each of these models described attitudes, biases, and behaviors associated with each identity status, with varying psychological consequences for persons of color and whites. For persons of color, a progression from nonacceptance to acceptance of racial identity is the ideal. For whites, the progression from unconscious racism to nonracist identity attitudes is a central developmental theme.

It seems that the greatest challenge is to assist all counselors toward achieving higher levels of consciousness about racial identity attitudes in order to improve their level of functioning as multicultural helping professionals. When counselors and clients hold opposing racial identity attitudes or world views, the chances of forming therapeutic alliances are reduced tremendously. Hopefully, the counselor's racial identity status is equal to or more advanced than the clients.

Helms (1993) suggested that white counselors in the United States have more difficulty in working with black clients as compared to clients from other ethnic groups. Perhaps some of this difficulty is due to the long history of racial oppression, violence, and tension that has existed between these two groups in the United States. It would seem reasonable that counselors should have a goal of exploring the implications of racial identity attitudes in the counseling dyad between members of whites and black Americans. In this way, members of both groups could examine how individuals in each respective group develop and achieve a nonracist identity and pride in one's racial group. Consequently, if an individual can feel a sense of security in one's own racial group, he/she can be more accepting of people who are of a differing racial group. Moreover, they can begin to appreciate each other rather than respond defensively in racist or acquiescent behaviors.

Experiential Learning Activities

Following are three experiential exercises, which have been successful in increasing awareness, skills and knowledge needed to become MCC counselors. The first two activities highlight personal awareness of contact with racial and ethnic diversity, and the third activity outlines how to develop action plans to increase knowledge of racial diversity themes.

1. Multicultural Experience Inventory

Objectives: The purpose of the *Multicultural Experience Inventory* (see Box 4.5) is to help participants explore and become more aware of the extent of their early and present life experiences with cultural diversity. The inventory consists of 16 items written in a sentence completion format. The first eight items cover early life experiences, while the last eight items (9–16) cover current experiences with various ethnic/racial groups.

Box 4.5

Multicultural Experience Inventory

Directions: Complete the 16 items below by selecting one of the five racial identity choices and fill in the blank with the appropriate number.

1 = Almost entirely my ethnic group
2 = Mostly my ethnic group with a few people of color from other groups
3 = Mixed (my ethnic group, whites, and other minorities about
    equally)
4 = Mostly whites, with a few people of color
5 = Almost entirely whites

---

1. The ethnic composition of the neighborhoods in which I spent most of my time was _____.
2. My childhood friends who visited my home and related well to my parents were _____.
3. The teachers and counselors with whom I have had the closest relationships were _____.
4. The people who have most influenced me in my education were _____.
5. In high school, my close friends were _____.
6. The ethnic backgrounds of the people I have dated were _____.
7. In the jobs I have had, my close friends were _____.
8. The people with whom I have established close, meaningful relationships were _____.
9. At present, my close friends are _____.
10. My close friends at work are _____.
11. I enjoy going to gatherings at which the people are _____.
12. When I study or work on a project with others, I am usually with persons who are _____.
13. When I am involved in group discussions where I am expected to participate, I prefer a group of people who are _____.
14. I am active in organizations or social groups in which the majority of members are _____.
15. When I am with friends, I usually attend functions where the people are _____.
16. When I discuss personal problems or issues, I discuss them with people who are _____.

Discussion Questions

Answer each question individually and join a small group for further discussion.

1. What impressed you most about your multicultural experience? Were there any surprises?
2. With regards to your multicultural experience, was there more homogeneity or more diversity? Explain.
3. Was there a difference in your multicultural experiences between your early life (items 1–8) and your present life (items 9–16)? Please explain.
4. How have your multicultural experiences impacted the development of your racial identity development?
5. How satisfied are you with your level of engagement with culturally diverse people?
6. What actions if any would you like to take to improve your level of involvement in multicultural experiences?

2. Influence of Racial Identity–A Self-Awareness Activity

1. Ethnic minority participants should review the R/CID and white participants should examine WRID until they identify the status that most closely represents their attitudes, feelings, perceptions, and behaviors. Biracial or multiracial persons may adapt these models as they see fit.
2. Think back over your life history and recall some of the life events that may have influenced the development of your racial/cultural identity attitudes and behaviors.
3. Consider some of the following factors to assist your recall:
   a. Messages you heard from your family about racially/culturally diverse people.
   b. Attitudes of your parents toward culturally diverse people.
   c. Attitudes of your peer group toward culturally diverse individuals.
   d. Positive experiences you had with culturally diverse persons.
   e. Negative experiences you had with culturally diverse persons.
   f. Portrayal of culturally diverse people through the media (radio, television, newspapers, and advertisement).

g. Opportunities (or lack thereof) for involvement with racially diverse individuals or groups.

Directions Guide for Group Leaders

1. After participants have had sufficient time to recall factors that influenced their racial/cultural development, ask participants to share or discuss any part of their recollections they choose.
2. Ask participants to share what they believe is a link between their current racial/cultural attitudes and their past experiences.
3. Help participants to identify and discuss common themes and life experiences that they share concerning their racial/cultural identity development.
4. Ask participants to share what they believe is the greatest influence on their racial identity development.
5. Ask participants to identify what they can do to advance their racial identity status.

3. Action Plans

Action plans are experiential learning activities that help you to learn, grow, change and understand yourself and others better. Action plans are a natural follow-up to self-assessment and understanding your racial identity development. Through action plans, you may strengthen areas of racial identity where growth and change are needed.

To begin the action plan process, determine your personal growth goals and select experiences from the following levels of involvement.

1. **Observation** (learning from a distance). Includes activities such as watching selected videos, films, reading literature, observing people in their environment, scanning the media for multicultural issues, trying out a new ethnic restaurant.
2. **Investigation** (learning with more personal contact). Includes activities such as interviewing people from culturally diverse groups, talking with community leaders, joining groups whose interests will support attaining your personal growth goals.
3. **Direct participation** (learning with interpersonal intimacy). Includes activities such as building friendships, volunteering in community service projects, visiting in the homes of culturally

diverse persons, being a conversation partner with someone learning English as a Second Language, and keeping a journal of reactions and feelings generated from these activities.

Given these guidelines, design a plan to meet your personal growth needs to advance your understanding of your racial identity development.

Sharing action plans. Discuss some of the following in small groups: Identify and discuss your personal growth goals and provide background relevant to your selected activities. Identify and discuss the three levels of action plans, providing brief descriptions of what you did, challenges you encountered, and what you learned about yourself related to your racial identity attitudes and development.

Examples of action plans developed by students in a multicultural counseling course included some of the following:

• Attended student assemblies and events: black, South Asian, LGBT, Rap music
• Attended Community Theater: *Jesus Jumped the A Train*
• Read books. *Why are all the Black kids sitting together in the cafeteria, and other conversations about race* by Beverly Tatum
• Visited a mosque
• Attended weddings
• Attended lectures on racism and relevant topics, e.g., LGBT in Nicaragua
• Interviewed a neighbor

Selected Films

Malcolm X: Directed by Spike Lee (1992). Malcolm X was a black liberation leader of the 1950s and 1960s noted for his militant and separatist rhetoric. He embraced the Nation of Islam while in jail, converted later to become a Sunni Muslim, and stopped his anti-white speech. He was assassinated and died as a Muslim martyr.

The Color of Fear: Produced and directed by Lee Mun Wah. Documentary film of an encounter weekend with black, Asian, Hispanic, Native, and European white men who confront and support each other in dealing with the effects of racism on their lives. Available online at http://www.stirfryseminars.com/pages/coloroffear.htm

Web Sites of Interest

Antiracism education and activism
http://www.Whiteprivilege.com/definition/
http://www.antiracismnet.org/main.html
Southern Poverty Law Center
http://www.splcenter.org/

REFERENCES

Abrams, L. and Trusty, J. (2004). African Americans racial identity and socially desirable responding: An empirical model. *Journal of Counseling and Development, 82,* 365–374.

Atkinson, D. R, Morten, G., & Sue, D. W. (1979). *Counseling American minorities: A cross-cultural perspective.* (3rd Ed.). Dubuque, IA: Wm. C. Brown.

Burkard, A. W., Juarez-Huffaker, M., and Ajmere, K. (2003). White racial identity attitudes as a predictor of cross-cultural working alliances. *Journal of Multicultural Counseling and Development, 31,* 226–244.

Burkard, A.W., Ponterotto, J.G., Reynolds, A.L., & Alfonso, V.C. (1999). White counselor trainee's racial identity and working alliance perceptions. *Journal of Counseling & Development, 77,* 324–329.

Carter, R. T. (Ed.) (2005). *Handbook of racial-cultural psychology and counseling: Theory and research, volume 1; Training and practice, volume 2.* Hoboken, NJ: John Wiley & Sons, Inc.

Cross, W. E., Jr. (1971, July). The Negro-to-Black conversion experience: Toward a psychology of Black liberation. *Black World, 20,* 13–27.

Cross, W. E. (1978). The Thomas and Cross models of psychological Nigrescence: A review. *Journal of Black Psychology, 5,* 13–31.

Cross, W. E., Jr. (1991). *Shades of Black: Diversity in African-American identity.* Philadelphia: Temple University Press.

Downing, N.E., & Roush, K.L. (1985). From passive acceptance to active commitment: A model of feminist identity development for women. *Counseling Psychologist, 13,* 695–709.

Greene, B. (1997). Ethnic minority lesbians and gay men: Mental health and treatment issues. In B. Greene (Ed.), *Ethnic and cultural diversity among lesbians and gay men* (pp. 216–239). Thousand Oaks, CA: Sage.

Hall, W. S., Cross, W. E. & Freedle, R. (1972). Stages in the development of Black awareness: An exploratory investigation. In R. L. Jones (Ed.), *Black Psychology* (pp. 156–165). New York: Harper & Row.

Helms, J. E. (1984). Toward a theoretical explanation of the effects of race on counseling: A Black and White model. *The Counseling Psychologist, 12,* 153–165.

Helms, J. E. (1985). Cultural identity in the treatment process. In P. B. Pedersen (Ed.). *Handbook of cross-cultural counseling and therapy.* Westport, CT: Greenwood Press.

Helms, J. E. (Ed.) (1990). *Black and White racial identity: Theory, research, and practice.* Westport, CT: Greenwood Press.

Helms, J.E. (1992). *A race is a nice thing to have: A guide to being a White person or understanding the White persons in your life.* Topeka, KS: Content Communications.

Helms, J. E. (1993). Toward a model of White racial identity development. In J. E. Helms (Ed.), *Black and White racial identity: Theory, research, and practice* (pp. 49–66). Westport, CT: Praeger.

Helms, J. E. (1995). An update of Helms' White and People of Color racial identity models. In J. G. Ponterotto, J. M. Casas, L. A. Suzuki, & C. M. Alexander (Eds.), *Handbook of multicultural counseling* (pp. 181–198). Thousand Oaks, CA: Sage.

Helms, J. E., & Carter, R. T. (1993). Development of the White Racial Identity Inventory. In J. E. Helms (Ed.), *Black and White racial identity: Theory, research, and practice* (pp. 67–80). Westport, CT: Praeger.

Helms, J. E. and Cook, D. A. (1999). *Using race and culture in counseling and psychotherapy: Theory and process.* Boston, MA: Allyn and Bacon.

Helms, J. E. & Pipir, R. E. (1994). Implications for racial identity theory for vocational psychology. *Journal of Vocational Behavior, 44,* 124–136.

McCarn, S. R. & Fassinger, R. E. (1996). Revisioning sexual minority identity development formation: A new model of lesbian identity and its implications for counseling and research. *The Counseling Psychologist, 24,* 508–534.

Ponterotto, J. G. (1993). White racial identity and the counseling professional. *The Counseling Psychologist, 21,* 213–217.

Poston, W. S. C. (1990). The biracial identity development model: A needed addition. *Journal of Counseling and Development, 69,* 152–155.

Sciarra, D., Chang, T., McLean, R., & Wong, D. (2005). White racial identity and attitudes toward people with disabilities. *Journal of Multicultural Counseling and Development. 33,* 232–242

Smith, E. J. (1977). Counseling Black individuals: Some stereotypes. *Personnel and Guidance Journal, 55,* 390–396.

Smith, E. J. (1985). Ethnic minorities: Life stress, social support, and mental health issues. *The Counseling Psychologist, 13,* 537–579.

Sue, D. W. & Sue, D. (1990). *Counseling the culturally different: Theory and practice.* New York: John Wiley & Sons.

Sue, D. W. & Sue, D. (1999). *Counseling the culturally different: Theory and practice* (3rd Ed.). New York: John Wiley & Sons.

Suyemoto, K. L. (2004). Racial/ethnic identities and related attributed experiences of multiracial Japanese European Americans. *Journal of Multicultural Counseling and Development, 32,* 206–221.

Vinson, T. S. and Neimeyer, G. J. (2003). The relationship between racial identity development and multicultural counseling competency: A second look. *Journal of Multicultural Counseling and Development, 31,* 262–263.

Vontress, C. E. (1971). *Counseling Negroes.* Boston, MA: Houghton Mifflin.

Chapter 5

UNDERSTANDING AND COUNSELING BLACK MALES

One ever feels his two-ness—an American, a Negro; two warring souls, two thoughts, two unreconciled strivings; two warring ideals in one dark body, whose dogged strength alone keeps it from being torn asunder.

W.E.B. DuBois (1903)

Abstract

This chapter was inspired by hearing the voices of black males speak through a qualitative focus group study on topics relevant for counseling. The chapter is organized around three themes: self-awareness of attitudes towards black men, understanding black men through hearing their voices, and implications for counseling. We have chosen to use the term *black male* to refer to all men of African descent, which is more inclusive, including those who are from the Caribbean, Latin America, and Africa.

INTRODUCTION

Black men have been vanishing from communities, schools, colleges and the work force at alarming rates (Kunjufu, 1995). Daily media paints a grim picture of black men with stories of substance abuse, incarceration, delinquency, homicide, suicide, low educational achievement, unemployment, and poverty. The issues and problems concerning black men are widely known and are well-documented (Gibbs, 1988; Johnson, 1985). In general, the mere presence of African American males often creates fear, anxiety, and suspicion among many individuals in our society. Many counselors and helping professionals have experienced similar fears. The negative forces of racism affect youth development and early intervention programs are warranted (Baggerly & Parker, 2005).

Oppressive social and economic conditions for African Americans still exist even though the Emancipation Proclamation legally freed them more than 143 years ago (Ani, 1994: Kambon, 1998; White & Cones, 1999). The physical and psychological consequences of being exposed to an oppositional world view remain a stumbling block to a healthy black male identity (Akbar, 1984; Lee, 1999). Lee proposed that black men may encounter at least six problems resulting from adapting to life in a racist society. They include (1) problems of aggression and control, (2) cultural alienation and disconnection, (3) self-esteem, (4) dependency issues, (5) help-seeking attitudes and behaviors and (6) racial identity issues.

Another major problem for black males is how they are portrayed in the media, social science literature, and popular culture. The tragedy of black men being stereotyped with labels such as "absent father, pimp, drug dealer, player, gangster and academic underachiever" is that these images are internalized and in many cases are integrated into their attitudes and behaviors. In a recent television interview, Mr. Charles Barkley, a well-known NBA basketball star and an outspoken critic on racism, supported the new NFL dress code which restricted players from dressing in the hip-hop fashion. His belief was that the hip-hop dressing practices of the NFL players had a negative influence on young black men. His rationale was that no one would hire young black men dressed as many professional black athletes do. Barkley also supported Mr. Bill Cosby's idea that black men should take personal responsibility for their actions (Barkley, 2005).

In a conversation in a black inner-city barbershop, black men discussed the plight of black males in America. One man stated that he was tired of all the negative labels thrust upon black men. Labels such as "black men are endangered, lazy and shiftless, or dangerous" seem to exist every where. Another man declared the problem with black men is that they don't know their history. He said, "When you don't know where you have been, you don't know where you are going." An elderly gentleman said that the problem is that young men "wear their pants too low around their knees and their caps backward. They would be OK," he said, "if they pulled their pants up and turned their caps around." Another gentleman said that he agreed with Maya Angelou, a keen observer of the black experience, who suggested that many young black males who roam the city streets are lost because they don't know their heroes and their "sheroes." Another customer said that although he did not want to sound paranoid, he agreed with people who believed that there was a conspiracy to destroy black boys. He reasoned that if there are no black men, no more black babies can be reproduced.

Some writers have identified and discussed the dilemma of black men in the American society. In his recent book, A. J. Franklin (2004) expounded on the work of Ralph Ellison, who viewed the problem of the black male as being invisible. Franklin provided an extensive definition of invisibility with the following points:

- Invisibility is an inner struggle with questioning whether one's talents, abilities, personality and worth are valued or recognized because of racism.
- Invisibility is a threat against the dignity of the black man.
- Invisibility requires the black man to protect his self-respect at all times.
- Invisibility requires vigilance at all times, being careful in evaluating opportunities, and being assertive about personal goals in spite of what others might think.
- Invisibility obscures personal vision, clouds judgment and changes one's ability to evaluate his stature and movement toward personal goals.

On the other hand, visibility occurs when one's true talents, abilities, personality, and worth are respected.

Franklin (2004) listed and briefly described below the seven elements of personal power needed to counteract invisibility:

1. Recognition—being acknowledged by others.
2. Satisfaction—being rewarded for what he does.
3. Legitimacy—having a sense of belonging.
4. Validation—feeling that others share one's views and values.
5. Respect—being treated as a person of worth.

6. Dignity—feeling like a person of worth and value.
7. Identity—feeling comfortable with oneself.

Given the depth of problems and concerns among many black men living in American society, there are many sincere attempts by individuals and groups to improve conditions with varying degrees of success. The population of black men is so vast and complex that no one method is sufficient to meet all of their needs. Unfortunately, many approaches to working with black men have been from a deficit model or from a negative perspective. We believe that there is a positive side to understanding and counseling black males, and we would like to present it in this chapter. Specifically, this chapter will cover three major themes. The first theme is counselor self-understanding, including a discussion on the role of counselor self-awareness, and an assessment of attitudes toward black males. The second theme in understanding the black male includes racial identity and understanding black males by hearing their voices. The third theme is delivering counseling services for black males, including a case presentation and discussion of strategies for helping counselors to connect with black males.

Self-Awareness

Successful or effective counseling in this area dictates that counselors are clear about their true feelings and attitudes toward black men. Although many counselors may attempt to mask or hide their true feelings and attitudes, they are often viewed by many black males as insincere. Black males are relatively good judges of those who are genuine and those who are not. They are often good judges of whether or not counselors or teachers are afraid of them. When black males determine that counselors are afraid or are not willing to challenge them to reach their fullest potential, they are likely to lose respect and may drop out prematurely. When black males lose respect for such counselors, they often feel insecure in the counselor/client dyad. Many black males respond positively to those counselors who are self-assured and who understand their world view. Hulnick (1977) emphasized the importance of counselors knowing their own issues, blocks, problems, prejudices, and stereotypic views before working with others. We agree with Hulnick that especially counselors who work with black males must know themselves if they hope to form therapeutic alliances. In particular, counselors need to become keenly aware of their own racial identity attitudes in order to develop empathy toward black male clients. Owning negative racial attitudes and feelings are often the first steps toward positive change. Gaining exposure to many different types of black males is one way to counteract fear reactions (Barkley, 2005).

To facilitate counselor self-understanding, we will present two assessment strategies designed to help you examine your experiences with black males and explore your level of comfort with black males in various situations. Following each assessment will be process questions for discussion and exploration.

Personal Experience Questions

The Personal Experience Inventory is designed to help you examine your past experiences with black males in order to become more aware of your own attitudes and feelings toward them. Through this inventory, self-knowledge and awareness of black males are enhanced by having you review your life and recall messages you heard about or experiences you had with black males. Questions are offered to jog your memory and heighten your awareness, see Box 5.1:

Box 5.1

Personal Experience Inventory

1. Identify your racial/cultural group(s) (e.g., biracial, American Indian, Asian, Latina/o, black, LGBT, white, Jewish, etc.) and tell briefly what it means to be a member of your group(s).
2. In which ways, if any, does being a member of your racial/cultural group(s) impact your relationship with black male individuals? For example, what messages had you heard from significant others (your family, relatives, peers, friends) about black males?
3. What generalizations do you believe black males have made about your racial/cultural group(s)?
4. Have your experiences with or perceptions of black men changed since early childhood? If so, what factors contributed to those changes?
5. What personal experiences with black males can you recall, if any?

Discuss your answers to these questions in small groups of four or five members each, following the suggested guidelines listed below:

1. Which themes emerged from the small group discussion?
2. How similar or different were your past experiences to those of others in your group?
3. What feelings emerged from taking the inventory or from participating in the group discussion?
4. Which questions, if any, did you find most challenging?
5. What did you learn about yourself from the discussion?
6. What would you like to do next regarding your relations with black men?

Black Male Comfort Index

The purpose of the Black Male Comfort Index is to help you explore your perceived comfort level in various situations with black males. Having an opportunity to imagine how you would feel in different situations with black males will help you become more aware of your strengths and weaknesses regarding your relations with them and to work toward changing any feelings or perceptions that may be negative (see Table 5.1). Please respond to these items based on your perceived or actual level of comfort in various situations involving black males, using a Likert scale ranging from 5 (high comfort level) to 1 (low comfort level).

Directions: After you respond to the fifteen items individually, discuss in small groups of four or five members each, and answer the following questions:

1. Which items represented your highest and lowest levels of comfort with black males?
2. Which items represented your actual experiences with black males?
3. Which items reflected your most challenging experiences with black males?
4. What factors do you believe have had the greatest influence on your comfort level with black males?
5. What do you believe you can do to increase your level of comfort with black men?

Self-knowledge and understanding by the helping professional are essential for building therapeutic alliances. We also believe that the counselor must be aware of the world view of the client. The next sec-

Table 5.1 Black Male Comfort Index

Item	High Comfort		Average Comfort		Low Comfort
1. Developing a friendship with a black male who doesn't place importance on race.	5	4	3	2	1
2. Selecting a black male to work on a class or work project.	5	4	3	2	1
3. Selecting a Black male as your family physician.	5	4	3	2	1
4. Being in a class or in a workshop where the leader is a black male.	5	4	3	2	1
5. Attending a church where the minister is a black male.	5	4	3	2	1
6. Voting for a black male for president of an organization.	5	4	3	2	1
7. Sharing membership in a social club with a black male.	5	4	3	2	1
8. Communicating with a black male who is Afrocentric (who has a black orientation).	5	4	3	2	1
9. Communicating with a Black male who is Eurocentric (who has a white orientation).	5	4	3	2	1
10. Reading a novel about the lives of black males.	5	4	3	2	1
11. Participating in recreational activities with black males.	5	4	3	2	1
12. Inviting a black male into your home for dinner.	5	4	3	2	1
13. Being a close friend of a black male.	5	4	3	2	1
14. Sitting next to an interracial couple in a theater.	5	4	3	2	1
15. Being alone on an elevator with a black male.	5	4	3	2	1

Scoring: 75 represents the highest possible level of comfort, 15 represents the lowest possible level of comfort.

tion is designed to help you learn more about the black male through the examination of ideas and beliefs. The experiences and voices of black males are expressed using a focus group study.

Understanding Black Males: A Qualitative Study

In order to elucidate contemporary attitudes among black men, we conducted a qualitative study using focus groups with black males. Our purpose was to better understand the strengths and coping strategies of black males, and their perceptions and expectations of counseling. The following series of questions provided an outline for discussion.

1. When you think of black males in general, what do you believe are their strengths?
2. What makes you proud to be a black male?
3. Who do you identify as your role model(s) (someone you would like to emulate; someone who inspires you) and why?
4. What, if anything, do you believe is particularly difficult or challenging about being a black male?
5 .What are your sources of social support and guidance daily?
6. Please share a story about facing a difficult situation or problem that had a successful outcome, and describe what worked.
7. What do you think keeps black males from seeking help from counselors, psychologists, psychiatrists or social workers?
8. How could a counselor, psychologist or social worker be most helpful to you?
9. Is there anything else you believe is important for counselors to know about counseling black males?
10. What can a counselor do to establish a meaningful, positive connection (relationship) with you?

Approximately 20 black males participated in four focus groups. Two groups were facilitated by one of the authors (W.M.P.) and two groups by black male leaders known personally by me. Participants were recruited through personal contacts; the age range was from 19 to 78 years. All had attended college or were college graduates, and were currently living in the south (Texas, Alabama, or Florida). The two Florida groups consisted of community college students and university faculty and staff, and a group of men known as community leaders. Each focus group was audiotaped and the findings are summarized in themes derived from each question.

1. When you think of black males in general, what do you believe are their strengths?

This part of the study covered their perceptions of strength, pride, and individuals they viewed as role models. They identified the following strengths:

• **Faith in God.** The older men consistently listed their faith in God as their primary strength. No matter how difficult the task, they believe that God will see them through. One man said, "I begin and end my day with prayer." They believe that God has been and will continue to be the key to their survival.

- **Perseverance.** Persistence and hard work characterize successful black men. They reported that there is no limit to what black men can do if they stick to the task and work hard enough. The fact that black men have survived and are still thriving is a living testimony to their ability to persevere. One group participant suggested that Black men inherited their perseverance qualities from their slave ancestors who worked from sunup until sundown.
- **Creativity and innovation.** Participants identified their creative, innovative and adaptive talents reporting that black men are able to make the most of minimal resources. Unable to hire plumbers, mechanics, or electricians, many black men creatively do whatever is necessary to get the job done themselves. One participant stated, "As boys growing up, we made our own toys, because our parents could not afford to buy them."

2. What makes you proud to be a black male?

The sources of pride including having the ability to counteract stereotypes, having a positive black racial identity, benefiting from a rich black heritage and being trailblazers for other black people.

- **Having the ability to counteract stereotypes.** Even though black men are labeled as "inarticulate, less intelligent, lazy, shiftless, and angry," one man said, "I am proud to show that I am just the opposite of those stereotypes." For example, they see themselves as intelligent men who can discuss a wide range of topics, and feel there is no limit to what they can do or become. One participant said, "As a black man I am strong physically, mentally, socially, spiritually, and intellectually. I feel proud I can hold my ground with the strongest white males or females in my unit."
- **Having a positive black racial identity.** Comments made by several men were exemplary of individuals with a positive black racial identity. For example, one gentleman said, "I am proud to be black and connected with the black community." A college student followed and said, "There is something special about being black." He said that the way black men conduct themselves in times of crisis is admirable. He stated, "I am proud to maintain my blackness while living in a complex, multiracial and multicultural society."

- **Benefiting from of a rich black heritage.** Several men said they were proud of, and benefited from, the hard work and struggles handed down by historical black men of high integrity who made monumental contributions to the development of the American society. One man said, "Because Frederick Douglas handed something down, I feel that I too must hand something down. I was proud to hand down my position of county commissioner to another black man."
- **Being trailblazers for black people.** Even though slavery has been abolished for 142 years, many career opportunities for black people are still not available. Some of the men in our study were proud to announce that they have opened doors to many new career opportunities for black people by being the first black individual to hold a position previously held by whites only. While one participant was the first black principal of a predominantly white school, another man was the first black Vice President for Student Affairs at a major university in the southeast. An elderly participant reported that over the past few decades, many men have been first in fields that include education, science, politics, sports, communications, and more.

3. Who do you identify as your role model(s) (someone you would like to emulate; someone who inspires you) and why?

One way to understand black men is to become more aware of the role models they emulate or by whom they are inspired. The term "role model" to some participants meant father. It was difficult for some of the participants to discuss role models if their fathers were absent or were negative influences. Contrary to the stereotype of the absent black father, however, most of the black men named their fathers as their role models for several reasons: One participant named his father for the sacrifices he made for his family in giving everybody an opportunity to receive an education. A stepfather was named because he treated his stepchildren as his own. "He worked by day and attended school by night to impress upon his children the value of education," said one participant. Another father was selected because he was viewed as a community leader who was respected by many for having a great deal of dignity. This participant said, "I really liked hearing people say positive things about my dad." One man said, "I followed my dad and did everything that he did. Since he has passed away, I find myself doing many of the things he did, such as washing clothes, cooking, ironing, mopping the floors, planting a garden, attending church, doing community service projects, spending quality time with the family and holding a steady job."

Some participants named other people such as aunts, uncles, grandparents, professionals and historical figures as their role models. Some selected their mothers because their fathers were not around. One said, "Women taught me the meaning of manhood such as self-respect, respect for others, competition, goal setting, hard work and sportsmanship."

Some participants suggested that role models did not have to be a member of their own race or gender, but rather could be anyone who cared about them and was willing to help. For example, one man stated, "My role model was an elderly white lady who was my English teacher and the first white person I ever trusted." He said, "She truly cared about me, encouraged me to attend graduate school, and has been a source of guidance and inspiration throughout my life."

4. What, if anything, do you believe is particularly difficult or challenging about being a black male?

Some of the themes that emerged from their discussion included: dealing with negative stereotyping, experiencing tokenism in the workplace, being isolated from black people, and dealing with racial conflicts.

Stereotyping. Stereotyping is manifested in many of the experiences discussed by the participants in this study. For example one participant stated, "I hate being watched by white people every second, and I hate being obligated to do certain things in the workplace that my white counterparts do not have to do." Some believed that there were unwritten expectations of black men before they were born, such as being expected to "run faster, jump higher, dance better, have the lowest test scores, get into more trouble, commit more crimes and avoid personal responsibility." One participant said, "My greatest challenge as a black man is to ignore the fact that I am expected to fail, to mess up and to give up."

Tokenism. Many institutions will hire one person of ethnic minority status as a token of diversity. Such persons often hold "out-group status" rather than being an integral part of the unit. One participant said, "I am the only black staff member in my unit, and I am becoming more and more isolated from black people." He said further, "I feel alone and sad that I cannot share my true feelings with white colleagues, some of whom believe that I should be happy in my role." He also said, "It is difficult for me to be my true self." Others spoke of frustrations of the token status, saying how tiresome it becomes when whites constantly ask questions about black people, i.e. "Why do black people do this or why do black people do that?"

Racial conflict. Several participants from each group saw racial conflict as a challenge because it is so pervasive and inescapable. One participant said, "I was walking on a treadmill recently at a fitness center when a white man working out next to me asked me why black men do not take advantage of all the opportunities this country has to offer them?" The questions continued, "How do black women put up with lazy, shiftless black men who are doing nothing but making the rest of the country look bad?" The questions continued, "How can Asian and other foreigners come to this country and in a very short time, educate themselves, find good jobs and contribute to the American economy?" The group participant responded, "I wondered how I could respond to these questions without becoming defensive and losing a teachable moment." He said, "I became petrified, confused, and more conflicted when the white man jumped off the treadmill and left shaking his head in disgust before I could respond to his questions."

Other participants experienced racial conflict based on perceived levels of blackness. For example, some men reported they were perceived as either "not black enough or too black." One professor stated, "I was seen as not black enough because I spoke Standard English, did not eat soul food, did not discuss black issues in every conversation and was not a member of the NAACP. One of my white colleagues was disappointed because he thought his department had not hired what he labeled, "a real black man." On the other hand, another participant reported that he had been written up by his supervisor for focusing on black issues too much. He said, "I complained that my department had not hired enough black people and those hired were given only menial positions. My office was adorned with black pictures and black art only. In addition, I never socialized with whites outside my work. My greatest racial conflict was being perceived by white people as raising my voice too loudly in heated discussions. One of my colleagues once said that she was frightened whenever I spoke up."

Finally, some participants experienced racial conflict through black people being too critical and too distrustful of one another. One leader said, "I am often accused by black citizens of not having their best interests at heart, and they often accuse me of being a sellout or traitor." A participant remarked that "Many blacks do not trust black craftsmen such as bricklayers, carpenters, electricians or black professionals such as doctors, lawyers, or accountants to do quality work. Rather, they tend to have more confidence in white craftsmen and professionals."

5. What are your sources of social support and guidance daily?

The church, the family and seniors in the workplace were identified and discussed as sources of support and guidance. In addition, one participant listed negative forces as his source of motivation. He said, "I was inspired to attend college and better my life when I noticed how my friends were hanging out, wasting their lives and doing nothing." Another man reported that he first looks within himself for guidance and support before seeking external help.

The church. Clearly, the church plays a major role in the daily lives of many black men. One man explained that "I pray at home and at work and I seek God's wisdom in major decisions that I make." Another participant said, "My church family confirms my existence, and validates me. Through faith in God and membership in my family of Christian believers, I am convinced that I am not alone in the world." These participants all seem to agree that no matter what happens in life, they can always count on God and their church family.

The family. The family plays a vital role in the lives of black men. Even though these men were all mature adults, they thought it was important to have a harmonious relationship with their parents. Married men referred to their wives as their best friends. One participant said, "My family is my real reason to exist. Without my family, nothing else matters." Some men viewed close friends as family since close friends are very important to them. One participant stated, "Men should have close friends who are males. For instance, there is no one I trust more than a male friend I have known all of my life."

Seniors in the workplace. Seniors were listed by some men as important because they provide leadership, knowledge and skills for new employees. Several participants recalled incidents where senior workers raised their level of inspiration in their time of need. One man said, "The wisdom of senior employees is not replaceable."

6. Please share a story about facing a difficult situation or problem that had a successful outcome, and describe what worked.

a. "I needed three thousand dollars to pay for tuition, but was turned down for a loan. Rather than give up, I sought assistance from the vice president for student affairs in a large community college. After seeing that I had a good attitude, good grades in school, and a clear plan for the future, she decided to help me get the aid for which I had applied." He added that others will help you after you have made an effort to help yourself.

b. "When I was a college student, two of my fraternity brothers and I were offered a weekend job 'pulling corn'. By midday, one of the fraternity brothers had gotten bored and left. By late afternoon, the second man decided to leave for a fraternity function before the work was completed. I remained working until nearly dark, when the employer returned to pick us up. He asked, 'Why are you still here while the others are not?' I replied that my father told me to always give 100 percent to any task. The employer was so impressed that he hired me for part-time work throughout my college years, and served as a reference for me when I graduated."

7. What do you think keeps black males from seeking help from counselors, psychologists, psychiatrists or social workers?

The primary issue with seeking mental health services is the stigma attached to mental illness. Secondly, they are socialized to handle their own problems. Other themes included pride, seeing help-seeking as a weakness, and religious faith. On the latter point, one member said, "God is our major source of help, the preacher is our counselor and prayer is the answer." Some individuals said that they would feel ashamed to admit that they had a problem. In addition, one participant stated that "Some counselors may not understand what he is trying to say, and may not fully understand his life experiences." Also, a major theme was not trusting counselors in general and white counselors in particular, and fears that there could be a breach of confidentiality. One participant said, "Personal problems are a fact of life that we all have to endure alone, without the help of any external sources." Another member agreed, "Problems are a part of life that makes you stronger."

One participant suggested counselors use the wrong techniques by just reflecting what they hear you say. "They cannot relate." Finally, some participants believed that in many settings there are insufficient black counselors available.

8. How could a counselor, psychologist or social worker be most helpful to you?

Upon hearing this question participants responded with a list of general guidelines that follow:

- Show mutual respect and honesty.
- Gain trust and be a good listener.
- Understand the black male and the life experiences.

9. Is there anything else you believe is important for counselors to know about counseling black males?

Participants offered the following suggestions concerning what counselors should know before counseling black men:

- When a black man comes for counseling, make sure he leaves with something other than idle talk and empty promises. As one of the focus group participant said, "when he comes, he means business and if he does not get anything, he probably will not return."
- Don't measure black men by the same yardstick as you measure white men. Rather, recognize differences as unique qualities to be celebrated, not as deficits.
- Assist black men to go as far as their dreams and aspirations will take them. Refrain from setting limits or "placing them in a box."
- Be careful about assumptions you make about black males. Get to know a variety of those with a wealth of knowledge who can serve as consultants or resource persons on black male issues and concerns.

10. What can a counselor do to establish a meaningful, positive connection (relationship) with you?

Focus group participants offered the following suggestions:

- Ensure that black males have mental health providers with whom they can identify.
- Provide outreach activities through churches, barbershops, residence halls, and other places where black males may congregate.
- Offer psychoeducational programs and workshops of special interest to black men, i.e., building positive relationships, accepting personal responsibility and so forth.
- Be visible throughout the community so that they understand that the counselor is also a caring human being who is part of the community.

• Be courageous in taking the first step toward relationship-building with black men.

In sum, this qualitative study was conducted to determine the strengths and coping strategies of black males, as well as with their perceptions and the expectations of counselors and counseling. As a result of this study, we found that the strengths of black men is their ability to survive through their spiritual beliefs, hard work, and perseverance. In the face of insurmountable odds, they still have been able to live productively in a complex, multiracial/multicultural society. Although men cited their fathers as role models, they accepted and appreciated anyone who showed genuine love and care for them. Being stereotyped as "low functioning, nonproductive individuals who encounter racial identity conflicts" were continuous challenges. These men looked to their families and churches for support. The participants were somewhat apprehensive about counselors and counseling because of the perceived stigma attached to the counseling process. The successful counselor for black males will need to exercise flexibility in their roles and functions. Additionally, counselors need to be aware of the life experiences and world views of black men.

Delivering Counseling Services for Black Males

Sanders-Thompson, Bazile, and Akbar (2004) identified barriers for blacks in seeking mental health services, including cultural beliefs, social stigma of mental illness, costs, and preferences for obtaining services within the black community. From their focus group study, some of the perceptions of white psychologists were that they were impersonal, untrustworthy, lacked involvement in the black community, and could not understand what it is like to live in a racist society. There is general agreement that there is underutilization of counseling and mental health services by some culturally diverse groups. Nevertheless, it has been our observation that black males still do not use counseling services to the same extent as their white counterparts. One possible reason for this low participation has been the inability of mental health professionals to make positive contacts or connections with these men. In this section, we will explore strategies to help counselors connect with black males. A case example with discussion questions completes this chapter.

It is generally known that it is challenging to provide consistent counseling services for black male clients. Parham (1999) and Sue and Sue (1999) proposed that counseling interventions based on Eurocentric norms and standards place cultural limitations on black males. These writers suggest that what is often missing in the counselor/ black male dyad is the African world view and African American value system. Case conceptualization of African American males' problems should consider African American world view and reality.

Over the past few years a few writers have attempted to address the counseling and mental health needs of African American men. They suggested that therapists examine their own biases, stereotypes, attitudes and behaviors toward black men. Second, they need to understand the limits of traditional theories and introduce culturally responsive interventions that evolve from cultural world views of African Americans. Parham (1999) also suggested counselor self-examination including: (a) awareness of their own biases; (b) working knowledge of history; (c) sense of their own cultural heritage; (d) awareness of how traditional counseling theories differ from Afrocentric perspectives; and (e) culturally sensitive counseling skills for African Americans.

A number of authors have advocated masculinity training for African American males. White and Cones (1999) presented fatherhood training, rites of passage programs, and cultural history education designed for helping African Americans males learn to become supportive fathers, committed husbands, loyal friends, culture-centered successful business men and compassionate brothers. An essential strategy of their training is intergenerational dialogue where African American boys have two-way conversations with older black men.

Still others have advanced the use of aesthetics, i.e., art, music, dance, poetry and other media to make counseling more appealing to black men (Lee, 1989; Pasteur and Toldson, 1982). Lee suggested that using music and art that is culturally relevant to black males requires a therapist that is culturally sensitive and who endorses an Afrocentric perspective. Watts and Abdul-Adil (2002) made use of media such as art, rap music and movies to promote discussion and to practice critical consciousness skills for young black males. Such skills were needed to help black males become more aware of the oppressive forces in their community that limited their potential growth and development.

A variety of techniques can be used to facilitate connections between counselors and black male clients, some of which are presented by

Parham (2002). First, a ritual may be used to develop a collective consciousness concerning the core issue the client presents. The ritual, which is just a symbol, may range from simple to complex and must be acceptable to the client. For example, rituals could be as simple as a handshake and as complex as burning old letters. Second, music can be used to connect the counselor and the black male client. Listening to music is a natural pastime for many black males and can be used as mechanisms of growth and change. Parham (2002) believed that since there is a natural rhythm to life, music helps men to connect in a rhythmic manner. One advantage of music is that it reflects the sociological context of the times, and the words to the music can be great conversation starters.

Some additional and practical strategies are presented here by W.M.P. based upon 30 years of work experience with black males. These actions were motivated by the need to promote greater utilization of counseling services by black men. A few of the strategies used are listed below:

1. Be visible in places that are frequented by black males.
2. Offer workshops on topics of interest.
3. Serve as faculty advisors for selected organizations and groups.
4. Participate in selected sports activities.
5. Organize mentoring programs for academic enhancement.
6. Provide a "walk in counseling service" where black men be seen without appointments.

A case example is in Box 5.2 and discussion questions follow.

Box 5.2

Case Example: The Incredible Education of Walter Lee Williams (fictitious name)

Walter is a 22-year-old black male college senior on the verge of graduating from college with a bachelor's degree in chemistry. He grew up in an impoverished area with little emotional or financial support from parents or relatives. Having grown up poor, neglected and abused, he is presently filled with many negative pent-up emotions. Because he moved from one relative's home to another as a child, he never felt secure and always worried that someday he would be abandoned again. Like many neglected children, he joined other troubled teenagers and had several encounters with the law for selling drugs and committing other delinquent acts. With mounting problems of crime and delinquency, he dropped out of the regular public school and completed high school through the GED program. Through observation, Walter determined that people who graduated from college had a better opportunity for socioeconomic advancement than those who did not. Having always competed with his cousins who planned to attend college, he decided that he should attend college if he did not want them to leave him behind. Therefore, he enrolled in the local community college where he completed his AA degree and later enrolled in one of the state universities.

By most standards, Walter would have been a statistic of failure rather than one of success. Fortunately, Walter is graduating from a major research university with a degree in chemistry and a bright future. Yet, he has many feelings to sort out and issues to clarify before entering the work force or advancing to graduate school.

As a college student, his main source of social support has been his white girlfriend which creates a whole set of different kinds of problems and issues for him. First, the girl's parents do not approve of the relationship, nor does his older cousin who provided a place for him to live until he left home. Second, his buddies from his old neighborhood think he has lost his mind for associating with white women. They believe that his dating a white woman is following the trend of other successful black men who marry white women in order to feel good about themselves. His older female cousin who helped to raise him, refuses to discuss the matter of the white girlfriend. In part, Walter does not care what others think about his relationship, because his white girlfriend has been the only person to show him any real compassion and support in his entire life. Yet he is somewhat conflicted about his real feelings about being rejected from all sides.

Because Walter is expecting to become a college graduate soon, some of his old acquaintances are beginning to show him respect they have never shown him before. Some of his relatives who mistreated him as a child claims to care about him now. How should he react to such relatives and old friends who pretend to care now that he has become successful? He ponders his feelings about his father who was absent when he needed him most.

Directions: Based on this scenario, discuss the following directives individually or in small groups.

1. Give a brief description of the client including age, gender, racial/ethnic background, physical features, marital status, school classification, or work status.

2. Provide a brief description of the client's psychosocial history and cultural background, including family members and their involvement with the problem. In addition, identify the client's racial/cultural affiliation including his experiences with racial/cultural diversity.

3. Identify the presenting problems and issues that brought the client into counseling or therapy. List what you believe are the core issues.

4. Do an informal assessment of the client's understanding and expectations of the counseling process.

5. Clarify the client's counseling goals and the purpose of the specific session.

6. Do an informal assessment of the client's racial identity (see Chapter 4 on Racial Identity) status and speculate if his status is related to his presenting problem.

7. Discuss multicultural issues that might be present in counseling if you were his counselor.

For the purpose of counseling practice and skill building, select a partner and role-play the scenario above in dyads. Within a 15-minute period of time each member of each dyad will take turns as counselor and client. A third person may join each dyad to provide feedback.

SUMMARY AND RECOMMENDATIONS

This chapter covered several themes essential for counseling black males. The first theme was counseling self-understanding, including the role of personal awareness and assessment of attitudes toward black males. The second theme was understanding the black male through hearing their voices through a focus group study. The third theme was delivering counseling services for black males, including strategies for connecting with black male clients. We recognize that there were some limitations with the focus group study in that all participants were college educated and successful, and their experiences may be different from black men who are from impoverished backgrounds. Even so, many of the participants had struggled to be successful and showed resilience in the face of economic and social barriers. They are truly an inspiration for overcoming adversity. We conclude with the following recommendations:

1. Understand that there is no monolithic black male (Lee, 1999). They differ by geography, class, and race.
2. Do not attempt to duplicate black dialect, slang or mannerisms (Franklin, 1989; Lee, 1999).
3. Provide services in a nonthreatening setting (i.e., churches, community centers etc.).
4. Offer nontraditional counseling services.
5. Understand the context of the black man by engaging in actions.
    a. Read some of these books:
       * *Native Son* by Richard Wright
       * *Brothers and Keepers: A Memoir* by John Wideman
       * *The Autobiography of Malcolm X* as told to Alex Haley by Attallah Shabazz
       * *Nigger: An Autobiography* by Dick Gregory
       * *Invisible Man* by Ralph Ellison
       * *Black Rage* by William Grier and Price Cobbs
       * *Who's Afraid of a Large Black Man?* by Charles Barkley
    b. Attend black history month programs.
    c. Visit black churches and mosques.
    d. Converse with black males from different backgrounds.
    e. Develop and execute action plans to attack any weakness you may have concerning African American males.
    f. Review articles from *The Journal of Black Psychology, The Journal of Blacks in Higher Education.*

Web Sites of Interest

The Black Collegian Online
http://www.black-collegian.com/african/aaprofil.shtml

REFERENCES

Akbar, N. (1984). *Chains and images of psychological slavery.* Jersey City, N. J.: New Minds.

Ani, M. (1994). *Yurugu: An African-centered critique of European cultural thought and behavior.* Trenton, N. J.: African World.

Baggerly, J. & Parker, W.M. (2005). Child-centered group play therapy with African American boys at the elementary school level. *Journal of Counseling & Development, 83,* 387–396.

Barkley, C. (2005). *Who's afraid of a large black man?* New York: The Penguin Press.

DuBois, W.E.B. (1903). *The souls of black folk.* Chicago: A.C. McClurg & Co.

Franklin, A. J. (2004). *From brotherhood to manhood*. New Jersey: John Wiley & Sons.

Gibbs, J. T. (Ed.) (1988). *Young, black, and male in America: An endangered species*. Dover, MA: Auburn House.

Hulnick, R. (1977). Counselor: Know thyself. *Counselor Education and Supervision, 17*, 69–72.

Johnson, R. L. (1985). Black adolescents: Issues critical to their survival. *Journal of the National Medical Association, 77*, 447–448.

Kambon, K. K. (1998). African/Black psychology in American context: An African-centered approach. Tallahasee, FL: Nubian Nation Publications.

Kunjufu, J. (1995). *Countering the conspiracy to destroy Black boys*. Chicago: African-American Images.

Lee, C. C. (1989). Counseling the Black adolescent: Critical roles and functions for the counseling professionals. In R. L. Jones (Ed.), *Black adolescents*. Berkeley, CA: Cobb and Henry.

Lee, C. C. (1999). *Counseling African American males: A guide to practice* (pp. 39–53). Thousand Oaks, CA: Sage.

Parham, T. A. (1999, August). *Counseling African Americans*. Paper presented at the annual meeting of the American Psychological Association, Boston.

Parham, T.A. (2002). *Counseling persons of African descent: Raising the bar of practitioner competence*. Thousand Oaks, CA: Sage.

Pasteur, A. B. and Toldson, I. L. (1982). *Roots of soul: The psychology of black expressiveness*. Garden City, NY: Anchor Press/Doubleday.

Sanders-Thompson, V. L., Bazile, A. & Akbar, M., (2004). African-Americans' perceptions of psychotherapy and psychotherapists. *Professional Psychology: Research and Practice, 35*, 19–26.

Sue, D. W., & Sue, S. (1999). *Counseling the culturally different*. New York: Wiley.

Watts, R. J. and Abdul-Adil, J. K. (2002). Enhancing critical consciousness in young African American men: A psycho-educational approach. *Psychology of Men and Masculinity, 3* (1), 41–50.

White, J. L., and Cones, J. H. (1999). *Black man emerging: Facing the past and seizing a future in America*. New York: Freeman.

Chapter 6

THE FIRST HOUR: ESTABLISHING A WORKING ALLIANCE

A journey of a thousand miles begins with the first step.
Lao-tzu

Abstract

In this chapter we address the question, "how are multicultural competencies integrated into intakes and initial counseling sessions?" We will highlight multicultural factors, which may be salient to clients' presenting issues. In this way, the culture of the client becomes foreground as an essential part of assessment, counselor assignment, and forming the working alliance.

INTRODUCTION

Unfortunately, many clients from diverse cultural backgrounds drop out of counseling after the first session. Counseling may be literally a foreign concept to some (especially internationals or recent immigrants), or perceived as an extension of the status quo for persons of color. We hope that building a knowledge and awareness base at intake will increase the accuracy of case conceptualization and facilitate building the working alliance. We will draw from the intercultural communication literature as well, to underscore the importance of understanding the importance of interpersonal processes inherent in counseling and psychotherapy.

121

This chapter is organized around the following topics: premature termination and resistances to counseling, establishing the working alliance, suggestions for multicultural intakes, guidelines for idiographic assessments, intercultural communication perspectives, and discussion of a case study. Cultural specific examples will be interspersed to illustrate theoretical points; remember that names are fictitious and details have been changed to protect confidentiality.

Premature Termination

The issue of premature termination of therapy is particularly salient for clients of color. Why do college students drop out of therapy? Curious about this trend, one of the authors (W.M.P) conducted a focus group with African American college students who started, but did not finish the counseling process. I asked students why they did not return after the first session. Quite a range of opinions was reported. One said "The counselor did not sound *real* in our interaction but rather sounded like she was reading directly from a psychology textbook." Another said that he did not like the atmosphere of the reception area. He said, "The reception area was a scary place where the lights were low and people spoke softly as though they were in a funeral home." A third student did not return because the counselor "blamed his mother for his stuttering problem." He told the focus group that his mother was the "nicest and sweetest person" in the world and he did not appreciate anybody saying bad things about her, even if the counselor was a doctor. Yet another student said the counselor was acting too nervous and did not seem to know what he was doing. "He kept biting his nails and looking at the floor and never once looked at me." Two of the students said they did not return because it seemed like a waste of their time. Some counselors seemed to have their own agenda, which did not address the issues of greatest concern to the client. Another student said that her counselor was O.K. except he was too eager to fix the problem rather than attend to the client's feelings of anger, hopelessness, and disappointment. She said that she just needed to vent, to be heard and to be supported. Finally, another focus group member perceived his counselor to have a superiority complex suggesting that the relationship would be like a master/slave relationship. This counselor said he would take care of all of his client's needs "as long as he did as he was instructed to do."

There are many reasons why culturally diverse clients do not return to complete the counseling process. We believe that what happens in the first hour can either make or break the development of a healthy counseling relationship. In the first session, the client makes internal evaluations about feeling safe and being helped. Similar to the early stages of group work, members decide whether they are *in* or *out* based largely on their feelings of security, safety and acceptance (Yalom, 1995). Their decision to return is based on the extent they believe their lives can be turned over to a stranger–the counselor.

Resistances to Counseling

The first hour of the counselor/client dyad is of decisive importance especially when the client and counselor come from racially and culturally diverse backgrounds. In the first hour many unspoken questions are raised and both the client and the counselor make many silent judgments. This internal dialogue embodies personal, family, and cultural messages about the efficacy of counseling. These negative thoughts have been identified as potential barriers to counseling effectively, and have been described in the *anti-counselor triad* training model (Pedersen, 2004). An example is demonstrated in the following client inner thoughts during a first session, "Why does the counselor only ask about my feelings? I know how I feel! I need help with passing my courses, with time and stress management, and with transportation to and from work in order to pay my bills so I won't get kicked out of school."

The following list represents some of the negative thoughts or resistances to counseling, which may be influenced by cultural backgrounds. Many of the myriads of questions raised in the client's mind include:

- Is it safe for me to discuss my personal business with this stranger?
- Does the counselor really care about me or is this just a job?
- What would my friends think if they knew that I had come to see somebody about a mental health issue?
- What would my parents think? Will they be disappointed that I did not discuss my problem with them?

Like the client, the counselor may have questions when he or she first encounters a culturally diverse client. Some of those questions include:

- I wonder what the client thinks of me, am I trustworthy?

- I wonder if racial/ethnic/cultural differences matter and should I bring them up?
- What if I make a racial/ethnic/cultural blunder?
- Will I be multiculturally competent?

An area of MCC skills includes being able to articulate some of these concerns in session with clients, to bring to the surface what is happening at a subtle or unconscious level.

We recommend practicing dialogues through role-plays, for example, using Paul Pedersen's (2004) *pro-counselor* and *anti-counselor* triad model training. In this training technique, three persons simulate a counseling session: one plays the counselor, one plays a client from a different cultural background, and the third person articulates the client's cultural messages, either in a supportive role *(for)* or disruptive role *(against)* the counseling experience (Neimeyer et al., 1986).

Sometimes counselors will need to explain how counseling works, clarify limits of confidentiality, and verbalize mutual expectations. These goals are accomplished in the context of managing first impressions and working towards establishing a working alliance.

Establishing the Working Alliance

Scott Miller and associates have summarized therapy outcome studies and concluded that clients' ratings of the therapeutic alliance are the best predictor of engagement and outcome. In addition, the clients' subjective experience of change early in the process is the best predictor of success in therapy (Duncan & Miller, 2000; Hubble, Duncan, & Miller, 1999). Multicultural factors play into establishing the working alliance from the first hour (Perez, Fukuyama & Case, 2005).

Sue and Zane (1987) summarized two dimensions that are helpful for establishing a working alliance–**credibility** and **gift-giving.** These process variables will be described as one way of defining strategies for a first session.

Credibility is defined as when the client views the counselor as an effective and trustworthy helper. Credibility is enhanced through:

- **Ascribed Status**-counselor demonstrates understanding of the position/role the client is assigned by others (based on race, class, gender, professional titles, and so on).

- **Achieved Status**-through counselor skills, client comes to have trust, hope, and confidence.
- **Conceptualization of the Problem**-counselor's view of the problem represents an integration of the problems and the client's belief system/world view.
- **Approach to Problem Resolution**-interventions towards change are congruent with the client's value system.
- **Therapeutic Goals**-client feels aligned with the counselor and feels essential aspects of his/her culture are affirmed (humanity/spirit).

Gift Giving refers to the client's perception that something was received during the therapeutic encounter. Meaningful "gifts" may include:

- Cognitive Clarity
- Normalization
- Reassurance
- Skills Acquisition
- Coping Mechanisms

These first session issues are important for all clients and may arise with mainstream clients also. For example: *Julie, a 20-year-old white college student of northern European descent, presented in an intake appointment feelings of anger and distress over her parents impending divorce. She also expressed concern that her anger was being taken out on her boyfriend and she didn't want to lose this relationship. She asks the intake counselor, "Can this be fixed?" The counselor reassures her by saying, "Yes, this sort of situation is fixable. It's normal when families are going through a divorce to have strong feelings about it, and counseling can provide you a safe space to express yourself."*

Sometimes it is important to begin *therapy* in the first session as part of gift-giving. Several reasons support this strategy in particular: First, some clients have exhausted all of their resources from their natural support system and are ready for immediate help when they arrive at the counselor's office. Second, some clients do not seek help until their condition has reached a crisis state, and they need interventions immediately. Third, since many culturally diverse clients are not accustomed to therapy, a little therapy in the first session provides the therapist with the opportunity to model the therapy process. Fourth, a sample of the therapy process may help the client to reduce some of his/her fears about what might happen.

Sometimes it is best to take advantage of the moment and collect the intake information in a later session. Beginning the therapy session immediately provides a *gift* the client can take home and the chances of the client's return are increased. *For example, the counselor sensed that Raul was ready to work when he said that he wanted to get to the heart of the matter. He said, further, that he had read all of the self-help books he could, but had not found the answer to his continuous anxious feelings.*

Finally, there are many strategies for instilling hope in clients, but Corey (1995) suggested that the most important one of all is the *person* of the counselor or therapist. *Who* the therapist is speaks louder than words. The genuineness of the counselor is important due to the value that many racial/ethnic group members place on relationships. Strupp (1970, 1973) suggested that while counseling techniques are valuable, especially those that are culturally relevant, the nonspecific attitudinal and relationship factors seem to be the most powerful components of the counseling experience.

In addition to the process variables of establishing credibility and gift-giving, intakes and initial counseling sessions encompass counseling assumptions and strategies. These will be discussed in the next two sections on intakes and *idiographic* assessments.

Suggestions for Multicultural Intakes

Don Locke (1998) constructed a comprehensive model for understanding ethnic cultural differences. He named ten elements for understanding within group differences and cross-cultural comparisons: acculturation, poverty and economic concerns, history of oppression, language and the arts, racism and prejudice, sociopolitical factors, child-rearing practices, religious practices, family structure and dynamics, and cultural values and attitudes. Utilizing this model, counselors may want to assess the elements that are salient to the client's presenting problem.

Gargi Roysircar (2005) at the Antioch New England Multicultural Center developed a multicultural intake checklist, and items adapted from her work can be found in Table 6.1. This list is intended to provide a broad framework for including a variety of multicultural variables when assessing client concerns. Of course, not all of the items may be

Table 6.1. Multicultural Factors in Qualitative Assessments at Intake

English Language Fluency
Individualistic-Collectivistic Worldview Orientation
Acculturation Adaptation (Integrated/ Bicultural; Assimilated; Traditional/Separated; Marginalized)
Acculturative Stress
Perceived Discrimination/Racism
Family/Extended Family Concerns
Intergenerational Issues
Identity (Racial/Ethnic, Gender, Sexual Orientation, Multiple Identities, Transgender)
Social/Network Resources
Loss of Face Issues
Issues of Privacy/Confidentiality
DSM-IV Cultural Considerations (e.g., Culture-bound Syndromes, Cultural V-codes, Axis IV Cultural Stressors)

Adapted from Roysircar, 2005, p. 34

covered in an intake, or even in the initial counseling sessions, but some may be important for consideration.

Many times these factors may be elicited by asking the client to tell their family story. Immigrants and children of immigrants or refugees often reveal emotionally rich details in their family backgrounds. As an example of assimilation, consider the description from Carlos Eire's memoirs in Box 6.1.

Box 6.1

Carlos Eire and his older brother Tony were airlifted from Havana to Miami in 1962, along with 14,000 other children *sans* parents, who could not get exit permits under Castro's new revolutionary regime. No one anticipated that it would be three years before they would be reunited with their mother in Chicago. In his memoirs *Waiting for Snow in Havana,* he described what it was like to acquire English as a second language.

Eventually, I acquired English. It's mine. All mine. I bought it word by word, on credit the American way. And English owns me, too. I think in English; I even dream in English, except when Louis XVI shows up [reference to his father]. Spanish stopped growing and is now a homely, misshapen dwarf. An all-wise and almost mystical dwarf, keeper of the keys to my soul, but a dwarf nonetheless. (Eire, 2003, p. 350)

Guidelines for Idiographic Assessments

Idiographic describes the uniqueness of the individual in the context of cultural dynamics. Ridley, Hill, Thompson, & Ormerod (2001) outlined guidelines for conducting idiographic assessments for clients. The authors emphasized taking a balanced approach to case conceptualization, including understanding culture specific knowledge, social-political contexts, and saliency of identity, in addition to psychological symptoms. The following discussion is derived from Ridley et al.'s work.

The authors proposed several core assumptions in working from the MCC perspective: (1) the person-in-context; (2) multiple identities; (3) a holistic view of the person; (4) the client experiences of trauma; and (5) clinical bias. These assumptions will be elaborated in the following discussion.

First, a *person-in-context* view examines situational factors. Traditional intakes include taking a family and medical history, exploring precipitating events, and elaborating symptoms. Situational factors may also include assessing the client's community resources, eliciting the family story related to immigration or refugee status, and evaluating cultural adaptation stress.

A second assumption is the concept of "multiple identities," which refers to the multiplicity of social identities. Here are some examples:

• Black gay male
• Upper middle-class white heterosexual male with physical disability
• Christian counselor of Haitian descent
• Jewish trans-female (male to female transgender) lesbian
• Biracial black-white male of Jewish descent
• Catholic Latino gay male

You can quickly see that the days of a single social identity are in the past. Part of integrating MCC related to identity is to think outside simplistic categories, and to recognize that people exist in multiple contexts, with multiple identities, which may or not be salient at various points in time. The multiracial identity process will be discussed further in Chapter 8.

For example, as an African American lesbian, Sherrie may not discuss her lesbian identity in the context of participating in her local church activities and political social causes. Her race/ethnicity is more salient in this social context. But when she attends a lesbian dance, her sexual orientation identity is more salient and affirmed. Persons with multiple social identities, especially persons of color, frequently adapt to the social context in a more fluid identity style (Fukuyama & Ferguson, 1999).

Third, we endorse a holistic view of the person. One of the limitations of the scientific world view is that people become reduced to parts and labels (i.e., medical model diagnoses). Instead of only labeling a client with a *panic disorder,* it is important to see him or her holistically as a person "consisting of a variety of assets, limitations, resources, and potentialities" (Ridley et al., 2001, p. 203). Other holistic approaches to health and wellness include exploring dimensions such as emotions, intellect, spirituality, physical body, social relationships, and career aspirations (for examples, see Bill Hettler, http://www.nationalwellness.org/; James Gordon, MD, http://www.jamesgordonmd.com/).

A fourth assumption is to examine the effects of trauma on the client. Maria Root (cited in Ridley et al., 2001, p. 204) identified three ways that trauma may be experienced. Trauma may be experienced in direct ways such as in natural disasters or war, indirectly through identification with victims of violence (e.g., women and fear of rape), and insidiously through social oppression (hate crimes, discrimination and prejudice). The latter form of trauma takes place in daily interactions for members of marginalized groups. The effects of oppression and ways to counteract it were discussed more fully in Chapter 3.

Examples of identification with the victim and insidious forms of trauma are illustrated in the following instance: *Eric and David are both of white European descent, upper middle class professionals. They have been partners for 8 years, yet they live in a fairly encapsulated lifestyle, socializing occasionally in gay community events like fundraisers, but otherwise working long hours or fixing up their home. They rarely go to gay clubs because they fear that they could be targeted on the street by hate crime. The tragic beating death of Matthew Shepherd, a young gay college student in Laramie, Wyoming, reinforced their perception that gay men are not safe.*

Another example of insidious trauma that affects daily life events is the racial profiling of Arabs as *terrorists*. Arab Americans or those who appear to fit a stereotype (such as Sikhs, a religious order from India in which the men wear turbans) are targeted as suspicious or disloyal. This prejudice is another example of how *the other* is cast by those in power. White males are not typically thought of as terrorists, yet the 1995 Oklahoma bombing which killed 168 and injured over 500 Americans was carried out by a white male.

The fifth and final core assumption is that counselors have their own biases that affect perceptions and interpretations of clinical work. Counselors are socialized just as everyone else in terms of mainstream culture, which may lead one to be biased for and against various cultural factors. For example, counselors have been known to favor the YAVIS client (Young, Attractive, Verbal, Intelligent, Successful), which reflects mainstream cultural values (Hollingsworth, 1985). Alternately, some counselors discriminate against culturally diverse clients and those who are poor. Sundberg (1981) labeled these clients as QUOID (quiet, ugly, old, indigent, or dissimilar culturally). These biases may lead to inaccurate clinical judgment and unconscious expressions of racism (Dovidio et al., 2002). Ridley et al. (2001) suggest that counselors develop cognitive complexity to avoid stereotyping and cultural blind-spots. Counselors need to consciously work to unlearn stereotypes and social biases.

Shonfeld-Ringel (2001) identified several domains that are essential to building a working alliance cross-culturally: empathy, mutuality, the dynamics of power and authority, the use of self, and the process of communication. Examples in each domain will be discussed further.

Traditionally, empathy refers to the counselor's ability to understand clients' feelings in relation to their identified concerns. A broader definition of transcultural empathy refers to the "ability to accept and to be open to multiple perspectives of both personal and cultural realities." (Ham, cited in Shonfeld-Ringel, 2001, p. 54.) In Asian cultures, Ham suggests that empathy is taught to children through folk tales, myths, and metaphors, and that empathy is an important basis for harmony in all relationships. Thus, she recommends studying culture-specific myths to learn intercultural empathy, particularly in counseling Asian clients. For a teaching example, see Box 6.1.

Box 6.2

The Magical Starfruit Tree by Rosalind C. Wang

A Chinese American author, who was born in China, grew up in Taiwan, and now lives in the U.S wrote this children's story. She wanted to share stories that she had heard growing up, and thus wrote this book based upon a Chinese folktale. From the book jacket description, "This

Chinese folktale tells the story of a greedy peddler, Ah-Di, a kind-hearted young boy, Ming-Ming, and an old beggar on a hot day. In spite of the heat and the old man's apparent thirst, the miserly peddler refuses to give him a juicy starfruit. Although he has little, Ming-Ming offers to buy a piece of fruit for the old man. The beggar gratefully accepts and eats the fruit, saving only one seed. Calling for someone to bring him a pot of hot water, he plants the seed. The old man uses his magic to make the seed grow, blossom, and bear fruit, all before the eyes of the bewildered crowd. In the end there is enough fruit for everyone, the peddler is chastised for his greedy ways, and Ming-Ming is rewarded for his generosity. *The Magical Starfruit Tree* teaches children the virtue of sharing and introduces the concept of respect for the elderly, which are cornerstones of Chinese philosophy and all-too-often overlooked in American culture."

The concept of mutuality in the therapeutic relationship suggests that it is a "collaborative, interactive, and dynamic process between client and therapist" (p. 55). Contemporary relational theories posit that the therapist's subjectivity, authenticity and personality influence the change process in an interactive way. This dynamic is especially of concern where there are genuine cultural differences between client and counselor, for example, when the counselor is focused on individuality and the client is from a collectivistic culture. The counselor may believe in egalitarian relationships when the client expects a hierarchical one.

The dynamics of power and authority in counseling are particularly important to consider, especially when the counselor is from the dominant culture and the client from a culturally diverse group, or again, when there are genuine cultural differences. **For example:** *Erica is a feminist therapist who strives to empower her clients by helping them discover their own voice. Her primary focus is on the individual and equal sharing of power in the therapy room. Chung is a male client who grew up in Taiwan. He expects the therapist to be an expert, and defers to her authority in the session. Additionally, his primary focus is on fulfilling parental expectations and achieving success in a career that reflects positively on his family.*

Discussion suggestion: Brainstorm and role-play ways in which counselors can express expertise (authority) and also empower clients to achieve their goals.

The use of self and counselor counter-transference are sources of information for the client's nonverbal communication or unarticulated affect. Counselors need to pay attention to their assumptions that are made about nonverbal cues, and to check them out with the client. Nonverbal communication concerns will be discussed further in the next section.

Finally, communication (both verbal and nonverbal) is an essential component of therapy, particularly complicated when counselor and client do not speak the same language. Intercultural communication competences require ongoing review to ensure that the counselor is being effective. English as a second language may lead to different understandings in therapy as well. For example, first language often accesses the emotions and childhood memories more effectively than English. On the other hand, English language may give the client a vocabulary to discuss difficult issues (such as sexuality and sexual orientation) that is not available in first language. Many factors influence communication styles. Several intercultural communication perspectives will be discussed next.

Intercultural Communication Perspectives

The intercultural communication field examines multiple factors that influence the communication process, and several of these will be discussed here, beginning with understanding the concept of low-context versus high context culture, followed by discussing individualism versus collectivism, and concluding with exploring intercultural skills building and nonverbal communication.

Low-Context and High Context Culture

Drawing from the intercultural communication field, the concept of *low context vs. high context* culture is a factor that may influence the counseling relationship from the first minute.

Here is a case example: *A 21-year-old female college student from Persia (Iran) makes an intake appointment for counseling. The intaker asks, "What brings you in today?" The student replies, "You mean I have to tell you what's bothering me already?!" The student proceeds to express high levels of discomfort with talking with a stranger about personal and intimate issues, and leaves the session after ten minutes.*

What just happened? In American culture, which is a *low context culture,* communication styles tend to be linear, that is, the best way to get from *point A* to *point B* is a direct straight line. This style of communication is effective for dealing with objective information; it focuses on issues, not the person. The meanings are communicated through words, and any conflict or differences are seen as an intellectual disagreement, It is a detached, not personal communication style. In contrast, many world cultures are *high context culture,* which means that communication is inferential, like a spiral or circle. The meanings are not in the words but in the context or process; i.e., "how you get to the point is more important than the point" (Bennett, 1996). This communication style tends to be vague, indirect, and requires intuitive listening skills. In conflict situations, the disagreement becomes personal, because it is an attached, relational style.

Arab cultures tend to be high context and verbally expressive, and involve an exchange in compliments and reciprocal giving. The indirect communication style is illustrated in this proverb: "It is good to know the truth, but it is better to speak of palm trees" (cited in Hammer, 2003, p. 9).

Let's assume the intake counselor recognized that the Persian female client may have a need to express herself in a more circular than linear way. Here is an alternative beginning, "Hi, my name is Dr. Fukuyama. I like to begin by us getting to know each other better. Can you tell me a little about yourself? What's it like to be in the U.S.? What are you studying in school? And what would you like to know about counseling and/or me?"

Other cultures have variations on this more circular theme, for example, Latino cultures may be represented by a fuzzy spiral, filled with words and indirect communication (D. Sermol, personal communication, July 27, 2005). The concept of *personalismo* suggests that Latino clients may prefer a more personal, warm and disclosive style of interactions with their counselors.

Individualism vs. Collectivism

Another area of cultural difference is found in comparing individualist versus collectivist cultures, and many social adjustment issues are related to understanding these anthropological concepts. Although cultures may vary in terms of emphasis, in general Northern European and English-speaking societies are individualist whereas Asian, Latin American, and Islamic societies are collectivist. This fact influences social relationships and interpersonal communication patterns widely

(Chen, Brockner, & Chen, 2002). For example, peer influence is stronger among individualists while parental influence is stronger among collectivists. Clinically speaking, a college student from a collectivist orientation may be striving to meet career goals based upon parental directives. Sometimes students feel conflicted between family wishes and personal interests, especially if the children are first generation in the U.S.

Individualist societies are equalitarian, democratic, and value human rights, whereas collectivist societies are hierarchical, authoritarian, and emphasize harmony and security. Individualists use guilt while collectivists use shame as a method of social control, hence, the Asian concern with *saving face*. Individualists value honesty and genuineness, whereas a collectivist may feel compelled to hide the truth or lie in order to save face for the family or group. It is not unusual for an Asian client to be referred to counseling after troublesome situations have worsened to the point of a crisis, for example, a student who had been failing classes for two semesters, but had not told anyone.

A business case study which illustrates the dimensions of individualist versus collectivist values is found in Box 6.3.

Box 6.3

A Business Case Study

Harris Friedman (2004) described a case study in which a Western expatriate manager did not understand collectivistic cultural norms. "The manager stated he had asked a local village chief to send three men to clear a field, with each man to receive a payment for eight hours' work. However, the entire group of 40 able-bodied men from the village showed up. The expatriate wanted only three and consequently asked the chief to send the remainder back to the village. The chief, however, requested that all 40 could do the work quickly and the payment could be made to the communal fund that helped all in the village collectively. Not understanding this collective approach, the expatriate sent all the men away and, instead, hired three Fijian Indian workers from the city who were more comfortable with an individual model of capitalism, illustrating the clash of different work values and productivity models. The result was that the manger's selection of the Fijian Indians fueled mutual resentments—from the native Fijians toward both the manager and the Fijian Indians whose competing labor deprived the village of needed resources, and back from the manager and Fijian Indians, who perceived the native Fijian behavior through the stereotypes of Western culture as laziness (i.e., not individually willing to do a "full day's work for a full day's pay"). Adding to the problem of competing economic models is a deep Western-based ethnocentrism that tends to deprecate native Fijian culture. (p. 120)

Intercultural Skills Building

Counselors need to be astute observers of human behaviors, especially in cross-cultural interactions. Ting-Toomey (1999) described a four-step process of developing cross-cultural observation skills (**O-D-I-S**). She suggested that by patiently **observing,** you prepare yourself to develop hypotheses about what is happening, a necessary step for understanding cultural differences and learning new behaviors. Secondly, she recommended that you **describe** what you experience using your five senses, holding a neutral position. Third, be aware of the natural impulse to label or **interpret** what you observe. It is natural to assign meaning to what you see or hear from your own cultural viewpoint, without knowing the meaning in the new situation. For example, "I *imagine* that the smile that I see on your face might mean that you are feeling anxious right now, is that so?" Finally, **suspend** judgment and evaluation, in order to avoid making premature generalizations about cultural behaviors.

This process is similar to the practice of mindfulness or Vipassana style meditation. Some counselor educators teach meditation (observational skills) in conjunction with studying multicultural counseling (K. Northsworthy, personal communication, May 17, 2000). Mindfulness meditation has also been shown effective in teaching patients how to cope with stress and illness (Kabat-Zinn, 1990).

Craig Storti (1990) adapted an Eastern meditation approach to coping with cultural adaptation. First, he noted that cross-cultural contact leads to anxiety, frustration, and confusion when people do not meet culturally-conditioned expectations for behavior. He analyzed the problem further by pointing out two natural responses to cultural differences: (1) people tend to assume that others are like themselves until those assumptions are confronted through difference, and (2) people tend to withdraw when they feel uncomfortable as a result of these unmet expectations.

Through learning self-observation skills, the ability to detach even momentarily allows the individual some time and space to understand the situation before becoming more reactive and judgmental. It also alleviates some of the stress and anxiety associated with the uncomfortable feelings which may accompany unfamiliar situations. He recommended that people need to have cross-cultural experiences to learn to change expectations. The only way to accommodate to the differences is through observation and understanding why the differences are disturbing.

Suggested Activity

One way to enhance your awareness of nonverbal communication is to watch a videotape of your counseling session with the sound turned off. Gather opinions from your supervisory group about the assumptions that are made from nonverbal cues alone. See Box 6.4 for more exercises to develop awareness of nonverbal communication.

Box 6.4

   Pair up with a partner and practice some of the following non-verbal communication exercises:

1. Greetings: what norms dictate how you greet a stranger, a friend, a relative, an elder, a child, (bowing, handshake, hugs, light kisses)? How have you experienced and adjusted to cultural differences in greetings?
2. Proxemics: refers to interpersonal spatial relationships, how comfortable people are in physical space with each other. U.S. Americans tend to prefer about a handshake distance apart when greeting strangers. Discover your personal space by experimenting with how close you like to stand to each other in conversation. How big is your *personal bubble?* What is communicated through positioning your body in relation to another? What social context factors influence your comfort zone (e.g., gender, role status)?
3. Eye contact: Practice with one partner averting eyes while the other maintains steady eye contact. What meaning do you ascribe to direct or indirect eye contact?
4. Facial animation: some cultures value emotional restraint in social situations and one way of doing this is by restricting facial expression. How do you interpret facial expression or restraint?

---

5. Silence: U.S. American culture does not tolerate silence in conversation well, and in some instances, people *talk over* one another, not even waiting for a pause. In Japanese culture, silence is valued; it is like listening to the reverberations of a meditation bell. In addition, as a high context culture, silence may be communicating something more powerfully than words. Practice having a conversation with intentional silence (e.g., count to 3 before speaking).
6. Discuss other factors: (tonality, loudness, and accents).

We complete this chapter with a case study which incorporates cross-cultural values.

Case Study

Dee is a 25-year-old graduate student in sociology, and first generation Vietnamese American. She presents with high levels of anxiety, including a recent history of panic attacks. She saw her family physician who prescribed medication for the panic attacks, but is uncomfortable with relying upon pills. Upon further exploration, the counselor learns that the panic attacks happen primarily in context of visiting her family where she is expected to work long hours in the family business, even though she is quite stressed by her graduate studies. Dee wants to help her family, and feels a strong obligation to do so. She is the oldest daughter. At some level, she feels that she has let her parents down by not pursuing a degree in medicine. In addition, she is hiding her relationship with a white American boyfriend, because she fears that they would not approve.

What are some of the contextual factors in the above case study? Clearly the family dynamics exist in the context of an immigrant family from Viet Nam. Their immigration history (e.g., the circumstances of their move to the United States), economic status, family roles, and acculturation are contextual factors which may be relevant and salient to this client. How are collectivist values being enacted? How does shame play a part in the problem? What are alternative interpretations of the problem beyond *panic attacks?*

CONCLUDING REMARKS

We have offered a set of guidelines and suggestions for counselors to navigate through the first session with culturally diverse clients (Perez,

Fukuyama, & Case, 2005). Unfortunately, it is not crystal clear when to collect basic intake data and when to begin the therapy process. Counselors generally gather information and make formal and informal assessments throughout the counseling relationship. It is critical for counselors to balance the amount of time for assessment and beginning therapeutic interventions in the first session.

Suggested Exercises

1. Counseling is often met with ambivalence. Discuss your own "push-pull" dynamics about becoming a counselor or psychotherapist to understand resistance.
2. Review a videotape of your counseling work (role-play, client tape) and analyze your responses from an Interpersonal Process Recall (IPR) perspective, e.g., what were you thinking when you responded in that way?
3. Formulate open-ended intake questions based upon Roysircar's list of cultural considerations in Table 6.1.
4. Interview someone who was raised in a collectivistic culture. How do his/her experiences compare to individualistic norms?

Web site to explore social bias and conscious and unconscious attitudes towards others:

https://implicit.harvard.edu/implicit/demo/selectatest.html

Books:

Eugenides, J. (2003). *Middlesex: A novel.* New York: Picador.
Fadiman, A. (1998). *The spirit catches you and you fall down: A Hmong child, her American doctors, and the collision of two cultures.* New York: Farrar, Straus & Giroux.
Kingsolver, B. (2003). *Poisonwood Bible: A novel.* New York: Harper-Torch.

REFERENCES

Bennett, M. (1996). *Better together than apart.* Lecture presented to the Intercultural Communication Summer Institute. [Videotape available from Intercultural Resource Corporation 78 Greylock Rd, Newtonville, MA 02160, http://www.irc-international.com or see http://www.intercultural.org/]

Chen, Y. R., Brockner, J, & Chen, X. P. (2002). Individual-collective primacy and ingroup favoritism: Enhancement and protection effects. *Journal of Experimental Social Psychology, 38* (5), 482–491.

Corey, G. (1995). *Group counseling* (4th Ed.). Pacific Grove, CA: Brooks/Cole.

Dovidio, J. F., Gaertner, S. E., & Kawakami, K. (2002). Why can't we just get along? Interpersonal biases and interracial distrust. *Cultural Diversity & Ethnic Minority Psychology, 8,* 88–102.

Duncan, B. L. & Miller, S.D. (2000). *The heroic client: Doing client-directed, outcome-informed therapy.* San Francisco: Jossey-Bass.

Eire, C. (2003). *Waiting for snow in Havana: Confessions of a Cuban boy.* New York: Free Press.

Friedman, H. (2004). Reframing the conflict in Fiji: Economic and transpersonal frameworks for peace. *The International Journal of Transpersonal Studies, 23,* 118–124.

Fukuyama, M. A., & Ferguson, A. D. (1999). Lesbian, gay, and bisexual people of color: Understanding cultural complexity and managing multiple oppressions. In R. M. Perez, K. A. DeBord, & K. J. Bieschke (Eds.), *Handbook of counseling and psychotherapy with lesbian, gay, and bisexual clients* (pp. 81–105). Washington, DC: American Psychological Association.

Kabat-Zinn, J. (1990). *Full catastrophe living: Using the wisdom of your body and mind to face stress, pain and illness.* New York: Delta.

Katz, J. H. (1985). The sociopolitical nature of counseling. *The Counseling Psychologist, 13,* 615–624.

Hammer, M. R. (2003). *Intercultural conflict style inventory. Individual profile ICS-IP, Interpretive guide.* Ocean Pines, MD: Mitchell R. Hammer.

Hollingsworth, D. K. (1985). The counselor and physical attractiveness: A response. *Journal of Counseling and Development, 63,* 488–489.

Hubble, M. A., Duncan, B. L., & Miller, S. D., (Eds.) (1999). *The heart & soul of change: What works in therapy.* Washington, DC: American Psychological Association.

Locke, D. C. (1998). *Increasing multicultural understanding: A comprehensive model* (2nd Ed). Thousand Oaks, CA: Sage.

Neimeyer, G. J., Fukuyama, M. A., Bingham, R. P., Hall, L. E., & Mussenden, M. E. (1986). Training cross-cultural counselors: A comparison of the pro-counselor models and anti-counselor triad models. *Journal of Counseling and Development, 64,* 437–439.

Pedersen, P. B. (2004). The triad training model. 110 *Experiences for multicultural learning* (pp. 153–156). Washington, DC: American Psychological Association.

Pedersen, P. B. & Ivey, A. (1993). *Culture-centered counseling and interviewing skills: A practical guide.* Westport, CN: Praeger.

Perez, R., Fukuyama, M. & Case, A. (2005, April). *Integrating multicultural competencies into intakes and initial counseling sessions.* Psychologist Continuing Education Workshops, Gainesville, FL

Ridley, C. R., Hill, C. L., Thompson, C. E., & Ormerod, A. J. (2001). Clinical practice guidelines in assessment: Toward an idiographic perspective. In D. B. Pope-Davis & H. L.K. Coleman (Eds.), *The intersection of race, class, and gender in multicultural counseling* (pp. 191–211). Thousand Oaks: Sage.

Roysircar, G. (2005). Culturally sensitive assessment, diagnosis, and guidelines. In M. G. Constantine & D. W. Sue (Eds.), *Strategies for building multicultural competence in mental health and educational settings* (pp. 19–38). Hoboken, NJ: John Wiley & Sons.

Sheu, H. B. & Fukuyama, M. A. (in press). Counseling international students from East Asia. In H. D. Singaravelu and M. Pope (Eds.), *Handbook for counseling international students.* Alexandria, VA: American Counseling Association.

Shonfeld-Ringel, S. (2001). A re-conceptualization of the working alliance in cross-cultural practice with non-western clients: Integrating relational perspectives and multicultural theories. *Clinical Social Work Journal, 29,* 53–63.

Storti, C. (1990). *The art of crossing cultures.* Yarmouth, ME: Intercultural Press.

Sue, S. & Zane, N. (1987). The role of culture and cultural techniques in psychotherapy: A critique a reformulation. *American Psychologist, 42* (1), 37–45.

Sundberg, N. D. (1981). Cross-cultural counseling and psychotherapy: A research overview. In A. J. Marsella & P. B. Pedersen (Eds.), *Cross-cultural counseling and psychotherapy* (pp. 29–38). New York: Pergamon.

Ting-Toomey, S. (1999). *Communicating across cultures.* New York: The Guilford Press.

Ting-Toomey, S. & Oetzel, J. G. (2001). *Managing intercultural conflict effectively.* Thousand Oaks, CA: Sage, 2001.

Wang, R. C. (1993). *The magical starfruit tree.* Hillsboro, OR: Beyond Words Publishing, Inc.

Yalom, I. D. (1995). *The theory and practice of group psychotherapy* (4th Ed.). New York: BasicBooks.

Chapter 7

COUNSELING LATINA/O FAMILIES

ANDRES NAZARIO, JR.

Con los pobres de la tierra
Quiero yo mi suerte echar . . .
With the poor of the land,
I want to share my destiny . . .

Jose Marti

Abstract

An overview of the Latin American immigrant in the United States is provided in this chapter, including census data characteristics and sociopolitical issues associated with different Latino/a groups, a brief review of the literature on Latina/o families in the United States, and suggestions for an approach for working with the variety of presenting problems Latino/as and Latina/o families bring to counseling.

INTRODUCTION

Latino/a individuals and Latina/o families seek counseling for a variety of difficulties. Recently, I worked with Latino/a individuals with

---

Note: I consider the term Latina/o, as opposed to Hispanic, to be more inclusive of all the people with roots in Latin America. It includes the African influence in many countries as well as the indigenous population. The term Hispanic excludes people from Central or South America and the Caribbean whose origin may not be related to the Spaniards, such as Afro-Cubans, Indo-Caribbeans, Haitians, and Brazilians. At times, the term Hispanic is used in this chapter in reference to original sources.

presenting problems such as adaptation to school, coming out as a gay man, depression, substance abuse, eating disorders, HIV and AIDS as well as a variety of court-referred cases. The Latina/o families with whom I work present difficulties such as parent-child conflicts, domestic violence, infidelity, separation and divorce, substance abuse, marital difficulties, depression, illness in the family, and death and dying. Therefore, for the most part, presenting problems for the Latino/a individual and/or Latina/o family are not that different from those presented by members of the dominant culture. It is the context in which these difficulties occur that requires added sensitivity and cultural awareness. The impact of racism, sexism, heterosexism, classism, ethnocentrism, and other forms of oppression need to be explored when working with Latino/as and Latina/o families.

An overview of the Latin American immigrant in the United States is provided in this chapter, including census data characteristics and sociopolitical issues associated with different Latino/a groups, a brief review of the literature on Latina/o families in the United States, and suggestions for an approach for working with the variety of presenting problems Latino/as and Latina/o families bring to the counselor's room.

Sociopolitical Issues

Latin America is comprised of a mosaic of different peoples, cultures, customs and even languages. Despite similar colonial experiences, diversity rather than uniformity characterizes the region that runs from Mexico to Tierra del Fuego and includes some Caribbean islands. Each nation was shaped by specific historical experiences following independence, and each has a particular cultural richness. Spanish is the official language for all of the region with the exception of Brazil, the largest and most populated nation in Latin America, where Portuguese is the official language, and Haiti, the poorest of the Latin countries, where Haitian Creole is spoken. Yet, most of these nations have one or more indigenous people with their own idioms.

A Brief Profile of the Latin American Immigrant

Different levels of economic growth place some Latin countries among the newly industrialized nations and others in the lower rank of the Third World. Political development has been successful in some countries and frustrating in others. Marked rivalries abound among neighboring countries, but the region is and always has been more stable than how it is generally perceived from the outside. Some shared political commonalities are perhaps the most pervasive: a tradition of *caudillismo,* or strong man rule, and a sense of vulnerability and dependence on outside powers, mainly the United States.

Latin American nationals in the United States represent a more cohesive group than perhaps the region itself, due to the shared characteristics of the immigrants. Most of the Latino/as born outside the U.S. and living in this country speak Spanish or Portuguese, even if with regional slang, rather than any of the indigenous languages. They are usually urban, of European or mixed descent, and rarely come from the lowest socioeconomic ranks of society since the indigenous populations hardly emigrate. With the exception of those who cross land borders, immigrants must have enough resources to buy an airline ticket or secure other means of passage. Exposure, even if limited, to the outside world is generally a precondition for leaving one's own country, as well as a willingness to work hard to achieve the expected opportunities for a better life that most immigrants perceive to be awaiting in the land of the dollar.

Poor and/or weak economies that offer very few incentives even for the most ambitious, be it unskilled workers or highly trained professionals, push the vast majority of Latin Americans in the United States out of their native country, and the highly industrialized and prosperous nation to the North pulls them in. The upper classes, which travel frequently to the United States, rarely stay, and the traditional middle class, which feels it can manage well in its own country, rarely leaves. Closeness to the United States, as in Mexico's case, influences the number of risk takers who are willing to cross over illegally. Many others, however, reach the United States legally, especially those professionals who are granted preferential visas, while still others overextend their stay when tourist or student visas expire.

The search for better economic and professional opportunities is not the only reason Latino/as come to the United States. Latino/as have also left their homelands for political reasons. Although most South Americans migrate seeking a chance for a better life, dictatorships in Chile, Argentina, Paraguay, Uruguay, Brazil, Peru, Ecuador, and Bolivia during the 1970s forced many people out. Some were expelled from their countries, while others were persecuted for their political activism. These groups, albeit small, represented part of the intellectual and political elite in their countries. Some exiles returned once democratic regimes took hold in the 1980s, but many preferred to remain there. In another South American country, Colombia, which in 2000 counted for over 1 percent of the total South American-born people in the U.S. (United States Bureau of the Census, 2000), decades of violence generated by guerrillas and drug cartels affected the security situation. An array of individuals, ranging from industrialists fearing kidnapping to judges prosecuting drug cases, were forced out of the country.

Central American nationals, whose presence in the United States soared from 1980 to 1990, were quite often pushed from the region by civil wars. It is not surprising that El Salvador and Guatemala account for almost 10 percent of the total foreign-born persons from Spanish-speaking Latin America in the United States in 1990 (United States Bureau of the Census, 1993). This trend continued, as Central Americans in the United States have become 4.8 percent of the total Latino population. Unlike most other Latin Americans in the United States, many of these Central Americans come from rural areas. They were caught in the rampage between armies and guerrillas and victimized by both, each side accusing them of cooperating with the other. Reaching the cities was not enough protection; the only sense of security came from leaving the country. Many traveled first to Mexico and then across to the United States. Although many received temporary permits, their immigration status was uncertain, pending on the direction both the conflicts and the U.S. government's support of those conflicts would take, notably in El Salvador and Guatemala. Nationals from Nicaragua, which in 1990 represented 2.3 percent of the Central Americans in the United States (United States Bureau of the Census, 1993), had similar experiences, except that the United States supported the insurgency rather than the Nicaraguan government. As Nicaragua became more stable, a significant number have returned home from the United States, and Nicaraguans now account for .5 percent of the Latino population (United States Census Bureau, Census, 2000).

Haitians come to the United States for the same reasons that many other immigrants have—the search for freedom and better economic opportunities. A long history of poverty and political oppression led Haitians to emigrate. The overthrow of the first ever-elected government in 1990 exacerbated the Haitians' frustration, resulting in a mass boat exodus to the Florida coast. By then, they were no longer welcomed in the United States and were housed in refugee camps for future repatriation. The condition of Haiti worsened as the United States reinstated the overthrown government years later and the economic situation continued to deteriorate.

The political situation of the Cubans granted them privileges not enjoyed by other political exiles or refugees in the United States. Large numbers of Cubans fled from the only Communist state in Latin America in the midst of the Cold War. In 1966, the United States government granted parole status to all incoming Cubans and facilitated the process for obtaining permanent residency. Many of them were professionals and entrepreneurs, although later flows reflected all sectors of the Cuban society. The special treatment ended in 1994, when the Clinton administration refused to accept a new influx of Cubans crossing the 90-mile Florida Straits on rafts. Instead, they were sent to safe havens, just as was being done with the Haitian refugees. (It is possible to imagine that such changes in United States policy were influenced by the darkening of the skin color of the Cubans coming in recent years, similarly to how skin color seems to have influenced the United States policy on Haitian immigrants). In 1990, Cubans represented 10 percent of all foreign-born Spanish-speaking Latin Americans in the United States (United States Bureau of the Census, 1993). The Cuban population in the United States increased by 18.9 percent from 1990 to 2000 (United States Bureau of the Census, 2000).

Other countries in the Caribbean exhibit completely different situations. Puerto Ricans, for example, are not immigrants. They are United States citizens and do not need a passport to fly to the mainland. Over three million Puerto Ricans are in the United States (United States Bureau of the Census, 2000), practically the same as the population left on the island. Many nationals from the Dominican Republic frequently sail to Puerto Rico, enter the U.S. there illegally, and falsify documents that show them as Puerto Ricans in order to come to the United States.

Puerto Ricans and legal immigrants can go back home and visit their families and friends left behind. Political exiles, illegal immigrants, and those with uncertain immigration status cannot. These family separations cause anguish, especially in cases of illness and death. Even in cases where couples and children are in the United States, the extended families are back home. In some instances, immigrants become the primary family providers and major sources of unrequited monetary transfers back to the country of origin. Illegal Central Americans may be subject to deportation now that most armed conflicts have ended, but the United States government took into consideration the effect that loss of remittances and the impact on unemployment would have on the budding stability of those countries.

Latino/as in the United States

There are 38 Latino/a groups in the United States (Flores, 1992). The Census Bureau counted 35.3 million Hispanics in 2000, an increase of almost 58 percent from the previous census. Ruiz (1981) reported 11.2 million Hispanics in 1975, citing references to gross underestimates at the time based on a variety of inaccurate practices. The 2000 total reported by the Census Bureau represents 12.5 percent of the nation's population. Persons of Mexican origin formed the largest Latino/a group, numbering over 20.5 million persons. The number of Mexicans in the United States is followed by Puerto Ricans with over 3.4 million, and Cubans with slightly over one million. These represent the three largest groups of Latino/as in the United States. Others are: Salvadoreans (655,000), Dominicans (764,000), Colombians (470,000), Guatemalans (372,000), Nicaraguans (177,000), Ecuadorians (260,000), Peruvians (233,000), Hondurans (217,000), Argentineans (100,000), and Venezuelans (91,000). All of these populations increased since the 1990 Census with the exception of Nicaraguans. Other South Americans account for 57,000 and the rest of the Central Americans for 103,000. The Latino population is fast growing. It grew 53 percent from 1989 to 1990, compared to 7 percent for non-Hispanics (U.S. Bureau of the Census, 1993), and again from 1990 to 2000 the Latino population grew by 57.9 percent as compared to an increase of 13.2 percent for the total U.S. population (United States Bureau of the Census, 2000).

Although Latino/as are found in every state of this nation, they are primarily concentrated in California, Texas, New York, and Florida. California, for example, has 32.4 percent Latino/a population, while Texas has 32 percent; New York has over 15 percent, and Florida has 16 percent (United States Bureau of the Census, 2000).

The United States Bureau of the Census (2000) reported that the Latino/a population in the United States tends to be younger than the rest of the nation. Its median age is 26 years compared to 35 among non-Latino/as. Over 35 percent of the Latino/a population was under 18 in 2000, as compared to 25 percent for the U.S. populations.

More than 85 percent of Latina/o households include children. About 76 percent of Hispanic families were headed by females in 2000, an increase of 10 percent from the previous census. Males, with no wife present, account for 48 percent of the Latino households (United States Bureau of the Census, 2000). The unemployment rate among Hispanics in 1990 was 11.3 percent, compared to 7.5 percent for the total population; this discrepancy in unemployment is higher than the one reported by Ruiz for 1974 (Ruiz, 1981). In addition, 20 percent of Hispanic families were below the poverty level in 2003, a decrease of 6 percent from the previous census (United States Bureau of the Census, 2000).

Latina/o Families

Latina/o families in the United States do not form a homogeneous group, and their level of adaptation and acculturation may vary even within a single family. As with any other oppressed group, there is always a danger in describing the characteristics of a group, which invites stereotyping. However, there are some shared characteristics applicable to most Latina/o families that can serve "as the basis for informed inquiry" (Vasquez, 1994, p. 114). The concepts of *respeto* (respect), *personalismo* (personalism), familism, *machismo* and *marianismo* have been described as applicable to most Latina/o families (e.g., Bernal & Shapiro, 1996; Boyd-Franklin & Garcia-Preto, 1994; Chin, 1994; Falicov, 1998; Garcia-Preto, 1996; Nazario, 198, 2003; Stevens, 1973; Vasquez, 1994).

Respect within the Latina/o family involves dutifulness and high regard for the family hierarchy, where "complimentary transactions between parents and children are stressed while symmetrical transactions are discouraged or tolerated only in jest" (Falicov, 1998, p. 169). I recently worked with a 33-year-old Mexican man studying in the United States. He had made significant strides in coming to terms with his sexual orientation and had developed a plan to come out to friends, relatives, co-workers and other important people in his life. In discussing not telling his parents, he clearly identified his *respeto* for his parents, which would not allow him to discuss with them such private matters.

In addition, respect acknowledges another's social worthiness and makes everything possible or impossible; it is the flywheel of interpersonal relationship (Garcia-Preto, 1996).

Personalism is the opposite of the white American concept of individualism (Garcia-Preto, 1996). It favors interpersonal relationships over concepts and ideas (Bernal & Shapiro 1996). Personalism is manifested in many different ways within the Latina/o relationships. Bernal & Shapiro (1996) reported *personalismo* as the informal manner in which Cubans tend to communicate with others. Instead of using the polite or formal pronoun *usted* (you), people from Cuba tend to use the familiar form tú in many interpersonal situations. This is viewed as an attempt to diminish distance and to establish familiarity and *personalismo*. The paradox of *respeto* and *personalismo* is often evident when Latino/a counseling clients address their nondoctoral counselors as doctor with the pronoun *tú*. Another form in which this manifests in relation to counseling is the attempt by many Latino/a clients to engage their counselors in social interactions outside the counseling room such as invitations to weddings, baptisms, and other family celebrations.

Familism (Bernal, & Shapiro 1996) refers to the Latina/o family tendency to value the family and to put the needs of the family above the needs of the individual. Family loyalty, respect for the family hierarchy, and the avoidance of airing family conflicts outside the family are part of this concept. For the Latino/a the notion of family goes beyond the nuclear family. Similar to the black family, in addition to the extended family, the family may include close or distant cousins, godparents, very close friends, and other individuals whose membership in the family may have happened through informal adoptions (Boyd-Franklin & Garcia-Preto, 1994).

Machismo is usually defined as a strong or assertive masculinity, characterized by virility, courage, and aggressiveness (Gurlanick, 1976). Chin (1994), discussing machismo in Hispanic cultures, identifies it:

> [A]s a socially constructed, learned, and reinforced set of behaviors comprising the content of male gender roles in Latino society. These behaviors include stoicism, varying levels of intimacy among men, attempts to avoid shame and gain *respeto* (respect) and *dignidad* (dignity) for self and family, the displacement of stress related to economic and social factors into the interpersonal and familial sphere, and at times, caricatured patterns of assertiveness and dominance. (p. 201)

Machismo does not necessarily imply the sexualization of women. Although machismo is very prevalent in the dominant culture, it is usually identified as a negative characteristic of Latino men. Marin and Marin (1990) suggested that there are positive characteristics associated with machismo, such as protection of one's family that are usually excluded from the discussion.

Marianismo was described by Stevens (1972) as the other side of machismo. It refers to women's roles within the Latina/o family. It emphasizes the value of virginity, the status of motherhood, and the expectation that women will deny their own needs in favor of their children and husbands (Chin, 1994). *Marianismo* derives from the influence of the Catholic Church and of the Virgin Mary in many Latin countries. It prescribes motherhood over sexuality and sex as an obligation rather than a pleasurable activity.

Women in Latina/o Families

Women's movements in Latin America have increased over the years. In several countries, women led the protest against dictatorships under which their sons and daughters and husbands either disappeared or were killed. The *Mothers of the Plaza de Mayo* in Buenos Aires, depicted as crazy by the Argentinean military, are recognized for the impact of their weekly protests in bringing down the dictatorship. They demanded to know the whereabouts of their disappeared loved ones. The *Arpilleras* in Chile embroidered in traditional folk art their silent protest against the Pinochet dictatorship, while women banged pots and pans in other countries to make their cases heard. These activities in which women used the tools of their womanhood as a way of rebelling could be considered an empowering aspect of *marianismo*. These movements have empowered women in some Latin American countries. Nonetheless, the overall conditions of women in most of Latin America remain deplorable (Fuentes, 1994). In the United States the status of most Latinas is characterized by lack of education, poverty, and unskilled blue collar and service occupations (Boyd-Franklin & Garcia-Preto, 1994). Latinas in the United States experience double oppression, the oppression of gender and the oppression of ethnicity. Espin (1994) clearly identified these issues as she discussed the failure of feminists in psychology to take into consideration "the oppression of women of color in a white-dominated society" (p. 265). She stated,

White racism combines with sexism in unique ways to influence the oppression of women of color. The poverty and lack of education and resources that many women of color suffer from are a consequence of centuries of racist denial of the opportunities this country is supposed to provide for all of its citizens. (Espin, 1994, p. 266)

Latina/o Families in Counseling

Latino/as usually do not like "to air their dirty linen in public." Counseling may not be the first choice for seeking solutions when difficulties arise. Seeking advice from the family physician, church, *curandera,* folk healer, *santero, espiritista* or other forms of healing more indigenous to the Latina/o cultures may take precedence. The diversity of Latino/a individuals and Latina/o families makes it difficult to suggest any one specific strategy as the appropriate one for working with this population. At the same time, the variety of presenting problems and concerns that Latino/as and Latina/o families bring to the consulting room require, as with other populations, adequate training, understanding of the culture, understanding of the influence of larger systems in the context of the client(s), and a willingness to challenge one's own biases and prejudices. Although Bernal and Flores-Ortiz (1982) suggested the contextual approach developed by Boszormenyi-Nagy as the most helpful in the evaluation and treatment of Latino/as, it is important to recognize that any approach that takes into consideration larger system influences and the context of the individual within the family may be helpful in working with Latina/o families. At the same time, in working with Latina/o families, who in general represent a marginalized segment of society, "we as clinicians must avoid negative and inappropriate stereotypes, and prevent the replication of the experience of discrimination in the therapeutic experience" (Vasquez, 1994, p. 135). It is important to keep in mind that it is impossible to work with the oppressed without discussing the impact of oppression in their lives (Hardy, 1992).

Oppression-Sensitive Family Therapy

At the Gainesville Family Institute we have been developing a therapeutic model appropriate for working with a variety of presenting problems and with diverse populations. This model, Oppression-Sensitive Family Therapy (Early, Nazario, & Steier, 1994), is primarily, but not solely, influenced by the feminist critique of family therapy (Ault-Riché, 1986; Goodrich, Rampage, Ellman, & Halstead, 1988; Hare-Mustin, 1978; Myers-Avis, 1985), the postmodern and narrative therapies of New Zealand and Australia (Epston, 1989; White, 1989; Waldegrave & Tamasese, 1994; White & Epston, 1990), and by the work of Kenneth V. Hardy (Hardy, 1992; Saba, Karrer, & Hardy, 1990). The approach has been successfully employed in working with Latina/o families. The model is health-oriented, gender-sensitive, and supports and affirms diversity in terms of ethnicity, race, cultural background, sexual orientation, and lifestyles (Early et al., 1994). It provides a broad umbrella of social justice under which many therapeutic techniques may be utilized.

Borrowing from the work of Hardy (1992), the model emphasizes the importance of organizing principles that influence our perceptions, attitudes, and behaviors in society. Hardy identified race, gender, class, religion, and culture as organizing principles by which our society operates and makes decisions. These principles also organize the therapeutic relationship. The oppression-sensitive model includes, in addition, ethnicity, age, sexual orientation and ability as additional sociopolitical organizing principles of existential meaning influencing society; therefore, those principles organize the therapeutic process in family therapy. These principles influence the attitudes, perceptions, and behaviors of clients, counselors and therapists, supervisors, agencies and institutions, and other larger systems. Several assumptions are derived from these ideas and should be made explicit:

1. Therapy is always contextual.
2. Therapy is political.
3. There is no such thing as neutrality in psychotherapy.
4. Sociopolitical organizing principles organize meaning.
5. Sociopolitical organizing principles organize therapy.
6. Reality is culturally defined.
7. The therapeutic system includes the therapist.
8. It is impossible to work therapeutically with oppressed people without addressing the impact of oppression on them (Hardy, 1992; Early et al., 1994).

Counseling or psychotherapy from an oppression-sensitive frame builds upon a philosophy of inclusion, with pluralism as its foundation.

A counselor, working from this model, demonstrates a total commitment to an open context promoting equality, social acceptance, and embracing of multiple views. It requires the creation of a therapeutic environment of inclusion rather than exclusion, wherein the client-family system and therapist work together in a collaborative manner, resulting in empowerment. This process takes place when we build upon the strengths of the client/family—when we recognize the inherent power differential that exists between client/family and therapist, yet, do not distant ourselves from the client/family as if we knew what is best for them. This therapeutic process also impacts the therapist providing an enriching transformative experience for her/him. The job of the counselor is to develop "an atmosphere of curiosity, openness, and respect" (Griffith & Griffith, 1992, p. 8.) in which discussion of the client/family's difficulties are nestled within the context of the social and political struggles of the Latina/o family, *vis a vis* the dominant culture. This openness requires the therapist to operate from what we have termed "therapy in the sunshine" (Nazario, 1993, p. 3.). This means that we talk with our clients in language that is understandable to them and not by the use of labels; that, whenever possible, we talk about our clients in their presence and with their participation in the process; that, when we discuss cases in case conferences, individual and/or group supervision, peer supervision or any other form of discussion about clients, we do so in language that is respectful of them and in such a manner that, if the clients were present, they would feel empowered by our presentation of them; that our records reflect this same idea of openness and that we invite our clients to participate in the annotation of what goes into the records; that, when a letter is requested by them or by anyone for whom they have signed consent to release information, we discuss the content of the letter with the client(s) and invite them to participate in the letter writing. These are just some of the specific actions we can begin to take when working with Latino/a families. The ultimate goal is to develop a therapeutic process that is transparent, in which client/family and counselor work collaboratively towards liberation from the oppressive nature of the presenting problem. This requires as much of the counselor as of the client/family. It places different demands on the counselor according to her/his own placement on a privileged-oppressed continuum based on the organizing principles of existential meaning. A white, middle-class, male, heterosexual, young, able, and Christian counselor would fall at one end of the continuum, while an older, poor, black Latina, physically challenged, Muslim, lesbian counselor would probably fall at the other end.

The Oppression-Sensitive model is a conceptual frame rather than a set of specific techniques. It requires, on the part of the counselor, the development of an awareness of the process of oppression. This awareness of the process of oppression is such that the oppressed and the privileged experience distinct yet separate stages reflecting their socialization (Early et al., 1994). The oppressed may lack awareness of the existence of oppression, but once this awareness begins to surface, a variety of feelings usually emerge, with anger at one's own sense of powerlessness taking strong hold. The slow pace with which social change takes place may generate depression and a sense of futility. This is the point at which the oppressed begin to identify the influence of oppression in one's life.

The privileged, on the other hand, usually lack awareness and sensitivity of their privileged position and their participation regarding the oppression of others. They may experience unexplained anger toward the oppressed. The privileged usually feel threatened by the potential loss of power and privilege. The recognition of a position of privilege may bring feelings of societal and/or individual guilt, which may then transform into two possible reactions: fighting back by entrenchment into a position of privilege or connecting with the pain of self and others and beginning to challenge dominant culture prescriptions.

Counselors fall within the broad spectrum of the oppression awareness continuum, but given the small number of minorities in our mental health professions, the vast majority of counselors in the United States may fall toward the privileged end of the continuum. For privileged counselors to work with a Latino/a and/or Latina/o family, it is important that they be willing to challenge their own position of power *vis a vis* the Latino/a client. They need to validate the personal and collective pain of the oppressed. The privileged counselor needs to recognize that "any group of people made to live in the periphery of a dominant culture hold within themselves a knowledge piece" (Waldegrave & Tamasese, 1994, p. 94), which is unknown to the privileged and that needs to be explored and validated. This is the framework upon which the therapeutic dialogue is constructed about all presenting problems.

When engaging Latina/o families, it is important to engage with the entire person and/or persons interviewed rather than with their presenting problem. Learn to pronounce their names, find out about their history both in terms of their roots in their Latin country of origin as well as their history in the United States. If they are recent immigrants, learn the reasons for their departure and the difficulties of adaptation they have encountered in the United States. "Although most people have access to their culture, for some their sense of belonging has been destroyed by war, political oppression, migration, or whatever" (Waldegrave & Tamasese, 1994, p. 96). If they are U.S. born, explore what they know of their family heritage. Regardless of the presenting problem, counselors are encouraged to open space for the discussion of the impact of racism, sexism, and other forms of oppression in their lives. The following case will illustrate some of these points.

> Johnny was a 28-year-old Latino man referred by the HIV Clinic at the Health Department because they were concerned about his lack of adherence to his medical treatment for AIDS. Our initial conversations with Johnny led to the discussion of his present context, married, with two children at home, HIV positive perhaps for 10 years, unemployed, and in severe financial difficulties. Over a period of several months Johnny was seen at times individually, at times with his wife, in a few sessions with his wife and children, twice with his HIV case manager, and in one session with a visiting sister. In working with Johnny, our primary goals were to get to know him and his relational system rather than to get him to comply with the medical treatment and then to explore, given his personal and familial context, his thoughts and feelings about HIV, AIDS, medical treatments, the impact of his condition on his family, and his aspirations for himself and his family. As we began to discuss his family, he reported that as a child he was physically abused by his father and that his mother's involvement with drugs precluded her from taking care of him. His parents did not live together; their marriage had fallen apart soon after they arrived in the United States. Spanish was the primary language spoken in both homes.
>
> Johnny went to a foster home at an early age, where he was sexually molested. After a series of unsuccessful placements, he returned home, and then back to foster care, after which Johnny ran away and began living on the streets. Johnny recalled with sadness his ambivalence about his cultural heritage. He cried, as he reported an incident in which as an adolescent in an attempt to "fit in," he participated with his Anglo peers at throwing eggs at the home of a Latino family. At age 15, out of school, he supported himself by running errands for small-time drug dealers. He reported this period of his life as one of fear and embarrassment, and by age 17 Johnny had found himself a job in a fast-food restaurant giving up

his involvement with drugs. Since then Johnny was able to maintain steady employment until his diagnosis of HIV six months prior to entering therapy. Johnny spoke of his parents both with resentment and love, and one of his goals for therapy became making peace with both of them. Johnny's story unfolded as the therapist supported his struggle. Johnny was very bright, and he was aware of his talent, yet he was poorly educated. He loved to write short stories but did not have command of the language to do so. A year or two prior to beginning therapy, he enrolled in an adult writing course and was crushed by the teacher's response to his essay. The therapist often made connecting statements identifying the struggles of Latinos both with language and culture.

As we focused on issues with HIV and medical treatment, Johnny identified not having money to put gas in his car as the reason for not attending some of his medical appointments, but he was embarrassed to let the medical personnel know about his financial condition. He was bicycling to the therapist's office, but the Health Department was too far for bicycling. Two issues emerged out of this conversation, Johnny's desire to get his GED as a legacy for his children about the importance of education and his desire to return to work to demonstrate to his family his sense of caring for them.

If we analyze Johnny's presenting problem, his difficulties were very similar to the ones presented by other individuals diagnosed with HIV or AIDS. The significant differences in working with Johnny centered on empowering him to tell his story. A stance of curiosity on the part of the therapist opened space for him to struggle with issues of prejudice, marginalization, connection to his wife and children, and relationship with his family of origin. It also provided a safe environment in which to address what it meant to him to be a Latino man. Therapy also provided an opportunity for Johnny and his wife to come to terms with the impact AIDS had on their lives and with her own struggles as a HIV negative woman living with an HIV positive man. The family hierarchy and cultural tradition was also respected in their decision not to tell their children the nature of their father's illness. Having been sexually molested as a child and suffering from a disease often associated with homosexuals, issues of masculinity, sexual orientation, sexual identity, and *machismo* were often part of the fabric of our conversations.

This therapeutic approach does not prescribe specific techniques or interventions but encourages therapists to attend to the meaning clients attribute to their difficulties within the context of the organizing principles of existential meaning.

Therapy with Latino/a families also brings into question issues of dual relationships. Since Latino/as tend not to air their difficulties in public, the more that they tell their story to a therapist, the more the therapist becomes an extension of their "family." Latino clients may introduce their therapist to their children as a very good friend; they may call their therapist, long after termination, for phone consultations as they would a family member; and they may invite you to important family activities such as weddings, baptisms, graduations, and other important celebrations. If they are in business, they may want to do everything possible to assist you with their services, and if they find you refusing those opportunities, they may feel rejected as they would by a family member. These are all generalizations, and we must be aware to recognize them as such; yet, when it comes to dual relationships, rather than to avoid them at all cost, it is important to think of them in terms of the potential for exploitation on the part of the therapist.

Learning Activities

Race, gender, class, culture, ethnicity, age, sexual orientation, spirituality, and physical and mental ability are sociopolitical organizing principles of existential meaning that influence the lives of our clients, students, and supervisees. They also influence the personal and professional lives of counselors. They influence our perceptions, attitudes, and behaviors. The following questions, developed by the Gainesville Family Institute Training Team (Early et al., 1994), are offered as an activity for personal and professional reflection or for an interactive dialogue:

• Have you looked at yourself and your therapeutic work in relation to any of the sociopolitical organizing principles listed above? Which ones have you considered? Which ones have you not?
• If you have, what encouraged you to take these steps?
• Has this been a painful or comfortable process?
• What have you found out?
• If you haven't considered any of these organizing principles in your therapeutic work, what has kept you from doing so?
• How do these organizing principles influence your interaction with your clients?
• How do they influence your expectations of relationships with clients and families?

- What experiences have you had in the past that have encouraged or restricted you from considering these organizing principles in your personal and professional life?
- What might be the cost or danger if you continue to explore these areas?
- What is your next step?
- How do you think exploring these areas will influence your appreciation of yourself as a person?
- What are your reactions to these questions?
- How do these issues most commonly present themselves in your therapeutic work?
- What do you find most challenging in your work in regard to these organizing principles?

Counseling with families from an oppression-sensitive model also embraces many of the *Just Therapy* ideas (Waldegrave 1990). For example, we encourage therapists to work with naming as a powerful tool, both for themselves and their clients. The poem by Kiwi Tamasese can be used as guidelines for engaging Latina/o families in the U.S. in an exploration leading to empowerment, see Box 7.1.

Box 7.1

Poem by Kiwi Tamasese

Name your name
Name your culture
Name its positioning within our societies.
Name your history.
Name your losses
Name your dead . . .
Name our discipline
Name its shortcomings
Name its strengths
Name its drawing of people into belonging.
Naming is indeed an act of courage, a political act, a costly act, an act ascribing belonging, drawing on sacredness.
Naming is an act of liberation.
Naming is indeed a therapeutic act.
   (cited in Waldegrave & Tamasese, 1994, p. 99)

Naming is a powerful tool in therapy. Naming provides an opportunity for making visible what is invisible (Early, 1992). In co-creating the therapeutic space in which Latina/o families may name the unspoken, we are attending to that which historically has not been attended to. Until such is done, we cannot begin to deal with Latina/o families in counseling within a framework of sensitivity to oppression. Counselors, please be aware: silence in the presence of oppression speaks loudly of complicity.

Selected Films (DeNeve & Condon, 2005)

El Norte (1985). Presents story of refugees/immigrants from Guatemala to the United States during civil war years, contrasts Latino and U.S. American values and behaviors such as family, interdependence, and gender roles.

LaFamilia (1995). Story of a Mexican American family's accomplishments in Los Angeles, shows stereotypes and clashes between Anglo and Mexican American cultures.

Maria Full of Grace (2004). Colombian story of economic survival for a 17-year-old woman who comes to the United States through the drug trade.

Motorcycle Diaries (2004). The story of young Che Guevara and the profound impact of his motorcycle trip throughout South America.

Real Women Have Curves (2002). Shows family relationships and generational differences between Mexican immigrant parents and their young adult children coming of age in the Untied States.

Strawberries and Chocolate (1993). Set in Cuba, tells a story of friendship between David, a conservative and Diego, his flamboyantly gay neighbor, and explores many Cuban issues since the revolution.

Tortilla Soup (2001). Story of a Mexican American father and his three grown daughters and shows transition into new values for second generation.

REFERENCES

Ault-Riché, M. (Ed.). (1986). *Women and family therapy.* Rockville, MD: Aspen Systems Corporation.

Bernal, G. & Shapiro, E. (1996). Cuban families. In M. McGoldrick, J. Giordano, & J. K. Pearce, (Eds.), *Ethnicity and family therapy*. 2nd Edition (pp. 155–168). New York: The Guilford Press.

Bernal, G., & Flores-Ortiz, Y. (1982). Latino families in therapy: Engagement and evaluation. *Journal of Marital and Family Therapy, 8,* 357–365.

Boyd-Franklin, N., & Garcia-Preto, N. (1994). Family therapy: The cases of African American and Hispanic women. In L. Comas-Diaz & B. Greene (Eds.), *Women of color: Integrating ethnic and gender identity in psychotherapy* (pp. 239–264). New York: The Guilford Press.

Chin, J. L. (1994). Psychodynamic approaches. In L. Comas-Diaz & B. Greene (Eds.), *Women of color: Integrating ethnic and gender identity in psychotherapy* (pp. 194–222). New York: The Guilford Press.

DeNeve, C. & Condon, J. C. (2005, July). Teaching Latino cultural variations through films. Workshop presentation at the Summer Institute for Intercultural Communication. Forest Grove, OR.

Early, G. (1992, April). *Power and gender: Making the invisible visible.* Florida Association for Marriage and Family Therapy Annual Conference. Gainesville, FL.

Early, G., Nazario, A., & Steier, H. (1994, April). *Oppression sensitive family therapy: A health affirming model.* American Orthopsychiatric Association. Washington, DC.

Epston, D. (1989). *Selected papers.* Adelaide, South Australia: Dulwich Centre Publications.

Espin, O. M. (1994). Feminist approaches. In L. Comas-Diaz & B. Greene (Eds.), *Women of color: Integrating ethnic and gender identity in psychotherapy* (pp. 265–286). New York: The Guilford Press.

Falicov C. J. (1998). *Latino families in therapy: A guide to multicultural practice.* New York: The Guilford Press.

Falicov, C. J. (1996). Mexican families. In M. McGoldrick, J. Giordano, & J. K. Pearce (Eds.), *Ethnicity and family therapy* (pp. 169–182). New York: The Guilford Press.

Flores, M. (1992, October). Latino acculturation and adaptation. In M. Watson, M. Flores, B. Larkam, H. Roberts, T. Martin & A. Nazario (Eds.), *Cultural and racial sensitivity: An ecological approach.* AAMFT 50th Annual Conference. Miami Beach, FL.

Fuentes, I. (1994, November 22). Un cuarto propio para las mujeres de hemisferio. *El Nuevo Miami Herald.*

Garcia-Preto, N. (1996). Puerto Rican families. In M. McGoldrick, J. Giordano, & J. K. Pearce (Eds.), *Ethnicity and family therapy* (pp. 183–199). New York: The Guilford Press.

Goodrich, T. J., Rampage, C., Ellman, B., & Halstead, K. (1988). *Feminist family therapy: A casebook.* New York: Norton.

Griffith, J. & Griffith, M. (1992). Owning one's epistemological stance in therapy. *Dulwich Centre Newsletter, 1,* 5–11.

Gurlanick, D. B. (Ed.) (1976). *Webster's new world dictionary. Second edition.* Cleveland, OH: William Collins + World Publishing Co., Inc.

Hardy, K. V. (1992, October). *Race, class and culture.* AAMFT 50th Annual Conference. Miami Beach, FL.

Hare-Mustin, R. (1978). A feminist approach to family therapy. *Family Process, 17,* 181–194.

Marin, B. V., & Marin, G. (1990). Effects of acculturation on knowledge of AIDS and HIV among Hispanics. *Hispanic Journal of Behavioral Sciences, 12,* 110–121.

Myers-Avis, J. (1985). The politics of functional family therapy: A feminist critique. *Journal of Marital and Family Therapy, 11,* 127–138.

Nazario, A. (2003). Latino cross-cultural same sex male relationships: Issues of ethnicity, race, and other domains of influence. *Journal of Couple & Relationship Therapy, 2,* 103–113.

Nazario, A. (1998). Counseling Latina/o families. In W. M. Parker, *Consciousness-Raising: A primer for multicultural counseling,* 2nd Edition (pp. 205–222). Springfield, IL: Charles C Thomas, Publisher.

Nazario, A. (1993, September). *Racial, ethnic and cultural diversity in counseling.* Workshop. Carolina Counseling Center, Rock Hill, SC.

Ruiz, R. A. (1981). Cultural and historical perspectives in counseling Hispanics. In D. W. Sue, *Counseling the culturally different* (pp. 186–215). New York: John Wiley & Sons.

Saba, G. W., Karrer, B. M., & Hardy, K. V. (Eds.). (1990). *Minorities and family therapy.* New York: The Haworth Press.

Stevens, E. (1972). Machismo and Marianismo. *Transaction-Society, 10* (6), 57–63.

United States Bureau of the Census. (1993). *Hispanic Americans today.* Washington, DC: U.S. Government Printing Office.

United States Bureau of the Census. (2000). *The Hispanic population.* Washington, DC: U.S. Government Printing Office.

Vasquez, M. J. T. (1994). Latinas. In L. Comas-Diaz & B. Greene (Eds.), *Women of color: Integrating ethnic and gender identity in psychotherapy* (pp. 114–138). New York: The Guilford Press.

Waldegrave, C. (1990). Just therapy. *Dulwich Centre Newsletter, 1,* 5-46.

Waldegrave, C., & Tamasese, K. (1994). Some central ideas in the "Just Therapy" approach. *The Family Journal: Counseling and Therapy for Couples and Families, 2,* 94–103.

White, M. (1989). *Selected papers.* Adelaide, South Australia: Dulwich Centre Publications.

White, M., & Epston, D. (1990). *Narrative means to therapeutic ends.* New York: W. W. Norton & Company.

Chapter 8

COUNSELING MULTIRACIAL PEOPLE: ATTENDING TO MULTIPLE SELVES IN MULTIPLE CONTEXTS

MARIE L. MIVILLE AND LELAINA ROMERO

Being biracial isn't hard because we're confused about our racial identity. It's hard because everyone else is confused. The problem isn't us—it's everyone else.

> From an interview with Chela Delgado,
> 14 years old (Gaskin, 1999, p. 15).

I have often said that my identity is a conversation, not a category.

> T. Israel (1996, p. 174)

Abstract

This chapter briefly outlines the history of multiracial people, particularly their marginalization, myths that affect them, and recent recognition in the larger society. Information about the psychological adjustment of multiracial people is outlined, demonstrating that, despite prevailing stereotypes, little evidence exists to indicate psychological maladjustment of multiracial people. Racial identity development models are reviewed as they apply to multiracial people, followed by a summary of counseling themes and guidelines for working with multiracial people. Finally, a case study of a multiracial client is presented.

Note: Correspondence concerning this chapter should be addressed to Marie L. Miville, Department of Counseling and Clinical Psychology, Teachers College, Columbia University, 525 West 120th Street, Box 73, New York, NY 10027 (Email: mlm2106@columbia.edu).

INTRODUCTION

In 2000, for the first time in United States history, multiracial people were able to identify themselves as such in the national census. This event marked a substantial movement forward in the recognition of the civil rights and social realities of multiracial people. The United States has had a long and painful history with regard to racism and racial discrimination, and multiracial people were affected by this history in a variety of ways. Examples of this historical impact include the use of the *one-drop rule* as a legal definition of racial heritage as well as laws passed by legislatures that made so-called interracial marriages illegal for many generations (Root, 1992). The *one-drop rule* refers to laws as early as 1660 attempting to maintain or promote so-called racial purity of white European immigrants; these laws prohibited marriages between male slaves of African descent with *freeborn English women* (for a review of historical events relevant to multiracial people, please see Wehrly, Kenney, & Kenney, 1999). Because of the predominant beliefs of both *Negroes* and *Indians* as being subhuman, the notion that a single drop of blood from a black person would contaminate a white person was codified into law by most states as the rule of hypodescent (Fernandez, 1996). The case of *Plessy v. Ferguson* in 1894 affirmed these beliefs at the federal level by ruling that a person who was one-eighth black could be classified as black. The Supreme Court struck down laws prohibiting interracial marriages in 1967 (Wehrly et al., 1999); the last of these antimiscegenation state laws was only repealed in 2000 (Hansen, 2001). Thus, the 2000 U.S. census marked a critical moment in which multiracial people finally began to gain governmental legitimacy with respect to their rich and complex racial heritage. Indeed, according to the 2000 census, nearly seven million people checked more than one racial category, representing 2.4 percent of the total U.S. population.

The terms *multiracial* and *biracial* generally describe individuals with two parents of different racial categories, irrespective of their personal racial self-identity (Rockquemore & Brunsma, 2002). These terms also can refer to individuals who have parents of the same socially designated race, if one or both of the parents are multiracial, or if there is an acknowledgement of cross-racial mixing in the family history (Root, 1996). *Multiracial* is a broader term that includes people who claim two or more racial backgrounds (e.g., black, white, Asian), as in individuals who have at least one parent who self-identifies as biracial and another parent of a different racial background (Root, 1996). Because of its more inclusive meaning, we use the term *multiracial* in the current chapter. To illustrate cultural complexity, one of the more visible multiracial sports figures, Tiger Woods, has called himself *Cablinasian* to represent his mixed ethnic heritage–Caucasian, black, Indian, and Asian.

Given the sociohistorical context described earlier, it is not surprising that there has been a lack of relevant literature in psychology and counseling on multiracial people. It is only within the past two decades that most theory and research describing the unique experiences of multiracial people has been proposed and conducted. With the publication of several book-length works (e.g., Brown, 2001; Rockquemore, 2002; Root, 1992, 1996), pioneering scholars recently were able to present a variety of theories, methodologies, findings, and suggestions for interventions regarding multiracial people in a single forum. Moreover, a number of conceptual models were proposed describing the racial identity development of biracial and multiracial people (Kerwin & Ponterotto, 1995).

Myths about Multiracial Individuals

In light of the controversial and ambiguous sociohistorical context in which multiracial people have existed, a number of myths were promoted in the larger society about multiracial people in the United States (Kerwin & Ponterotto, 1995). These myths have critical implications for counseling multiracial people as they may be aware of these myths or perhaps have internalized them. Several are described below.

- *Myth: The stereotype of the "tragic mulatto or marginal person" refers to the idea that multiracial people are destined to have long-lasting social and psychological effects due to the lack of a clearly defined racial group with which to identify.*
- **Reality:** Much research in this area has revealed few adjustment problems for this population (see Miville, 2005 for a review of empirical literature). When working with multiracial clients, it is important for counselors to be aware of their own ideas about their clients' well-being. Multiracial people may be all too familiar with being labeled as confused or even dysfunctional because of their racial identity. However, in light of the oppressive history of multiracial people in the United States described above, counselors also should be sensitive to

these clients' negative experiences, thoughts, and feelings around race.

- *Myth: "Multiracial individuals are forced to choose or identify with only one racial group" refers to the history of segregation and legalized discriminatory patterns in which social groups have been defined along rigid racial lines in the United States. As a result, individuals who have a multiracial heritage are forced to choose one racial group over another, also leading to the denial of their total heritage.*

- **Reality:** Recent research indicates that racial identity of multiracial people is fluid, dynamic, and at times transcendent of racial group labels (Root, 1998). Counselors should be aware of their desire to take apart their multiracial clients' identities, or worse, to force them to choose among monoracial categories. At the same time, although multiracial identity is fluid, multiracial individuals may have experiences in various contexts where their identity comes into question (e.g., being asked to "check one" box, or feeling pulled into racial conflicts within their families.)

- *Myth: "Multiracial people do not like to discuss their racial identity" refers to the notion that given the social and psychological difficulty of growing up multiracial and denying part of one's heritage, multiracial people learn to avoid discussion of this emotionally evocative topic.*

- **Reality:** Most research to date on multiracial people has been qualitative in nature, involving narratives and personal stories of multiracial people to derive a variety of identity models (Miville, Constantine, Baysden, & So-Lloyd, 2005). Counselors can work to build trusting relationships with their multiracial clients by challenging this myth and providing a safe space to dialogue about race and racial identity. Although it may be true that discussing race is difficult for multiracial people at times, the reality is that most people struggle with these dialogues because of racism. Multiracial clients may come to counseling seeking a safe space where they are accepted without having to ascribe to a singular identity. If counselors are having difficulty talking to a multiracial client about race, they should explore their own thoughts and feelings about race and how this may be affecting the therapeutic relationship.

The dismantling of these myths can play a significant role in counseling multiracial individuals. Providing a safe context for talking about race is crucial when working with multiracial people, as they may enter the counseling relationship wary of people who have misunderstood their identity (e.g., by pitying or exoticizing them). Counselors who are conscious of these myths and their biases about multiracial people are more likely to create an authentic dialogue with multiracial clients.

Psychosocial Adjustment of Multiracial People

As noted above, a common notion, even myth, about multiracial people is that due to their unique and multiple racial heritage (and the presumed lack of a coherent or stable community), they are at risk of becoming confused or somehow maladjusted. Thus, one primary area of emphasis in theory and research on these individuals has been the psychological functioning of multiracial people. This line of research portrays multiracial people as generally well-functioning, although at some psychological risk. For example, recent studies used a subsample of self-identified multiracial adolescents culled from the National Longitudinal Study of Adolescent Health (Cooney & Radina, 2000; Milan & Keiley, 2000). Results showed that multiracial participants reported higher levels of conduct problems, school problems, somatization, lower self-worth, and counseling use. However, other studies have shown little or no differences, leading scholars to comment on the resilience of multiracial individuals in the face of multiple stressors (Cauce et al., 1992; Mass, 1992; Phinney & Alipuria, 1996). A common problem of many of these studies is that research has been inconclusive as to how or why a multiracial heritage plays a role in psychological adjustment or maladjustment. Indeed, a major limitation of existing research on psychological adjustment of multiracial people is that identity variables (i.e., thoughts and feelings regarding racial and ethnic heritage) such as racial or ethnic identity were not included in any of these studies; instead, these studies used a self-identified multiracial label (Miville, 2005).

Racial Identity Development Models–Applications to Multiracial Identity

Many scholars today agree that notions of race are socially constructed, not biologically derived (Helms, 1995; Root, 1999, 2002). Race exists as a psychological and social reality, daily affecting both monoracial and multiracial people. Racial identity development (RID) models (Cross, 1991; Helms, 1990, 1995) were applied to the racial identity development of multiracial people (Helms, 1995). In general, RID models proposed that individuals do not react identically to conditions of discrimination or privilege but develop various schemas or statuses for interpreting these experiences.

For example, the **Person of Color (POC)** racial identity model (Helms, 1995) described racial identity development for people of color, according to their experiences with racial oppression and the capacity to relinquish external, generally negative views of people of color in favor of internal, more positive standards. Identity statuses included the following:

a. **Preencounter/Conformity,** when persons of color use society's more traditional, albeit negative, views of people of color to interpret race-related information,

b. **Encounter/Dissonance,** when as a result of new experiences, either with racial discrimination or positively-identified people of color, the capacity to question these views is developed,

c. **Immersion/Emersion,** involving a blend of idealization of membership in racial group(s), strong rejection of white-superior views, a search for positive definitions of self as a racial/ethnic being, and strong affiliations with racial group(s),

d. **Internalization,** in which persons of color are capable of conceptualizing themselves well as others by means of a positive definition of one's racial group(s), and finally

e. **Integrative Awareness,** reflecting the capacity of people of color to value all of their collective identities (based on race, gender) as well as to empathize more generally with oppressed groups.

RID models based on privilege were proposed by various multicultural scholars, one of the better known being the **White Racial Identity Development (WRID)** model (Helms, 1990). The WRID model described cognitive strategies associated with relinquishing power as an aspect of one's internalized racial identity. As with the POC model, the WRID model described racial identity statuses reflecting naïveté about racial issues (Contact), confusion and conflict regarding privileges based on race (Disintegration and Reintegration), and resolutions of these conflicts based on the adoption of a nonracist white identity (Pseudo-Independence, Immersion/Emersion, and Autonomy). Further discussion of racial identity is included in Chapter 4.

A current question regarding RID models is their applicability to multiracial people; indeed, some authors contend that RID models do not capture the authentic experiences of multiracial people in their identity development. For example, Root (2002) questioned the "assumption of some universal process affecting identity development in general" (p. 173), contending that such models are hierarchical and Eurocentric. Renn (2000) also stated that it is impossible for multiracial people to be "neatly separated for an Immersion experience" (i.e., becoming involved in a racial community, p. 3), a key aspect of RID models.

Because RID models address privilege (for white people) and oppression (for people of color) separately, they do not capture the nuances of both oppression and privilege experienced by some multiracial individuals. Depending on context, multiracial people may be able to pass as White and avoid overt racism at times, while still experiencing racism unique to their group. (e.g., the "What are you?" question often asked of multiracial people). It is crucial for counselors working with multiracial people to understand both the overt and covert forms of racism that may affect their clients.

RID models likely do not describe important aspects of racial identity of multiracial people. However, these models highlight critical commonalities of identity development for monoracial and multiracial people (Helms, 1995). As noted by Miville and Helms (1996) as cited in Miville, 2005, general common racial identity processes might be described as (1) Emergence/Conflicts of Identities and (2) Resolutions, either Internal or External. Thus, RID models do not necessarily preclude the development of more specific racial identity models for multiracial people. For example, the *immersion/emersion* phase may be applicable to multiracial people but perhaps in a different way than for monoracial people of color. Thus, rather than identifying with a group of multiracial people and excluding monoracial group values, a person with a white mother and black father may seek identification with a diverse community of people or with another racial group entirely. RID models may help to identify critical common factors or processes that multiracial people, along with people of color in general, in the United States must negotiate in their development of a positive racial identity. Such processes relate to experiences with overt racism and finding supportive others in the community with whom to identify. RID models based on privilege also might be examined for their validity and relevance with multiracial people.

Multiracial Identity Development Models

Beginning with Poston (1990), other multicultural scholars have proposed unique racial identity models for multiracial people. For example, Poston (1990) proposed a five-stage model of multiracial identity development, suggesting that all multiracial individuals will experience some conflict and subsequent periods of maladjustment during the identity development process. In the first stage of Poston's model, *personal identity,* which usually occurs in childhood, multiracial individuals are not aware of their mixed-race heritage. During the second stage, *choice of group categorization,* numerous societal, communal, and parental influences compel individuals to choose one racial or ethnic group identity. In the third stage of his model, *enmeshment/denial,* individuals' feelings of guilt and disloyalty about choosing one racial group over the other may predominate. Unable to resolve feelings of guilt and disloyalty, these individuals may deny the racial differences and subsequently identify with both groups. In the fourth stage, *appreciation,* individuals may remain committed to one racial group but might explore the previously ignored racial group as they experience increased awareness and knowledge of the ignored group. In the fifth stage of Poston's model, *integration,* individuals may still identify with one racial group but value the integration of their multiple racial identities.

Kich's (1992) conceptualization of multiracial identity development emphasized movement from dissonance between choosing a monoracial self-identity toward adopting an integrated multiracial self-identity as a function of age progression. In Kich's three-stage model of multiracial identity development, individuals move from incongruent feelings between self- and external perceptions (Stage One–3 through 10 years of age), through struggles for social and self acceptance (Stage Two–8 years old through young adulthood), until they fully internalize a bicultural and multiracial identity (Stage Three–late adolescence or young adulthood).

Kerwin and Ponterotto's (1995) model of multiracial identity development used age-based developmental markers to illustrate progression in racial awareness. However, unlike the above models, Kerwin and Ponterotto's conceptualization acknowledged that there is variance in identity resolution styles (e.g., establishing a public racial identity that differs from a private one) that is influenced by personal, societal, and environmental factors. Their model also differed from the other models in that they acknowledged that multiracial individuals may experience exclusion from groups of color as well as from whites. The developmental stages are described below:

In the **preschool** stage, which occurs up to five years of age, multiracial children recognize similarities and differences in physical appearance, and this awareness may be a function of the degree of parental sensitivity to and addressing of race-related issues.

In the **entry to school** stage, multiracial children are in greater contact with social groups and may be asked to classify themselves according to a monoracial label.

In the **preadolescence** stage, there is an increased awareness of social meanings ascribed to social groups as characterized by skin tone, physical appearance, ethnicity, and religion. Environmental factors, such as entry into a more diverse or more monocultural context, and direct or vicarious exposure to racism also may heighten these young adolescents' sensitivity to race.

As multiracial children enter **adolescence,** pressures to identify with one social group may be intensified by expectations of identification with the racial group of a parent of color.

In the **college/young adulthood** stage, there may be a continued immersion in a monoracial group, accompanied with an acute awareness of the contexts in which race-related comments are made.

The **adulthood** stage is characterized by a continued exploration and interest in race and culture, including self-definitions of racial and cultural identities and increased flexibility in adapting to various cultural settings.

A limitation of some multiracial identity development models is the assumption that a fully integrated multiracial identity is the desired end-state and that this identity must address aspects of racial identity singularly and somehow separately before integration (Root, 1998). Root (1998), however, has suggested alternative resolutions of the multiracial identity development process. She proposed an ecological meta-model for understanding the potential influences of inherited influences (e.g., parents' identities, nativity, phenotype, and extended family), traits (e.g., temperament, coping skills, and social skills), and socialization agents (e.g., family, peer, and community) on resolution of racial identity for multiracial people. Different sources of experiential conflict lead to feelings of alienation and marginality, discrimination, and ambiguity that challenge the development of a healthy sense of self. Root (1996)

also noted that multiracial individuals can negotiate identity development concerns through four possible border crossings or comfort in,
across, and between racial categories:

1. Carrying multiple cultural perspectives simultaneously.
2. Having a situational identity, or shifting racial identity with
   regard to context or environment.
3. Claiming an independent multiracial reference point.
4. Maintaining a monoracial identity when entering different cultural environments.

Border identity, or identification with both or many racial groups
(Root, 1998), may be positive when personality and sense of self remain
constant across racial contexts, although social validation of racial identity may be specific to regions of high concentrations of multiracial people. This model of multiracial identity development can be very helpful
when counseling multiracial people. Through understanding that multiracial people can come to an identity resolution in various ways, and
that this process may be context-dependent, counselors can be more
open in their work with multiracial people, allowing them to tell their
stories without pathologizing them.

Despite disagreements among scholars, common themes across racial
identity models (e.g., RID, ecological meta-model) can be noted (Miville,
2005). Most important are the emphases on race as a social construction
and identity development as nested in a social context affected by
sociopolitical history. Further, although scholars generally agree that
racial identity is developmental (i.e., changes over time and with experience), current theories have moved away from describing invariant
stages, instead emphasizing strategies of identification, affected by cognitive and affective processes and social interactions. Theories diverge in
their differing emphases on the dynamic interplay of variables and the
recognition that multiracial people can and do adapt a variety of positive
and healthy ways of identifying themselves; that is, the internalization or
integration of identity is dynamic, fluid, and ongoing and is affected by
such variables as physical appearance and language.

Implications for Professional Practice

Due to their unique sociopolitical history in the United States, multiracial people are likely to face a number of stressors. Of primary con-

cern is finding community or social networks that will provide meaningful support, particularly in the face of overt racism regarding both their monoracial and multiracial heritage (the oft-asked "What Are You?" question). Multiracial people may come to define themselves in ways that are unique from their parents, siblings, and peers (Root, 1996). These self-definitions also will be multiple and fluid over time and situation. Thus, finding support for engaging in this dynamic process of self-definition and adoption of multiple meaningful self-labels will be critical to developing a healthy multiracial identity. A variety of resources are listed at the end of this chapter, which are supportive to this end.

Mental health professionals working with multiracial individuals need to be aware of the impact of multiple racial labels among their clients. For example, themes of cultural mistrust typically evident in cross-racial dyads may be exhibited with multiracial clients. Moreover, therapists and counselors who have been trained in existing models of racial identity development and multicultural counseling may conceptualize multiracial clients' situations from these monoracial racial identity frameworks without a more holistic understanding of clients' experiences. In other words, although mental health professionals may attempt to use racially/culturally sensitive frameworks in counseling, their interventions and conceptualizations may not be congruent with clients' public and private understandings of their own racial or cultural identity.

Root (in Wehrly, 1996) identified six key themes that may affect multiracial clients in counseling:

1. **Uniqueness,** a predominant theme that likely interacts with other clinical issues. A sense of uniqueness may lead to behaviors misdiagnosed as pathological or maladjusted. For example, a context adaptive focus for many multiracial individuals may lead to a more detail-oriented communication style that may be misinterpreted as compulsive or paranoid. Moreover, as Wehrly (1996) noted, "Living as a unique individual all of one's life sometimes leads to strong feelings of isolation and depression" (p. 128).

2. **Acceptance and belonging.** As a multiracial participant in a study by Miville et al. (2005) noted, "I think a lot of us are chameleons," meaning that many multiracial people can fit into a number of social groups, but perhaps never fully participate or

feel connected to any one group, except perhaps other multiracial people. Social barriers to full group membership may give rise to feelings of loneliness, anxiety, and depression.

3. **Physical appearance.** A unique physical appearance can lead to multiple experiences of being openly stared at or questioned, for example, as to the matching of their name with their physical presence. Constant questioning of who or even what someone is may be associated with feelings of being judged or negatively evaluated by others. These issues may be more predominant for multiracial women than men, given the premier emphasis on physical appearance for women in general.

4. **Sexuality.** The exotic nature with which multiracial individuals, particularly women, are viewed in the larger society, as well as a presumption of promiscuity, may lead to outright discrimination as well as feelings of evaluation and objectification by others. Relationship issues may occur for both multiracial individuals and their partners in dealing with internalized stereotypes or fantasies based on prevailing sexual myths about multiracial individuals.

5. **Self-esteem.** Being or feeling different or unique may lead some (though not all) multiracial individuals to struggle with their self-esteem and to strive to excel to feel better about themselves. Wehrly (1996) cautioned that a clinical consequence of this struggle might be a fragile sense of self, due to an external directedness. At the same time, it is important for counselors not to presume that low self-esteem is automatically a concern for their multiracial clients and to explore positive feelings their clients might have about being who they are (different and unique as well as parallel with others).

6. **Identity.** As noted earlier, identity issues may be of concern for multiracial clients. However, it is important to support clients in their efforts to identify and emphasize strengths of their multiracial heritage. As participants in the study by Miville et al. (2005) described, one strength may be their ability to negotiate with a variety of social groups and settings and to cross rigid social boundaries, along with an awareness of the importance of doing so. Another finding from the study by Miville et al. was that these individuals may privately identify as multiracial while publicly identifying as a member of a particular racial/ethnic group (e.g.,

Black or Asian). Thus, part of facilitating identity development is supporting the multiple labels multiracial people may adopt for themselves as well as helping them connect with similar and supportive others who can provide a social network.

Sue and Sue (2003) provided the following guidelines for practice with multiracial individuals:

1. Become aware of stereotypes and preconceptions about interracial marriages and multiracial people.
2. Understand the history surrounding multiracial people, such as the one-drop rule, and issues of marginality and ambiguity (the "What are You?" question).
3. View multiracial people in holistic terms rather than as fractions of a person.
4. Help contextualize potential feelings of loneliness and marginality, should these be present, within a perspective of racial prejudice and social injustice.
5. Emphasize positive attributes and advantages of being multiracial.
6. Incorporate family counseling, where possible, to help educate parents.

The following section presents a case example that highlights potential presenting themes of multiracial clients, along with suggestions for conceptualization and intervention.

Case Example

Lillian is a 29-year-old multiracial (Filipina/African American) woman coming to therapy at a community mental health center because she feels anxious and wants to stop procrastinating. She is attending a local community college part-time, working toward her Associate's degree, and she works full time as a teacher's aide at a preschool. She lives with and cares for her mother, who is chronically ill. Her parents divorced when she was very young, and she is estranged from her father and his extended family. Lillian also lives with two younger brothers, ages 18 and 19, from her mother's second marriage. During the course of treatment, Lillian expresses frustration with her mother and her aunts, who expect her to be constantly available to them and who often chastise her for the amount of time she spends at work and school. She also begins describing a feeling of not fitting in with her mother's family at times and a desire to know her father's family. The client discloses that her mother is Filipina, and while Lillian has always played an important role in her family as the oldest daughter, she often feels as if her extended family treats her differently than her other female cousins, who are pure *Pinay*. Her father is black/African American, and she has always longed to know his family. She feels that her mother's family is "too traditional–it's suffocating!" and wonders if her father's family is different because they are "from the States."

Lillian describes close friendships with a few people from work and school. She is dating a Puerto Rican American man whom she met at an event sponsored by a multicultural club on campus. She states that she is grateful for her friends and boyfriend, but lately she does not have the time or energy for these relationships. Her mother has been confined to the house because of her illness for the past month, which means that she is cooking for her brothers and mother more frequently. Lillian states that she is having trouble sleeping at night, but when she gets home from work or school, "all I want to do is pass out." When she does have the time and energy to do her schoolwork, she sometimes has trouble breathing because all she can think about is what she is going to do when she graduates with her Associate's degree. Lillian would like to go on to a Bachelor's degree in education but is worried that she will not be able to handle the stress because of her family obligations and her need to work to support herself.

Therapeutic Issues and Strategies

Lillian's presenting concerns reflect anxiety, and possibly some depression, about her family roles and obligations and her identity, as well as ambivalence regarding her upcoming graduation. She feels criticized and overworked by her family as well as emotionally disconnected or different from them because she is not *pure Pinay*. Some of Lillian's conflicts also may revolve around how she identifies herself. Lillian's racial-ethnic identity likely reflects her Filipina heritage, given her immersion into this cultural group by living with her maternal relatives. At the same time, Lillian expresses curiosity about her black/African American heritage, perhaps due to her current stress and feelings of frustration and confinement regarding family obligations.

Her curiosity also may stem from a normative process of simply wanting to know all of who she is, particularly since her father may have been absent from her daily life. That Lillian has a number of close friends as well as a boyfriend indicates that she has been able to build relationships outside her family, a major source of strength for her. Although it appears that Lillian is immersed in the Filipino community, she may be experiencing a second immersion of sorts at her community college and through her friends. Lillian's situation demonstrates how, for many multiracial people, immersion into a one or more monoracial groups may not be necessary for identity development.

Lillian also is experiencing anxiety and ambivalence regarding her educational achievements, perhaps because this experience may further distance her from her family, and she may be unsure how to negotiate changes in her family roles that arise from these achievements. It will be helpful to know more about Lillian's childhood and adolescence to understand her racial and cultural socialization throughout her life. She is now almost 30 years old and may be struggling to integrate a new racial-cultural identity into a self-concept that was formed at a younger age. On the other hand, counselors' understanding of identity as a life-long, fluid process may validate Lillian's struggles in the context of racism and society's stereotypes about multiracial people.

Strategies for helping Lillian may include discussion of her frustrations regarding family obligations while simultaneously acknowledging how she might want to maintain strong connections with her family in ways that are culturally and psychologically meaningful to her (i.e., articulate the *push/pull* many families exert on individuals). Providing support for Lillian's curiosity about her father's family may help her develop a more holistic sense of who she is. This process also may lead to a more complex sense of who she is (multiple labels or selves for multiple settings) that may be adaptive for Lillian. A more complex sense of self also may help protect Lillian from further tension that arises in her maternal family regarding role obligations as well as her multiracial heritage. Strategies regarding Lillian's ambivalence about her educational endeavors might include helping Lillian articulate what obtaining an education means for both herself and well as her family, perhaps contextualizing the educational experience as a means of defining herself as an adult within her family system (i.e., how to be a dutiful daughter and a responsible adult).

Counselors working with Lillian should be aware of their beliefs about blacks and African Americans, Filipina/os, and multiracial people, including an understanding of their own biases. Throughout their work with Lillian, counselors should be aware of the ways in which Lillian has internalized racial constructions that may be harmful to her self-identity. What are Lillian's ideas about blackness, in light of the fact that she has no contact with this part of her family? Is she idealizing blackness because she longs for contact with her father? How might this affect her beliefs about being Filipina? Counselors should be aware of their tendencies to pick apart Lillian's identity. Multiracial people are often viewed as parts of a person, rather than being viewed holistically. Counselors should create a safe space where Lillian can explore her feelings and identity as a whole person, both racially and in light of the multiple roles she plays.

In addition, it is important to understand Lillian's experiences with gender and social class along with her multiracial identity. As stated earlier, the racism that multiracial women experience often involves being labeled exotic. While Lillian may derive strength from her unique racial identity, it is possible that this identity was sexualized by men (and certainly by the media). In addition, Lillian may face stereotypes related to social class because both of her parents are people of color. She also may struggle with self-esteem because of the low expectations for education that may have been communicated to her by family, friends, the school system, and so on.

CONCLUDING REMARKS

Much change has occurred in the last two decades regarding the societal recognition of the rights and realities of multiracial people. This evolution was paralleled in the social sciences by an increasing emphasis on better understanding the lived experiences of multiracial people. Multicultural researchers and practitioners focused on the struggles and strengths of multiracial people by listening to the spoken stories of these individuals, rather than imposing myths and stereotypes. Recent models regarding identity development (Rocquemore, 2002; Root, 1999) of multiracial people are more closely linked to these experiences, reflecting authenticity, rather than rigid theorizing that only serve to continue and promote harmful myths.

Multiracial people have unique stressors and strengths. In this chapter, we identified a number of potential concerns that multiracial clients may bring to their counseling sessions. The challenges of constructing a positive racial identity as a multiracial person occurs in a social context historically embedded in struggle, oppression, survival, and resilience. The specific constellation of identity challenges no doubt changes with each individual and his or her unique blending of race and culture, family system, and so on. It is critical for researchers and practitioners to recognize both the unique challenges faced by multiracial people, as well as the common struggles shared with others considered as minorities in the United States, such as from overt racism and discrimination or invisibility or negative visibility in the larger media.

Review Questions

1. How did the 2000 census impact the history of multiracial people in the United States?
2. What are some societal myths about multiracial people? How do these myths relate to racial oppression?
3. How do monoracial identity development models differ from multiracial identity development models?
4. Compare and contrast the three multiracial identity development models discussed in this chapter (Kerwin & Ponterotto, 1995; Kich, 1992; Poston, 1990; Root, 1998).
5. Identify and discuss three themes that may affect multiracial clients.
6. Give three examples of ways that counselors can be effective in working with multiracial clients.

Additional Resources

Books

Burnt Bread and Chutney: Growing Up Between Cultures: A Memoir of an Indian Jewish Childhood by Carmit Delman
What Are You? Voices of Mixed Race Young People by Pearl Gaskin
Atul's Quest by Nader Habibi
How Did You Get to be a Mexican: A White/Brown Man's Search for Identity by Kevin R. Johnson

Property by Valerie Martin
The Salaryman's Wife by Sujata Massey
The Color of Water: A Black Man's Tribute to his White Mother by James McBride
Caucasia by Danzy Senna
Black, White, and Jewish: Autobiography of a Shifting Self by Rebecca Walker

Web Sites

http://mavinfoundation.org/
An organization dedicated to building healthy communities that celebrate and empower mixed heritage people and families.
http://www.swirlinc.org/
Swirl, Inc., an anti-racist, grassroots organization serves the mixed heritage community and aims to develop a national consciousness around mixed heritage issues to empower members to organize and take action towards progressive social change.
http://multiracial.com
An online newsletter called *The Multiracial Activist,* news that concerns multiracial people, and more.
http://www.fusionprogram.org
Program for mixed heritage youth.
http://www.amerasianworld.com/
A web site dedicated to persons of Asian and American ancestry, specifically those fathered by American servicemen with Asian women in Asia. Historically, the first Amerasians were born in Japan and Korea, and subsequently, Vietnam and the Philippines.
http://www.seaweedproductions.com/hapa/
The Hapa Project, a creative arts project by Kip Fulbeck, nationally known artist and faculty member at UC, Santa Barbara.
http://www.hapas.com/
Online community for Eurasian, biracial, multiracial, Amerasian, mixed Asian, Blasian, hafu, half-Asian, and hapa people.
http://www.whatareyou.com/
Comments and reviews about the book *What Are You?* by Pearl Gaskin. Author's website.
http://users.arczip.com/xmen3/bfnchicago/
The Biracial Family Network, a nonprofit public benefit corporation organized to help eliminate prejudice and discrimination by assisting

individuals and families of diverse ethnic ancestry to improve the quality of their intercultural relationships via education and social activities.

Films

Anomaly available online at http:www.Anomalythefilm.com. Documentary in production
Banana Split documentary by Kip Fulbeck
Café au lait (also known as Métisse), 1993, directed by Mathieu Kassovitz
Catfish in Black Bean Sauce, 1999, directed by Chi Moui Lo
Chasing Daybreak (documentary about mixed race in the U.S.), 2005, directed by Justin Leroy
Do 2 Halves Really Make a Whole? 1993, directed by Martha Chono-Helsley
Rabbit-Proof Fence, 2002, directed by Phillip Noyce
The Nephew, 1993, directed by Eugene Brady

REFERENCES

Brown, U. M. (2001). *The interracial experience: Growing up Black/White racially mixed in the United States.* Westport, CT: Praeger.

Cauce, A. M., Hiraga, Y., Mason, C., Agilar, T., Ordonez, N., & Gonzales, N. (1992). Between a rock and a hard place: Social adjustment of biracial youth. In M. P. P. Root (Ed.), *Racially mixed people in America* (pp. 207–222). Newbury Park, CA: Sage.

Cooney, T. M., & Radina, M. E. (2000). Adjustment problems in adolescence: Are multiracial children at risk? *American Journal of Orthopsychiatry, 70,* 433–444.

Cross, W. E., Jr. (1991). *Shades of Black: Diversity in African-American identity.* Philadelphia: Temple University Press.

Fernandez, C. A. (1996). Government classification of multiracial/multiethnic people. In M. P. P. Root (Ed), *The multiracial experience: Racial borders as the new frontier* (pp. 15–36). Thousand Oaks, CA: Sage.

Gaskin, P. F. (1999). *What are you? Voices of mixed race people.* New York: Henry Holt and Company.

Hansen, S. (2001). *Mixing it up.* Retrieved December 7, 2005, from http//archive.salon.com/books/int/2001/03/08/sollors/print.html

Helms, J. E. (1990). *Black and White racial identity: Theory, research, and practice.* New York: Greenwood Press.

Helms, J. E. (1995). An update on Helms's White and people of color racial identity models. In J. G. Ponterotto, J. M. Casas, L. A. Suzuki, & C. M. Alexander (Eds.), *Handbook of multicultural counseling* (pp. 181–191). Thousand Oaks, CA: Sage.

Israel, T. (1996). Conversations, not categories: The intersection of biracial and bisexual identities. In A. R. Gillem & C. A. Thompson (Eds.), *Biracial women in therapy: Between the rock
of gender and the hard place of race* (pp. 173–184). New York: The Haworth Press.

Kerwin, C., & Ponterotto, J. G. (1995). Biracial identity development: Theory and research. In
J. G. Ponterotto, J. M. Casas, L. A. Suzuki, & C. M. Alexander (Eds.), *Handbook of multicultural counseling* (pp. 199–217). Thousand Oaks, CA: Sage.

Kich, G. K. (1992). The developmental process of asserting a biracial, bicultural identity. In M.
P. P. Root (Ed.), *Racially mixed people in America* (pp. 304–317). Newbury Park, CA: Sage.

Mass, A. I. (1992). Interracial Japanese Americans: The best of both worlds or the end of the
Japanese American community? In M. P. P. Root (Ed.), *Racially mixed people in America* (pp.
265–279). Newbury Park, CA.: Sage.

Milan, S., & Keiley, M. K. (2000). Biracial youth and families in therapy: Issues and interventions. *Journal of Marital and Family Therapy, 26,* 305–315.

Miville, M. L. (2005) Psychological functioning and identity development of biracial people: A
review of current theory and research. In R T. Carter (Ed.), *Handbook of racial-cultural psychology and counseling, Volume I: Theory and research* (pp. 295–319). New York: Wiley.

Miville, M. L., Constantine, M. G., Baysden, M. F., & So-Lloyd, G. (2005). Chameleon changes:
An exploration of racial identity themes of multiracial people. *Journal of Counseling Psychology, 52,* 507–516.

Phinney, J. S., & Alipuria, L. L. (1996). At the interface of cultures: Multiethnic/multiracial
high school students and college students. *Journal of Social Psychology, 136,* 139–158.

Poston, W. S. C. (1990). The biracial identity development model: A needed addition. *Journal
of Counseling and Development, 69,* 152–155.

Renn, K. A. (2000, April). *Tilting at windmills: The paradox of researching mixed-race.* Paper presented at the annual meeting of the American Educational Research Association, New
Orleans, LA.

Rockquemore, K. A. (2002). *Beyond Black: Biracial identity in America.* Thousand Oaks, CA.:
Sage.

Rockquemore, K. A., & Brunsma, D. L. (2002). Socially embedded identities: Theories, typologies, and processes of racial identity among Black/White biracials. *Sociological Quarterly,
43,* 335–356.

Root, M. P. P. (1992). *Racially mixed people in America.* Newbury Park, CA: Sage.

Root, M. P. P. (1996). *The multiracial experience: Racial borders as the new frontier.* Thousand Oaks,
CA.: Sage.

Root, M. P. P. (1998). Experiences and processes affecting racial identity development: Preliminary results from the Biracial Sibling Project. *Cultural Diversity and Mental Health, 4* (3),
237–247.

Root, M. P. P. (1999). The biracial baby boom: Understanding ecological constructions of racial
identity in the 21st century. In R. Hernandez Sheets & E. R. Hollins (Eds.), *Racial and ethnic identity in school practices: Aspects of human development* (pp. 67–90). Mahwah, NJ.:
Erlbaum.

Root, M. P. P. (2002). Methodological issues in multiracial research. In G. C. N. Hall & S.
Okazaki (Eds.), *Asian American psychology: The science of lives in context* (pp. 171–193). Washington, DC: American Psychological Association.

Sue, D. W., & Sue, D. (2003). *Counseling the culturally diverse: Theory and practice* (4th Ed.). New
York: Wiley.

Wehrly, B. (1996). *Counseling interracial individuals and families.* Alexandra, VA: American Counseling Association.

Wehrly, B., Kenney, K. R., & Kenney, M. W. (1999). *Counseling multiracial families.* Thousand
Oaks, CA.: Sage.

Chapter 9

INTRODUCING SPIRITUALITY INTO MULTICULTURAL COUNSELING

ANA PUIG AND CHRIS ADAMS

The important thing is that somehow or other [spirituality] has come into existence, and is widespread, and does not disappear from the mind with the growth of knowledge and civilisation.

C.S. Lewis, *The Problem of Pain*, p. 8

Abstract

This chapter begins by addressing the field of spiritual counseling from a broad historical perspective, defining spiritual counseling, and discussing the contextual issues inherent in spirituality and culture. Spiritually-based multicultural counseling competencies are reviewed. The chapter also discusses assessment, goals, and the process of change in spiritual counseling. Applications and practices are discussed through a case example and research perspectives are discussed. Spiritually-based activities are suggested to help counseling students explore multicultural spiritual experiences. Finally, the chapter concludes with a discussion of how multicultural spiritual counseling may be integrated into existing psychotherapy approaches.

INTRODUCTION

The increased diversification of cultures in the United States has challenged the counseling profession to develop multicultural com-

petencies (Sue, Arredondo, & McDavis, 1992). As a counseling professional, you can expect to encounter clients from a variety of cultures different from your own. Specifically, as the North American landscape
shows increasing diversity and interest in spirituality and spiritual practices, the clients with whom you work may come from a variety of religious and spiritual traditions that are part of their cultural heritage.
Fukuyama & Sevig (1999) offer a comprehensive view of critical factors
present at the intersection of religion, spirituality, and culture and
extend an invitation to explore its counseling implications, likening this
learning process to the human journey of "self-exploration, growth and
service to others . . . the spiritual journey invites us to deeper levels of
understanding self, expanded consciousness, and service; similarly, the
multicultural journey challenges us to shift perspectives and to encompass different points of view" (O'Hara, 1998, p. 19).

Throughout this human journey, issues of meaninglessness, emptiness, listlessness, and vague depression are but a few of the presenting
problems borne of the spiritual dimension (Moore, 1992). All of these
concerns speak to the inherent human need for transcendence and pur-
posefulness (Maslow, 1998). Western society's value-orientation emphasizes "doing" over "being" and this emphasis may contribute to an
individual's sense of loss of self, values, faith, or meaning (Sue & Sue,
2003). This may be particularly relevant for clients who come from
diverse cultures as they are faced with these Western values. Multicultural spiritual counseling addresses these and other issues holistically,
attending to all aspects of the individual: mind, body, emotions, and
spirit (Clinebell, 1995) and includes attending to cultural and other contextual factors influencing the clinical presentation.

Spirituality and Culture: Historical Context and
Conceptualizations

Psychology and counseling have historically emphasized the cognitive, behavioral, emotional, and biological factors that influence personality development and psychological distress. The human experience of
the numinous (i.e., the divine, mystical or deeply spiritual realm), until
recently, remained largely untouched by psychology and the counseling profession, despite the Humanistic movement of the 1960s and
1970s. Although a focus on spiritual and transcendental elements was
present during this movement, the spiritual lives of clients have typical-

ly been thought to be personal, intimate aspects of the individual that fell outside the scope of clinical practice and belonged to representatives of organized religion or pastoral counselors. The debate about "the appropriateness of mixing spirituality and counseling, defining a relationship between spirituality and religion, and the status of the church-state separation in the United States" (Faiver, Ingersoll, Brien & McNally, 2001, p. 8) has become an active part of clinical discourse. However, many counselors opt not to discuss spiritual or religious issues in sessions, addressing these only when raised by the client. Others may only include a spiritual assessment component in their structured intake assessment process.

Nonetheless, a number of writers have laid the foundation for the exploration of spiritual and religious themes in counseling. Carl Jung (1933) is arguably one of the first to propose that the spiritual life of clients must be attended to in session, resulting in Jung's "exile from the Freudian psychoanalytic world" (Scotton, 1996, p. 39). In addition, influential psychologists including Erik Erikson, William James, Gordon Allport, Abraham Maslow and Viktor Frankl all underscored the importance of the religious and spiritual domains and contributed to our understanding of the roles of spirituality and religiosity in people's lives (Frame, 2003).

Other writers, as well, have acknowledged the critical role of spirituality and religious beliefs in human experience. For example, Kroll and Sheehan (1989) reported that more than 90 percent of individuals living in the United States believe in the existence of a Higher Power (e.g., God). Stanard, Sandhu, and Painter (2000) described spirituality as "a pervasive force in contemporary American society [that] is deeply influencing several helping professions such as counseling, education, medicine, nursing, psychology, [and] social work" (p. 204). As such, innovative treatment interventions are being proposed, developed, and researched which transcend the realm of traditional psychotherapeutic practices and address the role of spirituality in emotional and psychological healing (Katra & Targ, 2000). In addition, some research suggests potential benefits of incorporating spirituality into clinical practice (Larimore, Parker, & Crowther, 2002). However, most mental health practitioners continue to remain relatively unaware about the positive role of spiritual and religious beliefs in regard to psychological well-being, as well as reluctant to address such beliefs with their clients. In addition to understanding the benefits of spirituality and religion, it is also necessary for clinicians to understand the negative aspects of spirituality and religiosity and to carefully consider the client's cultural background in addressing these issues.

Religion, spirituality and culture have been conceptualized as "intertwined and interrelated" constructs (Fukuyama, Siapoush & Sevig, 2004, p. 123). Despite the acknowledged importance of spiritual and religious beliefs for many people, spiritually-based counseling remains an emerging specialized practice (Cashwell & Young, 2004; Ceasar & Miranti, 2003), although a greater acceptance of spirituality as part of counseling has been documented in recent years. In a thematic review of family therapy journals, Rivett (2000) reported that spirituality is a significant emergent issue for counseling practice. Further evidence of this trend may be found in the appearance of religious or spiritually focused divisions of the American Psychological Association and the American Counseling Association. For example, the American Association of Pastoral Counseling (AAPC) was founded in 1963 to ensure responsible spiritual counseling. Organizations such as the Association for Spiritual, Ethical, and Religious Values in Counseling (ASERVIC), chartered in 1974 and the Psychology of Religion (APA, Division 36), chartered in 1976, were created to explore the role between wellbeing and spirituality and religion. In addition, graduate programs and institutes specifically focused on the study of spiritual and religious approaches in psychotherapy training are also gaining popularity among counseling students. There is a sample list of web sites for these educational institutions at the end of this chapter.

Definitions of Spirituality

Historically, the reluctance to address spiritual issues in counseling may be due to its inherently complex and abstract nature. Although there are many ways to describe and conceptualize spirituality, there is no agreement on a single definition of the concept (Maher & Hunt, 1993). Adding to the confusion, the terms spirituality and religion, because of their interrelatedness have often been used interchangeably. Another layer of complexity in this issue are the critical roles of race, ethnicity, culture, and national origin in personal spiritual development. Finally, although spirituality and religion serve as sources of strength, support, and healing for many (Fukuyama & Sevig, 1999; Kelly, 1995), some clients have had negative and toxic religious experiences, and counselors may feel hesitant to address such experiences. However, these negative religious experiences–called religious wounding or toxic religiosity–may be a presenting problem for some clients.

The definition of spirituality is as varied as its many disciplines. Stanard, Singh, and Painter (2000) envisioned spirituality as a concept that includes "transcendence, self-actualization, purpose and meaning, wholeness, balance, sacredness, altruism, universality, and a sense of a higher power" (p. 213). Anderson & Worthen (as cited in Rivett & Street, 2001) explained that religion, on the other hand, "solidifies [spirituality] into particular forms, rituals, sacred scriptures, doctrines, rules of conduct, and other practices" (p. 460).

Spirituality may be also defined in individual or contextual ways. For example, Hinterkopf (1998) proposed an intrapersonal definition of spirituality as "a subtle, bodily feeling with vague meanings that brings new, clearer meanings involving a transcendent growth process" (p. 11). Hinterkopf further reported that her definition takes into account Gendlin's (1961; 1964) theory of experiencing, where therapeutic process and content are acknowledged as distinct, important aspects of psychotherapy that counselors must attend to during sessions. Griffith and Griffith (2002), on the other hand, provide a definition of spirituality as a contextual and relational experience: "a commitment to choose, as the primary context for understanding and acting, one's relatedness with all that is." They added that "with this commitment, one attempts to stay focused on relationships between oneself and other people, the physical environment, one's heritage and traditions, one's body, one's ancestors, saints, Higher Power, or God" (pp. 15–16). Clearly, spirituality and its contextual cultural dimensions have been deemed as important, subjective, personal, intimate, and powerful aspect of individuals' lives.

Spiritually-Based Counseling Competencies

Although there appears to be general consensus in the helping professions that spirituality is "a universal phenomenon that can act as a powerful psychological change agent" in clients' lives, there is no clear set of principles to guide spiritual counseling practice (Ceasar & Miranti, 2003, p. 244). The following concepts may be characterized as humanistic in nature and provide a foundational understanding of clients' spiritual and religious lives, including their sociocultural, systemic contexts. These, in turn, inform spiritual counseling practice:

1. Spirituality can be a change agent and assist human beings to achieve their full potential.
2. Spirituality is an innate, subjective, individual, collective, and universal life force.
3. Spirituality is one dimension of a holistic view of human life that also includes body (physical dimension), mind (cognitive dimension), and emotions (affective dimension).
4. The spiritual domain inherent in all humans encompasses issues of: altruism, transcendence, connection (with self, others and a higher power), consciousness of being and nonbeing, values, and the capacity for creativity, compassion, meaning, love, and hopefulness.
5. Spirituality holds the interconnectedness of all living things.
6. Spirituality and religion are social construction: there is a sociocultural systemic context to spiritual, religious, faith traditions, mandates, and practices. (Ceasar & Miranti, 2003, p. 244)

In 1995, members of the Association for Spiritual, Ethical and Religious Values in Counseling set forth a series of competencies to help counselors appropriately address clients' religious or spiritual issues. They concluded counselors need to be able to:

1. Explain the relationship between spirituality and religion.
2. Describe religious and spiritual beliefs and practices in a cultural context.
3. Engage in self-exploration of one's religious and spiritual beliefs in order to increase sensitivity and acceptance of a variety of religious and/or spiritual expressions in their communication.
4. Identify limits of one's understanding of a client's religious and/or spiritual expressions and demonstrate appropriate referral skills and possible referral sources.
5. Assess the relevance of the religious and/or spiritual beliefs in the pursuit of the client's therapeutic goals as befits the expressed preference. (cited in Ceasar & Miranti, 2003, p. 243)

These spiritual counseling competencies clearly underscore the importance of cultural context. Additionally, they emphasize that counselors helping clients explore spiritual or religious concerns must have clear awareness of their own spiritual beliefs. Counselors bring into session their own lived experiences of spirituality and religion. Counseling professionals who lack sensitivity regarding the influence of their own religious beliefs may inadvertently impose their own values on a client. Thus, the counselor's role begins with a clear understanding of him or her self just as he or she strives to maintain an open and unbiased stance toward the client's spiritual and/or religious life.

Kelly (1995) warned that avoiding religious or spiritual themes in counseling sessions may rob the client of an opportunity to explore the potentially healing and beneficial aspects of deep spiritual engagement and practice, including religious affiliation and community involvement. He added "counselors need to take care that a personal discomfort with the earthiness and sometimes quirkiness of concrete religions does not blind them to other peoples' positive regard for and involvement in traditional religions and religious practice" (p. 7). However, counselors who clearly recognize the presence of barriers to spiritual counseling (e.g., inability to accept a client's religious or spiritual affiliation) are ethically bound to acknowledge this limitation and refer out whenever a client asks to explore issues related with this domain (Thayne, 1997).

From a spiritual perspective, the client/counselor dyad is informed by fundamental spiritual values: a belief in the connection among all beings, a spirit of compassion, mutual respect, acceptance, and the capacity for forgiveness (Fukuyama & Sevig, 1999). True to its humanistic roots, the counseling relationship values and affirms human dignity, the potential for growth and change and the human being's need to manifest her true self in the world. In keeping with these principles, the interactions between client and counselor seek to increase openness to seeing the self, others and the world in authentic ways and with a sense of integrity. In traditional psychotherapy approaches, issues of power, control, authority and client/counselor expectations can emerge in session. In multicultural spiritual counseling this is also true; however, the spiritual nature of the interaction may help in navigating this challenging aspect of the client/counselor relationship.

The nature of the client/counselor relationship may also be informed by the client's particular religious affiliation and cultural background. It is important to keep both multicultural and spiritual competencies in mind when approaching client issues in particular ways. Whether you approach the relationship as a teacher, guide, leader, or collaborator, your role as counselor will help define how the client responds to specific interventions and techniques.

The dogma and faith tenets of a particular religious denomination are usually interpreted by their religious leaders. In some methods of therapy guided by religion, the relationship may take the form of teacher and student or guide and student. Most organized religious faiths have clear ethical and moral behavior guidelines based on scripture or sacred texts; for those who accept these as absolute (e.g., a fundamentalist or orthodox world view) counseling is more a process of working with an expert in order to live by these rules and religious principles. For example, an Orthodox Jewish Rabbi may rely on Torah text to offer direction and guidance to a practitioner, while a Pastoral Counselor in a Southern Baptist Church may cite biblical passages to help counsel a church member. Religious counselors with a less fundamentalist or orthodox point of view may practice counseling that is more similar to traditional psychological counseling. Divinity Schools across the United States offer Master's degrees in counseling geared toward pastoral care, usually in various Christian faith denominations (Tisdale, 2003).

In spiritual counseling, as in traditional psychotherapy, the counselor-client dyad is a crucial aspect of the helping process. The counselor's role is to assist the client explore spiritual or religious issues in open, nonjudgmental, and meaningful ways and to help manifest the human potential for growth and development. The counselor can only achieve this by learning about other religious and spiritual traditions, exploring his or her own spiritual and religious beliefs, and remaining aware of biases or limitations that may interfere with the counseling process. These premises underlie basic humanistic and multicultural spiritual approaches to counseling.

Assessment, Goals, and the Process of Change

Counseling professionals addressing spiritual or religious issues with clients need to accurately assess and seek to understand the role that spirituality and/or religion play in clients' lives; this has been deemed an important part of mental and physical health care delivery (Kelly, 1995; Fukuyama & Sevig, 1999; Stanard, Sandhu, and Painter, 2000; Wolf & Stevens, 2001; Woods & Ironson, 1999). Spiritual assessment serves multiple purposes. It helps counselors to understand the client's world view and social/familial context whence they come. In a way, counseling begins with the assessment process since it facilitates client self-exploration and disclosure. In the process of asking questions about client history and background, the client begins to open up about issues or concerns that brought him or her to counseling. Assessment also helps counselors diagnose problems and explore how the client might use religion and/or spirituality as a personal resource. Conversely, some clients use religion and/or spirituality in detrimental ways. Counselors can also assess the degree of pathology present in the client's belief system, and help uncover religious and/or spiritual problems affecting the client's life. A particularly useful tool to help assess family dynamics and possible spiritual issues is the spiritual genogram (Frame, 2000). Finally, assessment can help determine the appropriate interventions to be used, given the client's presenting problems (Frame, 2003).

According to Richards and Bergin (1997) there are nine religious or spiritual domain areas that warrant counselor exploration. They are:

1. **World View:** How does the client see the world and what does he/she believe about spirituality and religion?
2. **Religious Affiliation:** Is the client currently involved in organized religion? Has there been a recent or remote change in religious affiliation?
3. **Level of Orthodoxy:** How closely does the client follow the tenets of his/her faith? Is his/her lifestyle congruent with these faith principles?
4. **Approach to Religious Problem-Solving:** How does the client approach life problems? Does the client rely on inner guidance? Does the client turn the problem over to a Higher Power or God? Does the client work in partnership with God to solve his/her problems?
5. **Spiritual Identity:** How does the client see him or herself in relation to God and to the world? Is the client strong in his or her sense of self-worth? Does he or she feel loved by God? Does he or she feel unworthy of God's love?
6. **God Image:** How does the client view God: benevolent, angry, detached, loving, punishing . . . ?
7. **Value-Lifestyle Congruence:** Is the client acting in ways that support what he or she believes is important, ethical, or valuable in her life?
8. **Doctrinal Knowledge:** Does the client have accurate information about his/her faith tradition's doctrine and teachings? Is

he/she privy to this information or misguided about the tenets of his/her religious affiliation?

9. **Religious and Spiritual Health and Maturity:** What is the client's religious orientation? Does he or she rely on intrinsic values or extrinsic forces to help inform his/her lifestyle decisions?

All of these domains can provide invaluable information about a client's spiritual and religious life. The importance of self-awareness in the counseling process in general and multicultural spiritual counseling in specific cannot be overstated.

The goals of spiritual therapy will vary according to the client's presenting problem. In general, a client presenting with spiritual or religious concerns may be experiencing a number of psychological, emotional, and physical problems: cognitive dissonance, negative or irrational beliefs, psychic numbness, anxious preoccupation, unresolved fear, anger, resentment, depression, sadness, grief and/or psychosomatic problems. The goal of therapy is to help the client restore a sense of peacefulness and functionality to daily life and to explore ways to incorporate spirituality toward resolution of current struggles.

Frequently, spiritual issues brought by clients revolve around interpersonal or intrapsychic anxiety that is often related to specific spiritual or religious conflicts; incongruence between deeply held spiritual or religious beliefs; social or familial pressures related to spiritual, religious, and lifestyle issues; loss of faith or belief in God due to traumatic life events; and changes in religious denomination or faith due to spiritual development or change in marital status, among others. The DSM-IV-TR has a category that can be used when the focus of clinical attention is a religious or spiritual problem (V62.89). Examples include problems associated with conversion to a new faith, or questioning of spiritual values that may not necessarily be related to organized religion (Diagnostic and Statistical Manual of Mental Disorders, 2005). In addition, many seemingly nonspiritually-based problems (e.g., academic concerns) may be best understood within the context of an individual or family's spiritual/religious background.

Kelly (1995) warned that a religious or spiritual focus may be masking nonspiritual or nonreligious problems that are the real crux of the client's challenges. In such instances, avoidance of psychological issues for religious reasons may be described as a *spiritual by-pass* (Battista, 1996). As is the case with traditional psychotherapies, achievement of counseling goals is a function of the therapeutic relationship, the therapy process and the techniques applied by the counselor during session.

The process of therapeutic change in multicultural spiritual and religious counseling is deeply embedded in the spiritual dimensions of meaning-making, ethical living, personal values and beliefs, connectedness among all living things, the human experience of suffering, and transcendence of the body-self. Additionally, from a Western, Judeo-Christian perspective, this meaning-making may include a personal relationship with God. Therapy is about transformation of the self (self-awareness), connection with a higher power or being outside oneself (transcendence), and creating meaning in our lives (meaning-making) (Fukuyama & Sevig, 1999). The process of therapy aims to remove psychic obstacles to the attainment of these three goals. Fear is a common reaction to the introduction of this process.

As we have discussed in this chapter, western ideals of psychotherapy tend to emphasize individual personal power and control over one's thoughts, emotions and behavior. In a way, multicultural spiritual counseling asks the client to let go of preconceived notions of self, others and the world, and to open up to experiencing the transcendent, the numinous. Kelly (1995) proposed that counselors could be instrumental in the transformational process by cultivating these areas: awareness, benevolence, connectedness, unconditional and hopeful openness, and transcendent meaningfulness. These domains tend to be counter to more traditional counseling theories and as such, create some discomfort within student counselors. Remaining open to your development as a counselor and embracing a spirit of self-acceptance are attitudes that will assist you to access your "true-self," a necessary prerequisite to spiritual counseling (Fukuyama & Sevig, 1999).

Spiritually-Informed Techniques/Practices

Spiritual and religious counseling techniques must be applied in context and only after a client's openness and readiness to attempt or receive them. The counselor must also feel comfortable and capable to include these topics and practices. The number of techniques related to spiritual and religious counseling is vast; although not an exhaustive list, we offer some of the most common interventions here (adapted from Faiver et al., 2001):

1. **Blessing:** Intentional honoring and caring about the client.
2. **Disputing:** Disputing or confronting incongruence between the client's actions and professed beliefs; especially useful when clients are struggling with 'toxic religiosity' or self-deprecating beliefs.
3. **Forgiving and Releasing:** Conscious letting go of long-held resentments or grudges toward others; embracing the reality of what occurred; includes self-forgiveness and self-acceptance.
4. **Guiding:** Engaging the client's trust and serving as guide and teacher; a more directive intervention.
5. **Praying:** Praying on behalf of the client, silently or outside of session, in order to ask for guidance from a Higher Power or God; or asking for guidance from God to help guide the client or, less frequently, the act of praying with the client. The latter is more common in pastoral or Christian counseling practices.
6. **Relating:** Forming a therapeutic alliance and offering comfort and understanding to the distressed client.
7. **Meditating:** Participating in prolonged periods of silence and self-reflection that may bring about insights or discoveries for client and therapist alike.
8. **Ritualizing:** Creating and participating in ritualized activities that provide meaning, transformation, and affirmation to a client's experience; particularly useful for accessing the sacred, promoting transcendence, facilitating transitions, and grieving losses.
9. **Supporting:** Standing alongside the client to encourage continued engagement in the growth process; complements disputing of irrational, self-defeating or unhealthy beliefs.
10. **Teaching:** Providing information to the client in order to expand their knowledge, understanding and awareness.
11. **Creating:** Engaging the creative self through activities such as journaling, painting, drawing, dancing, music, and so on (Gladding, 1998: Puig, Lee, Goodwin, & Sherrard, 2005).

Counselors who attend to the spiritual and religious dimension of individual clients are navigating, in a way, relatively complex and uncharted territory. Although spiritual development models have been proposed to help explain the evolution of human beings' spiritual lives, no exemplary or definitive paradigm has emerged. As usually happens with any theory of personality or human development, how people come to identify themselves as spiritual beings is a function of biology, family, society, culture, and life events.

The techniques presented here may assist clients manage and explore many of the presenting problems we have already delineated. These are but a few of the creative ways that spiritual or religious counselors may assist client in the resolution of spiritual or religious dilemmas and unresolved issues. As you become further involved in learning and understanding the principles behind these approaches, your exposure to counseling techniques and applications will continue to grow. Finally, an increasing number of scholarly publications offer in-depth descriptions of spiritual, religious, and transcendental theories and approaches to psychotherapy that also attend to diverse cultural and contextual issues (Cashwell & Young, 2004; Faiver, Ingersoll, O'Brien, & McNally, 2001; Frame, 2003; Fukuyama & Sevig, 1999; Kelly, 1995; Scotton, Chinen & Battista, 1996).

APPLICATIONS

The application of multicultural spiritual counseling interventions can take many shapes. Let us review the case of David to further explore how a counselor might assist a client struggling with existential issues.

Case example. *David, a 48-year-old marketing executive is in counseling because he feels dissatisfied with his life. He has been married to Susan for 12 years and they have a nine-year-old daughter, Rebecca. He describes his family life as normal and says they get along fine. Although he is fairly successful in his line of work, he has been feeling discouraged and listless of late. His primary complaints are feelings of meaninglessness and alienation from everyone around him.*

Counselor: David, you have told me that you have been feeling alone and empty inside, like something is missing and you can't quite put your finger on it. I was just wondering, what has brought meaning to your life in the past?

David: I guess my family and friends. You know, when I was a young boy, my family was very religious. We attended services every Friday night. I loved the rituals and the prayers. . . . As I grew older, life sort of got in the way. I moved away to go to college and before I knew it, I stopped going to temple, got busy and other things became more important . . .

Counselor: I remember our first session when I asked about your spiritual or religious life you said you were "a holiday Jew." Now I am wondering, how do you think this change you described may be contributing to the way you are feeling now?

David: I hadn't thought about it. I do miss it. I used to feel good about my faith, my family traditions. I am not quite sure how I got away from it all . . .

Counselor: Could it be that this feeling of emptiness, this sadness you feel may be related to the spiritual disconnect from your religious roots . . . ?

Here, the counselor is helping David explore meaning-making as it relates to his religious background. Clearly, he has somehow lost his connection to practices that brought him spiritual fulfillment in the past.

Discussion Questions

1. How might you proceed with this exploration?
2. What are some key questions you could ask David to help him move closer to a more meaningful life?
3. Would you consider inviting David's wife Susan, into session?
4. What other therapeutic interventions might you consider using to help advance David's process?

Research Perspectives

The number of research studies focusing on the effects or influence of spirituality and religion has boomed over the past 30 years. This is especially true of research in the areas of spirituality, religiosity and health outcomes (for a review see Thoresen & Harris, 2002). A number of institutes across the United States have been founded with the sole aim of researching these themes (e.g., the Spirituality and Psychology Research Team–SPiRiT–at Bowling Green State University, the Fetzer Institute, the Center for the Study of Religion/ Spirituality and Health at Duke University; and the Templeton Foundation).

In a research study aimed at providing a spiritually based therapeutic intervention to cancer patients, Cole & Pargament (1999) developed a pilot psychotherapy program named *Re-Creating Your Life: During and After Cancer.* The authors made a case for integration of spirituality in psychotherapy programs aimed at addressing existential dilemmas raised by a cancer diagnosis. The program addressed four existential concerns believed to affect cancer patients: control, identity, relationships, and meaning. Their group intervention was developed within a holistic healing framework to assist cancer patients cope with their disease. They utilized an emotion-focused coping approach, believed to be more helpful than problem-focused coping for this patient group (Strentz & Auerbach as cited in Cole & Pargament, 1999). The authors concluded "a program that explicitly integrates spiritual resources into the psychotherapy process may hold considerable promise for this population [and] the benefits of such a program may even exceed those offered by traditional psychotherapy" (p. 405). Research results such as this one clearly indicate that attending to clients' spiritual lives is an important aspect of counseling practice (Puig, 2005).

Learning Activities

As a counselor who may work with individuals from various spiritual and religious backgrounds, it may be important to develop an understanding of their spiritual and religious traditions. One way to do this is through immersion in spiritual or religious practices that are unfamiliar to you.

Diversity Experience. In order to increase your knowledge of spiritual and religious diversity, find a classmate who is of another spiritual or religious heritage than yourself and is active in their spiritual/religious community. Ask that classmate if you could attend a spiritual/religious service with her/him. Or you could contact a campus spiritual/religious organization and arrange to attend a service or event sponsored by that organization.

Meditation Sample Exercise. Many spiritual or religious traditions engage in reflective practices such as prayer or meditation, and recent literature suggests that such spiritually-oriented practices may have physiological and psychological benefits (see Shapiro & Walsh, 2003; Thoresen & Harris, 2002). This activity is designed to introduce you to one such practice, a form of meditation that involves focusing on a mantra—a repeated sound or word that helps to focus the mind.

Directions: Select a sound or word that has personal meaning for you. The sound or word should not produce anxiety, but should be something that holds positive connotations for you. Take five minutes to engage in slow and deep breathing, becoming aware of how you feel physically and mentally with each breath. As you begin to relax, bring your selected sound or word to awareness. Mentally or verbally repeat this continuously for another five minutes. As you do so, begin to notice the qualities of the sound or word you are repeating (e.g., how does it sound in your mind, or what does it "look" like?). After you have done this for approximately five minutes, take a few minutes to bring your attention back to your breathing. When you are ready, slowly blink your eyes open and reawaken yourself. How do you feel physically and mentally? How did you feel during the experience? What, if any, thoughts or emotions did you experience? How comfortable would you be practicing this activity–or a similar one–with a client? Discuss your reactions with a friend or small group.

Suggestions for Self-Reflection Journaling

1. Many spiritually-based models of well-being encourage altruism. Think of an experience you had that involved giving of your time and energy to a cause important to you. *What effect do you believe serving others had on your mental and physical health?*
2. Spiritual counseling requires self-awareness and understanding of your own spiritual or religious beliefs. *Do you have a sense of your personal spirituality? Can you imagine ways in which this personal spirituality (or the lack thereof) may help or hinder your ability to counsel clients of spiritual/religious/cultural backgrounds different from yours?*
3. Counselors have limits to their understanding of client's diverse religious and/or spiritual traditions, beliefs, and expressions. *What do you see as growing edges (possible limitations and challenges) to your own multicultural spiritual and religious counseling abilities? In what areas are you more comfortable with your skills and competencies?*

CONCLUSION

Integrating spirituality into counseling theories. Basic knowledge and awareness of traditional psychotherapy approaches and techniques does not automatically prepare you to conduct multicultural spiritual counseling. Remember our caveat about spiritual counseling competencies as you consider integrating spiritual counseling to other, more traditional counseling techniques. Interestingly, a recent national survey of CACREP (Council for Accreditation of Counseling and Related Educational Programs) accredited programs' faculty representatives concluded that although 69 percent of programs address spiritual counseling and related issues within their curriculum, only 46 percent of faculty representatives felt *prepared* or *very prepared* to integrate the spiritual or religious material into their teaching or supervision work (Young, Cashwell, Frame, & Belaire, 2002). Fortunately, over the past decade a fair number of textbooks addressing the integration of multicultural spiritual and religious issues into secular counseling have begun to emerge in a continued attempt to bridge this gap (Cashwell & Young, 2004; Faiver, Ingersoll, O'Brien, & McNally, 2001; Frame, 2003; Fukuyama & Sevig, 1999; Griffith & Griffith, 2002; Kelly, 1995).

Multicultural spiritual counseling emphasizes the interconnectedness of mind, body, emotions, and spirit. When one aspect is unattended, all are affected. Therefore, spiritual counseling adopts a holistic and contextual view of the person and attempts to educate the client about these themes. Multicultural spiritual counseling also seeks to help alleviate psychological and emotional distress by assisting the individual come to terms with and develop congruence between their cultural background, beliefs and faith tradition principles, if any, and how they are living life. Multicultural spiritual counseling is in line with humanistic and existential theories in that it sees the human being as essentially good, full of potential and capable of inner growth. It is a versatile approach that could be adapted to other counseling theories simply by incorporating the sociocultural and spiritual dimensions to whatever treatment interventions the particular theory espouses. This includes brief therapy models currently popularized by the advent of managed care. However, it should be noted that spiritual counseling interventions emphasize lifestyle changes over time and as such, are not intrinsically short-term in nature. Ideally, a client would remain in treatment as long as spiritual distress symptoms remain in the clinical picture.

Spiritual theories of counseling offer alternative ways to view mental health concerns that are markedly different than many traditional models of psychotherapy. Spiritual counseling may adopt an individualistic or collectivistic view of the person, depending on the counselor's theoretical grounding and approach. Many counselors who include spirituality in their practice emphasize the client's relationships to self, other people in his or her life, including God or a Higher Power, and his or her relationship to all of creation (e.g., the world). In this sense, unlike most Western theories of psychology that tend to be individualistic in their orientation, multicultural spiritual counseling strongly emphasizes the interconnection of the individual with the environment. In addition, spiritual schools of thought are holistic in nature, and do not separate physical health from mental health, as most Western theories do. Finally, spiritual models of well-being are congruent with the current emphasis on multiculturalism and pluralist, post-modern thought increasingly emphasized in counseling theory and practice.

In conclusion, we would like to echo and underscore Fukuyama and Sevig's (1999) contention:

> We do not believe it is possible to understand or transmit understanding of spirituality without some experiential base. We therefore invite those who desire further understanding of spirituality to engage at the appropriate level for self in activities that support, nurture, and expand their individual bases of understanding. . . . Multiculturally and spiritually speaking, true empathy is accomplished by "walking in another person's shoes" across cultures. (p. 166)

Bearing witness to client's struggles can be a deeply moving spiritual experience. As you attend to your client's presenting issues and their personal life journey, take care to be mindful of your own path; remaining open to your own cultural and spiritual influences, transitions, and struggles as you embark in the process of helping others explore theirs.

ADDITIONAL RESOURCES

Popular Books

Borysenko, J. (1997). *7 Paths to God: The ways of the mystic*. Carlsbad, CA: Hay House.

Chodron, P. (1997). *When things fall apart: Heart advice for difficult times*. Boston: Shambhala.

Chodron, P. (2001). *The places that scare you: A guide to fearlessness in difficult times*. Boston: Shambhala.

Chodron, P. (2004). *Start where you are: A guide to compassionate living.* Boston, MA.: Shambhala.

Fontana, D. (2001). *Discover Zen: A practical guide to personal serenity.* San Francisco: Chronicle Books.

Kabat-Zinn, J. (1994). *Wherever you go, there you are: Mindfulness meditation in everyday life.* New York: Hyperion.

Katra, J. & Targ, R. (2000). *The heart of the mind: How to experience god without belief.* Norato, CA.: New World Liberty.

Kushner, H. S. (1989). *When bad things happen to good people.* New York: Avon Books.

Lesser, E. (1999). *The seeker's guide: Making your life a spiritual adventure.* New York: Villard Books.

Myss, C. (1996). *Anatomy of the spirit: The seven stages of power and healing.* New York: Harmony.

Samuels, M. & Rockwood Lane, M. (2000). *Spirit body healing.* New York: John Wiley & Sons.

Walsh, R. (1999). *Essential spirituality: Exercises from the world's religions to cultivate kindness, love, joy, peace, vision, wisdom, and generosity.* New York: John Wiley & Sons

Wilber, K. (2000). *Grace and grit.* Boston: Shambhala.

Yungblut, J. R. (1988). *The gentle art of spiritual guidance.* New York: Continuum.

Zukav, G. (1989). *The seat of the soul.* New York: Fireside.

Web Sites

Association for Spiritual, Ethical, and Religious Values in Counseling (ASERVIC): http://www.aservic.org/
California Institute for Integral Studies: http://www.ciis.edu
Duke University Center for Spirituality, Theology and Health: http://www.dukespiritualityandhealth.org/
Institute of Noetic Sciences: http://www.noetic.org
Institute of Transpersonal Psychology: http://www.itp.edu
Kripalu Center: http://www.kripalu.org
Naropa Institute: http://www.naropa.edu
Omega Institute: http://www.eomega.org
Psychology of Religion (APA, Division 36): http://www.apa.org/about/division/div36.html

University of Florida, Center for Spirituality and Health: http://www.spiritualityandhealth.ufl.edu/
University of Massachusetts Medical School, Center for Mindfulness in Medicine, Health, and Society: http://www.umassmed.edu/cfm
University of Minnesota, Center for Spirituality and Healing: http://www.csh.umn.edu/

Videos

American Psychological Association
750 First St, NE
Washington, DC 20002-4242
800-374-2721 or 202-336-5510
A series of videos featuring mindfulness-based cognitive therapy, spiritual awareness psychotherapy, and theistic integrative psychotherapy produced by the American Psychological Association may be accessed through: http://www.apa.org/videos/series6.html

Integrating Spirituality into the Counseling Process

This video illustrates how spirituality can be effectively integrated into the assessment, client conceptualization, and treatment planning aspects of the therapeutic process. Additional information may be accessed through: http://www.emicrotraining.com/spirituality.html

Journals and Magazines

Spirituality & Health
The Soul/Body Connection
74 Trinity Place
New York, NY 10006

Science & Theology News
Eastern Nazarene College
162 Old Colony Ave.
Quincy, MA 02170

Counseling and Values
American Counseling Association
5999 Stevenson Avenue
Alexandria, VA 22304-3300

Journal of Transpersonal Psychology
Association for Transpersonal Psychology
P.O. Box 50187
Palo Alto, CA 94303

Monitor on Psychology (2003, Dec)
American Psychological Association
750 First Street, NE
Washington, DC 20002-4242

Review Questions

1. Discuss the historical and contextual forces that have helped shape multicultural spiritual counseling to date. As a group, discuss the paradigm shifts that have occurred as a result of these changes.
2. Spiritual counseling competencies ask that you be able to explain the relationship between spirituality and religion. As a group, discuss your own conceptualization of each. Compare/contrast your ideas.
3. Review the spiritual techniques presented in this chapter. As a group, answer and discuss the following: Which techniques would you be most comfortable using in your own sessions? Which might be more challenging or anxiety producing for you?

REFERENCES

Battista, J. R. (1996). Offensive spirituality and spiritual defenses. In B. W. Scotton, A. B. Chinen, & J. R. Battista (Eds.), *Textbook of transpersonal psychiatry and psychology* (pp. 250–260). New York: Basic Books.

Cashwell, C. S., & Young, J. S. (Eds.). (2004). *Integrating spirituality and religion in counseling.* Alexandria, VA: American Counseling Association.

Ceasar, P, & Miranti, J. (2004). *Counseling and spirituality.* In D. Capuzzi & D. R. Gross (Eds.), *Introduction to the counseling profession* (4th Ed.). New York: Allyn & Bacon.

Clinebell, H. (1995). *Counseling for spiritually empowered wholeness: A hope centered approach.* New York: The Hearth Pastoral Press.

Cole, B., & Pargament, K. (1999). Re-creating your life: A spiritual/psychotherapeutic intervention for people diagnosed with cancer. *Psycho-Oncology, 8,* 5, 395–407.

Diagnostic and Statistical Manual of Mental Disorders (2005). Retrieved December 1, 2005, from http://www.psychiatryonline.com/content.aspx?aID=11442#11442.

Faiver, C., Ingersoll, R. E., O'Brien, E., & McNally, C. (2001). *Explorations in counseling and spirituality: Philosophical, practical, and personal reflections.* Belmont, CA.: Wadsworth/Thomson Learning.

Frame, M. W. (2000). The spiritual genogram in family therapy. *Journal of Marital & Family Therapy, 26,* 2, 211–216.

Frame, M. W. (2003). *Integrating religion and spirituality into counseling: A comprehensive approach.* Pacific Grove, CA.: Brooks/Cole.

Fukuyama, M. A. & Sevig, T. D. (1999). *Integrating spirituality into multicultural counseling.* Thousand Oaks, CA: Sage Publications, Inc.

Fukuyama, M. A., Siapoush, F., & Sevig, T. D. (2004). Religion and spirituality in a cultural context. In C. S. Cashwell, & J. S. Young (Eds.), *Integrating spirituality and religion in counseling* (pp. 123–142). Alexandria, VA.: American Counseling Association.

Gendlin, E.T. (1961). Experiencing: A variable in the process of therapeutic change. *American Journal of Psychotherapy, 15,* 233–245.

Gendlin, E. T. (1964). A theory of personality change. In P. Worchel & D. Byrne (Eds.). *Personality Change* (pp. 102–148). New York: Wiley.

Gladding, S. T. (1998). *Counseling as an art: The creative arts in counseling* (2nd Ed). Alexandria, VA.: American Counseling Association.

Griffith, J. L. & Griffith, M. E. (2002). *Encountering the sacred in psychotherapy: How to talk with people about their spiritual lives.* New York, NY.: Guilford Press.

Hinterkopf, E. (1998). *Integrating spirituality in counseling.* Alexandria, VA: American Counseling Association.

Jung, C. (1933). *Modern man in a search of soul.* (W. S. Dell & C. E. Baynes, Trans.). New York: Hartcourt.

Katra, J., & Targ, R. (2000). *The heart of the mind: How to experience god without belief.* Norato, CA.: New World Liberty.

Kelly, E. W. (1995). *Spirituality and religion in counseling and psychotherapy: Diversity in theory and practice.* Virginia: American Counseling Association.

Kroll, J., & Sheehan, W. (1989). Religious beliefs and practices among 52 psychiatric inpatients in Minnesota. *American Journal of Psychiatry, 146,* 67–72.

Larimore, W. L., Parker, M., & Crowther, M. (2002). Should clinician incorporate positive spirituality into their practices? What does evidence say? *Annals of Behavioral Medicine, 24,* 69–73.

Lewis, C. S. (1940/1996). *The problem of pain.* New York: Harper Collins.

Maher, M. F., & Hunt, T. K. (1993). Spirituality reconsidered. *Counseling & Values, 38,* 21–28.

Maslow, A. (1998). *Toward a psychology of being* (3rd Ed.). New York: Wiley.

Moore, T. (1992). *Care of the soul.* New York: Harper Perennial.

O'Hara, M. (1998). Gestalt therapy as an emancipatory psychology for a transmodern world. *Gestalt Review, 2,* 154–168.

Puig, A. (2005). The efficacy of art therapy to enhance emotional expression, spirituality, and psychological well-being of newly diagnosed, Stage I and Stage II, breast cancer patients (Doctoral dissertation, University of Florida, 2004). *Dissertation Abstracts International, A 66/01,* 98.

Puig, A., Lee, S. M., Goodwin, L., & Sherrard, P. A. D. (in press). The efficacy of art therapy to enhance emotional expression, spirituality, and psychological well-being in early stage breast cancer patients. *International Journal of the Arts in Psychotherapy.*

Richards, P. S., & Bergin, A. E. (1997). *A spiritual strategy for counseling and psychotherapy.* Washington, DC: American Psychological Association.

Rivett, M. (2000). The family therapy journals in 2000: A thematic review. *Journal of Family Therapy, 23,* 423–433.

Rivett, M., & Street, E. (2001). Connections and themes of spirituality in family therapy. *Family Process, 40* (4), 459–467.

Scotton, B. W. (1996). The contribution of C. G. Jung to transpersonal psychiatry. In B. W. Scotton, A. B. Chinen, & J. R. Battista (Eds.), *Textbook of transpersonal psychiatry and psychology* (pp. 39–51). New York: Basic Books.

Shapiro, S. L., & Walsh, R. (2003). An analysis of recent meditation research and suggestions for future directions. *Humanistic Psychologist, 31,* 86–114.

Stanard, R. P, Sandu, D. S., & Painter, L. C. (2000). Assessment of spirituality in counseling. *Journal of Counseling & Development, 78* (2), 204–214.

Sue, D. W., Arredondo, P., & McDavis, R. J. (1992). Multicultural counseling competencies and standards: A call to the profession. *Journal of Counseling and Development, 70,* 477–486.

Sue, D. W., & Sue, D. (2003). *Counseling the culturally diverse: Theory and practice* (4th Ed.). New York: Wiley & Sons

Thayne, T. R. (1997). Opening space for client's religious and spiritual values in therapy: A social constructionistic perspective. *Journal of Family Social Work, 2,* 4, 13–23.

Thoresen, C. E., & Harris, A. H. S. (2002). Spirituality and health: What's the evidence and what's needed? *Annals of Behavioral Medicine, 24,* 3–13.

Tisdale, T. C. (2003). Listening and responding to spiritual issues in psychotherapy: An interdisciplinary perspective. *Journal of Psychology and Christianity, 22,* 3, 262–272.

Wolf, C. T., & Stevens, P. (2001). Integrating religion and spirituality in marriage and family counseling. *Counseling and Values, 46,* 66–75.

Woods, T. E., & Ironson, G. H. (1999). Religion and spirituality in the face of illness: How cancer, cardiac, and HIV patients describe their spirituality/religiosity. *Journal of Health Psychology, 4* (3), 393–412.

Young, J. S, Cashwell, C., Wiggins Frame, M., & Belaire, C. (2002). Spiritual and religious competencies: A national survey of CACREP-accredited programs. *Counseling and Values, 47,* 22–33.

Chapter 10

SYNTHESIS: WEAVING A WEB OF CULTURAL COMPLEXITY

Be the change you would like to see in the world.

Gandhi

Abstract

In this chapter, a brief review and synthesis of materials covered in this book are provided. After reviewing future trends, we discuss the intersection of multiple social identities and present a conflict resolution model from the intercultural communication field. We conclude with an invitation for you to connect with your passion and share your legacy for MCC work.

INTRODUCTION

As a primer for consciousness-raising on multicultural counseling, we have included historical perspectives on the development of multicultural counseling competencies (MCC), focused on counselors' emotional work inherent in facing social oppressions like racism, reviewed racial identity development that is relevant for counselor-client matching and therapy, and explored basic intercultural communication concepts that enhance the therapeutic alliance.

In addition to these culture-general MCC themes, chapters on listening to Black male voices, counseling Latino(a) families, and understanding multiracial persons have provided culture-specific examples to enhance MCC awareness, skills and knowledge.

In this final chapter, we reflect upon the material covered in this book and offer several ways to synthesize these concepts and understand layers of complexity. We will highlight future trends, revisit the importance of exploring multiple social identities, examine conflict resolution, and close the chapter with eliciting your multicultural legacy.

Future Trends

Just as we began this book with a view of the changes in the field in the past thirty years, the current state of affairs in multicultural counseling is dynamic and ever changing. Even by the time this book is published, new issues will have surfaced. In this section we highlight the following trends: mainstreaming and expanding MCC theoretical and empirical knowledge, evolving MCC metaphors, dealing with backlash, recruiting diverse students, understanding globalization and international psychology, deepening social justice movements, and applying MCC to organizational change.

Mainstreaming and expanding. MCC is becoming more mainstreamed into mental health training; especially as national organization adopt guidelines for MCC. The MCC social science literature is expanding at an exponential rate, which mirrors the changing demographics of the United States and globalization. In addition to empirical social science research, qualitative studies and critical theory offer alternative ways of *knowing* that enriches the MCC literature. The emergence of interdisciplinary cooperation and dialogue will assist the development of MCC, including experts in the intercultural communication field, cultural anthropology, social psychology, and sociology, in addition to counseling and psychology. Although MCC is receiving more attention in the field, empirical research and building of new MCC theories takes time and may not be fully developed for years to come.

In perspective, the multicultural literature has expanded to include many disenfranchised groups. An emerging group that is sometimes included under the LGBT umbrella is that of transgendered persons, those who self-identify more comfortably with being the other gender, and/or who have a more fluid gender identity than society's dichotomous categories (Sager, Gustafson, & Byrd, 2006). This emerging area likewise deserves attention in the counseling field. It is subject to misinformation and stereotypes, has its own specialty knowledge and vocab-

ulary, and requires training to become a gender specialist (Israel &
Tarver, 1997). However, one cannot assume expertise in dealing with
transgender issues even when knowledgeable about Lesbian/Gay/
Bisexual issues, for instance (for more information, see
http://www.ifge.org/). Consider a case study of Jo (see Box 10.1) who
began transitioning from male to female while in college.

Box 10.1

Jo, a trans-woman, comes to counseling during her sophomore year
because she is ready to begin living as a woman and needs a letter to
explain her situation to the Housing staff in order for her to live in a residence hall that is suitable. She described the challenges of using the
men's restroom and having had an embarrassing encounter with the jan-
itorial staff. Jo comes from a Latino family background and is struggling
for acceptance in the family. Her mother has expressed grief and self-
blame, and her father is not talking to her. However, her sister is supportive and they keep in touch through email and phone. Jo would like to
start some aspect of the transition process, such as hormone therapy, but
she has limited funds and no medical provider. Jo started attending a
Transgender Support Group and finds most of her support in the LGBT
community. Jo wants to date women, and yet has experienced prejudice
in the lesbian community when some are uncomfortable when she
attends woman-only parties.

Discussion Question: What resources are needed to assist transgendered college students, and to what extent has this issue been explored
in your community?

Evolving metaphors. These changes in theoretical perspectives are
reflected in the metaphors and symbols used to explain MCC phenomena. For instance, identity development theories have shifted from linear stage models to circular, spiral or cyclical models. Some theorists
have changed conceptualizing MCC constructs from being on a continuum to concentric circles or a cube model, incorporating three-dimen-
sions (Sue & Sue, 2003). We can expect new models to emerge as
cultural complexities are explored more deeply. It will be more typical
to explore the intersection of multiple identities and oppressions rather
than focusing on only one social dimension. This trend is reflected in
the theme for the National Multicultural Conference and Summit 2007,

The Psychology of Multiple Identities: Finding Empowerment in the Face of Oppression (Retrieved January 26, 2006 from http://www.multicultural-summit.com/). The conference organizers stated that "while we acknowledge the vast diversity of cultures within the dimensions of age, race, ethnicity, and geographic region, the 2007 conference specifically addresses the *intersection* of the dimensions of race and ethnicity, sexual orientation, social class, age, ability, and gender." (Email communication, William Liu, January 18, 2006).

Dealing with backlash. We maintain a positive attitude about MCC and its integration into the counseling field, even as resistance and backlash are also part of the picture. A positive reframe on these negative reactions is to believe that in fact, MCC is having an impact and making a difference in the dominant culture. One expression of tensions in becoming a multicultural and pluralistic society can be seen in media reports of *culture wars* in the United States, where differences and values clash in the public arena. A simple but emotional example was visible during the December holiday season in recognizing the cultural celebrations of Winter Solstice, Hanukah, Christmas, and Kwanzaa. Businesses tried to be inclusive and consumers lobbied for their specific religious views. In our local community, controversy emerged from selling *Holiday trees* instead of *Christmas trees!* A truly pluralistic paradigm makes room for all views equally, but this model has yet to be fully accepted in a society that is accustomed to winners and losers.

Recruiting diverse students. In addition, MCC will be enhanced by recruiting and retaining culturally diverse students in mental health professional training programs. Over the past five years, we have observed that small numbers of students from diverse backgrounds are admitted to graduate programs in counseling and in psychology. Howard-Hamilton and colleagues suggested 10 ways to recruit culturally diverse students:

1. Contact them while they are still undergraduates.
2. Provide information about the benefits of graduate school. Invite student leaders from graduate programs to speak to undergraduate classes.
3. Provide workshops on how to enter graduate programs.
4. Provide role models with whom culturally diverse students can identify.
5. Introduce culturally diverse undergraduate students to research opportunities.

6. Recruit culturally diverse alumni who may want to attend graduate school.

7. Explore creative ways of predicting success of culturally diverse students other than the traditional standardized test.

8. Involve alumni students of color to discuss positive aspects of the program.

9. Assist culturally diverse students in the publication process by providing opportunities for co-authorships and by making sure they have at least one publication before graduation.

10. Serve as an ally or as an advisor to culturally diverse graduate students to help them feel a sense of belonging (Howard-Hamilton, Ferguson, & Puleo, 1998).

Understanding globalization and international psychology. It is tempting to think that Western ideals that are being exported are shaping international relations in a positive direction. A truly ethnocentric perspective would suggest that one's own values, culture and norms are best. But if a truly ethno-relativist position is adopted, as recommended in Chapter 2 using Bennett's model of intercultural sensitivity, each culture finds it has much to learn from other cultures as well. As forces of capitalism are loosening national boundaries, so may concepts of citizenship and cultural affiliations. Just as there are *doctors without borders,* there is a trend to have *counselors without borders* who provide services in areas of special needs, such as disaster relief following Hurricane Katrina (Kennedy, 2006). These trends call for multicultural ethics and guidelines for negotiating new territory (Pack-Brown & Williams, 2003).

The field of international psychology has a reputable history originating with cross-cultural psychology studies (see *Journal of Cross-Cultural Psychology* available online at http://www.ac.wwu.edu/~culture/jccp.htm). It is likely to be a hot topic as more international students attend U.S. universities and more U.S. American students study abroad. In addition, more and more U.S. Americans will be working for multinational corporations and global businesses. In keeping with the spirit of the Peace Corps, U.S. Americans working in other countries can learn much about self and home culture as well as share resources in developing countries. Many lessons are to be learned about U.S. American privilege when traveling, study and working abroad (Fukuyama, 2004). U.S. Americans need to become more aware of their role and impact in the world at large, and to realize that the

United States (and its citizenry) are a wealthy resource in relation to global needs (see http://www.globalrichlist.com/).

Deepening social justice. A natural development from the MCC movement is one of social justice. Social justice refers to the "fair and equitable distribution of power, resources, and obligations in society. . . . Fundamental principles underlying this definition include values of inclusion, collaboration, cooperation, equal access, and equal opportunity" (Hage, 2005, p. 286). Studying the impact of oppression leads one towards seeking systemic change through empowerment and advocacy efforts (Toporek, Gerstein, Fouad, Roysircar, & Israel, 2005).

Grace Boggs and John Maguire, freedom fighters and cohorts of The Rev. Martin Luther King Jr. shared their thoughts about social movements. We offer their observations to advance your thinking about the complexity of social change at the macro level, movements that embrace social transformation and evolution, see Box 10.2.

Box 10.2

Seven Great Ideas for Movement Builders

1. Suffering and oppression are not enough to create a movement. A movement begins when the oppressed begin seeing themselves not just as victims, but as new men and women, pioneers in creating new, more human relations, thus advancing the evolution of the human race.

2. Movement builders are able to recognize the humanity in others, including their opponents, and therefore the potential within them for redemption and the possibility of work-through-change.

3. Movement builders are conscious of the need to go beyond slogans and to create programs of struggle that transform and empower participants. At the heart of movement building is the concept of two-sided transformation, both of ourselves and of our institutions.

4. Thinking dialectically is pivotal to movement building because it prepares us for the contradictions that inevitably develop in the course of the struggle. A struggle that starts with the need of a particular racial, ethnic, or social group only becomes a movement if it creates hope and the vision of a new society for everyone. But because great hopes can also lead to great disappointments, movement participants must be in touch with elements that sustain them through dark times as well as bright.

> 5. Movement building is intergenerational and involves children and youth, as well as adults, in community building and productive activities.
>
> 6. Movement building is essentially counter-cultural. It is a struggle to transform both ourselves (the way we think and act in relationship to one another and the Earth) and institutions. Radical organizing, by contrast, is mostly about distributive justice, making demands on the system in order to redistribute the products of the society (wages, healthcare, education, etc.) more equitably. Genuine movement building is about restorative justice, new ways of thinking and being that restore community and advance us another step in our evolution as human beings (Boggs, 2005).

Working towards social justice is a process which spans generations. Society at large is the last to make a shift in consciousness, yet individuals and groups do make a difference through sustained effort. During World War II, over 110,000 Japanese Americans, two-thirds U.S. citizens, were imprisoned in U.S. internment camps for the duration of the war (Tateishi, 1984). An official government apology and reparations were not forthcoming until some 50 years later, after a long lobbying campaign and official hearings were conducted (see Japanese American Citizens League available online at http://www.jacl.org/).

Today, the consensus of those who studied this issue would agree that the incarceration of Japanese Americans during WWII was unjust and an act that was caused by war hysteria and racism. George Takei, an actor famous for his role as Sulu in the popular *Star Trek* TV series, was a child in the camps. Recently he came out publicly as a gay man and observed that LGBTs are subject to "invisible barbed wires of legality" that deny LGBTs full justice and freedom, just as Japanese Americans were imprisoned with barbed wire in the camps under unjust circumstances (Human Rights Campaign, 2006).

Applying MCC to organizational change. Organizational change takes a long time but is achievable. We are as interested in systemic changes as we are in individual consciousness raising, and can imagine that you will play a critical role in making changes in organizations. Sue et al. (1998) described the processes by which organizations develop MCC in Box 10.3.

Box 10.3

Based on the works of Cross, Bazron, Dennis, & Isaacs (1989), six stages of cultural competences for care-giving organizations such as mental health agencies were identified.

1. *Cultural Destructiveness:* Characterized by attitudes, policies and practices which are destructive to cultures and to individuals within cultures. Examples include repression of first language usage and forced assimilation policies.
2. *Cultural Incapacity.* Holds a monocultural view of the world, with beliefs that one's culture is superior to all others. May take a paternalistic attitude towards minorities.
3. *Cultural Blindness.* Assumption of no difference, "people are all the same," and the dominant cultural worldview fits all. Presumes that the culturally different are deficient.
4. *Cultural Pre-Competence.* Beginning level of developing cultural competencies, "talk the talk." Tokenism in hiring practices.
5. *Cultural Competence.* "Walk the walk." Show continued self-assessments to develop more sophisticated multicultural competencies. Higher levels of staff hiring, awareness of issues, and skill development. Working towards bilingual/bicultural levels in providing services.
6. *Cultural proficiency.* High levels of competency, seek to add to MCC knowledge in the field, hire MCC specialists, all levels of the organization are sensitized to MCC mission, social advocacy roles.

Additionally, Sue et al. (1998) suggest the following characteristics describe a MCC organization:

• Values diversity,
• conducts cultural auditing and self-assessments,
• clarifies its vision,
• understands the dynamics of difference,
• institutionalizes its cultural knowledge,
• adapts to diversity in meeting local community needs (pp. 108–109).

Systemic change takes time and requires support from the top-down (Fukuyama & Delgado-Romero, 2003; Perez, Fukuyama, & Coleman, 2005). Even with strong MCC support, some areas of sensitivity may be lacking. For example, heterosexism is a pervasive attitude that permeates the helping professions (Fukuyama, Miville, & Funderburk, 2004).

Suggested Activity

Conduct an interview with a mental health professional about their agency or departmental strategies to address multicultural competencies. Questions may include some of the following:

1. Does your agency have a multicultural mission statement?
2. What is the number of culturally diverse employees hired?
3. How are services extended to clients who typically underutilize traditional psychological services? What culturally diverse clientele are served?
4. Do you have bilingual staff?
5. What sorts of training to you provide for staff on MCC?

In the remainder of this chapter, we will demonstrate how to weave a web of complexity that is multi-layered when approaching social issues in a multicultural context. In specific we will discuss the intersection of multiple identities and conflict resolution.

Multiple Social Identities

Cultural complexity in the new millennium includes exploring more than one social identity status and concurrently considering more than one type of oppression. The intersection of social consciousness movements can be both creative and dissonant (Funderburk & Fukuyama, 2001). For an example, consider the opening lines of a poem by Kristie Soares (2005, p. 7) in Box 10.4.

Box 10.4

Cuban, Brazilian, Bisexual Me
By Kristie Soares

I've come to realize that I hate my own people
Because I have no people.
Friday night is *Fiesta Latina,*
The Cubana in me is nowhere to be found.
Wednesday night is *Festo Brasileira,*
The Brasileira in me is feeling just too queer to go out.
 But on Saturday night, which is gay night,
she's just not queer enough.

> She's not American enough for White night,
> which is every night in this town.
> Not smart enough to just stay home . . .
>
> Reprinted by permission of the author

For persons with multiple social identities, including ethnicity and sexual orientation, the questions of "who am I" and "where do I belong" are salient in late adolescence and early adulthood. Clearly society's labels and dichotomies do not apply, and young people like Kristie are involved in a dynamic, creative process of claiming their lives and expressing their voices, as she concludes her poem: "And by the power vested in me, by the hetero-centric, racist society that hates you, I validate your presence in this world" (p. 10).

As suggested in the discussion of how to become an ally in Chapter 3, assessing your privilege and power across domains is important for cultivating empathy and learning empowerment strategies. Additionally, we recommend a review of Chapter 8 on counseling multiracial persons as an example of negotiating multiple identities. As Miville and Romero suggest, internalization or integration of identity is dynamic, fluid, and ongoing. The saliency of various social group memberships may shift from one social context to another and over the lifespan (Fukuyama & Ferguson, 1999).

Considering the influences of post-modernism, Jandt (2004) has suggested that the United States is now in a *post-ethnic era,* in which individuals no longer adhere to ethnicity by birth, but rather, voluntarily construct multiple social identities. "Post-ethnicity recognizes that groups based on affiliations are as substantive and authentic as groups based on blood and history" (p. 458). Following this line of reasoning, social group identities are another expression of culture. One could say that he or she identifies with LGBT culture, women's culture, disability culture, and/or combinations of same, based on interactions of persons who share social norms and join against a common oppression.

A case example may illustrate these points. *Jean was a 20 year old biracial Chinese/Anglo American, 3rd generation in the United States. She began to explore her ethnicity while in college, but didn't feel that she fit into the Chinese Club. Most of her friends were Latina, and they invited her in their social events. Eventually, Jean was considered to be an "honorary member" of the Latina organization.*

Another influence of post-modernism and critical theory is deconstructing the *other* and understanding power. Hopefully we have been successful in this book towards breaking down barriers that have historically contributed to creating the *other*. Such goals are not achieved without dealing with discomfort and at times, conflict. We once again draw from the intercultural communication field and discuss conflict resolution in the next section.

Intercultural Conflict Resolution Styles

Engaging with cultural differences often entails dealing with conflict, whether internalized (intrapersonal) or with other people (interpersonal). It is not unusual for client problems to be associated with conflicts (disagreements, differences in communication styles, as examples). The intercultural communication field offers ways to conceptualize cultural differences in conflict resolution styles. Intercultural conflict has been defined as the emotional frustration in conjunction with perceived incompatibility of values, norms, face orientation, goals, scarce resources, processes and/or outcomes between two parties from two different cultures in interaction (Ting-Toomey, & Oetzel, 2001).

For instance, persons with a strong individualistic orientation may prefer for conflict to be dealt with openly and directly, and be satisfied only when goals or outcomes are achieved. Persons with a strong collectivistic orientation are influenced by in-group/out-groups norms and may be more concerned with face-saving strategies and relationships than with achieving explicit goals.

Mitch Hammer (2003) developed an *Intercultural Conflict Style Inventory,* which explores two possible dimensions of difference: direct or indirect communication and emotional or nonemotional expressiveness. Taken in combination, four communication styles were identified that are illustrated in Figure 10.1: **Discussion** (high direct, emotionally restrained), **Engagement** (high direct, emotionally expressive), **Accommodation** (indirect, emotionally restrained), and **Dynamic** (indirect, emotionally expressive). Hammer suggests that no one approach is inherently better than another, that each has its strengths and weaknesses as perceived by those who prefer other styles. In fact, he recommends that one try to solve problems using all four styles.

The strengths of persons who prefer the **Discussion Style** include the ability to confront problems, elaborate arguments, and hold a calm

Figure 10.1. Intercultural Conflict Style Model (Developed by Mitchell R. Hammer, Ph.D.)

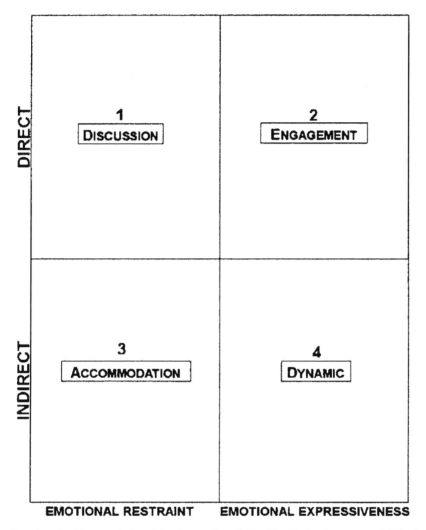

atmosphere. The downside includes having difficulty in reading between the lines. One may appear logical but unfeeling, or may be uncomfortable with emotional arguments. A typical statement from someone who prefers this style may sound something like: *Let me explain my position on this matter, I believe that it's best to approach conflict with logical, well thought-out arguments, and I don't understand your ration-ale for disagreeing with me.*

Those who prefer the **Engagement Style** are able to provide detailed information and explanations, express opinions and show feel-ings. The downside is that they may appear unconcerned with the feel-ings of others, may come across as dominating or rude, or may be uncomfortable with viewpoints that are non-emotional. Here is a sam-ple statement, *I've already told you a thousand times, you know how I feel about this issue, it's better to get our feelings out on the table and then we can discuss our differences!*

Persons who prefer the **Accommodation Style** have strengths such as the ability to consider alternative meanings when the situation is ambiguous, able to control emotional outbursts, and sensitivity to feel-ings of others. In some Asian family situations, a third party (example, an elder uncle) may be invited to negotiate and help resolve differences (Sheu & Fukuyama, in press).The downside is that they may have diffi-culty voicing opinions, appear uncommitted or dishonest, or have dif-ficulty in providing elaborated explanations. In keeping with the sample conversation above, *OK, let's sit down and have some tea, it's been quite a while since we've had a chance just to sit down with each other.*

Finally, the strengths of those who favor the **Dynamic Style** include the use of third parties to gather information and resolve conflicts, skill at observing non-verbal behavior, and comfort with strong emotional displays. The downside is that they may be perceived as rarely getting to the point, and may appear unreasonable, devious, or too emotional (see Hammer, 2003, p. 13). Sample reply to the above statements, in loud tones, *I'm not sure that anyone here really understands me; I can hardly stand being here! You're not listening!*

Imagine the challenges for a group of employees who come from dif-fering backgrounds and are dealing with a major conflict. Contradicto-ry behaviors may actually aggravate an already tense situation. Family members may also represent differing styles, whether due to culture or personality traits (or both), as illustrated in the following case example.

Case example: *Alice and Grace are middle-aged and have lived together in a committed lesbian partnership for five years. Alice is from a collectivistic culture, values harmony in relationships, and favors an accommodation style (emotionally reserved, indirect). Grace is from an individualistic culture, values assertiveness and direct expression of feelings in an engagement style. In a con-flict situation, the more Grace expresses her feelings, the more Alice seeks to* *accommodate and avoid confrontation. At times like this, both partners feel frustrated, disrespected and threatened. Grace uses humor to diffuse their tensions by comparing their relationship to being like an inter-species relationship—a bouncy puppy and a cool cat!*

Suggestion: Brainstorm ways to enhance communication in this relationship situation seeking compromises with both conflict styles (engagement and accommodation).

Sometimes these intercultural conflicts are internalized within the person, mirroring external values differences. Sorting out values conflicts is a common issue for those who are bicultural or dealing with multiple oppressions as described in Box 10.5.

Box 10.5

Case example: Amir is a bicultural 23-year-old of Iraqi descent. He has lived in Europe and the United States while growing up. Now enrolled at a large state university, he is having difficulty fitting in socially. His internal dialogue sounds something like this:

You should go out and make friends, don't sit home and feel sorry for yourself!

But I just want to have a few close friends; students here seem so superficial and shallow.

You have to speak up and make the first move; no one is going to come to you.

I miss my family and friends back home, I wish I could find someone like me.

Suggestion: Role-play the above dialogue, continue to develop it, and discover ways to problem-solve Amir's social isolation.

Discussion Activity

Recall how conflicts were approached in your family of origin, and/or within your cultural group/community. What approach do you personally tend to favor? Perhaps this preference varies with social-cultural context; if so, what factors influence your communication style preferences?

The Intersection of Religion and Sexual Orientation

The intersection of religion and sexual orientation is another hot topic in the field of multicultural counseling. If one were to believe the media coverage on LGBT issues, it appears that to be gay and religious is an oxymoron. The polarization by ultra-conservatives on homosexuality and religion has oversimplified and politicized issues related to freedom of religion and sexual orientation. Conservative religious groups have rallied around this issue as a symbol for moral values. However, upon closer investigation, there is a wide range of opinion and attitudes related to sexual orientation and religion that varies from ultra-conservative on one end of a continuum to radical on the other. This range of beliefs and attitudes towards LGBTs is presented in Table 10.1.

Resolving religious differences is yet another layer of multicultural complexity. Religious diversity in the United States is broadly defined, including literally thousands of denominations and approaches that range from fundamentalist to liberal. Working through and clarifying religious values and beliefs are both personal and communal, and especially poignant for LGBT individuals due to negative attitudes perpetuated in the media (Haldeman, 2004). Interestingly, even though the climate appears chilly towards LGBT persons from religion, there are LGBT support groups available based in many religious denominations (Thumma & Gray, 2005).

In counseling clients who struggle with forming a sexual orientation identity in the context of religious beliefs and values and ethnic identity, it is important to focus not on choosing one identity over the other, but rather how to best manage, integrate, and affirm multiple identities as a religious and spiritual LGBT person (Perez, in press).

The case study in Box 10.6 presents multiple social oppressions. Individuals vary on how they manage oppression, and cultural context may be a significant factor.

Box 10.6

Case Example

Carolina is a 30-year-old single mother of a 4-year-old daughter who is coming out as a bisexual woman. She is of Puerto Rican descent and Catholic upbringing, and lives in an urban setting in the Northeast. She had strong female role models in her family and yet is respectful of authority and sees her father as the head of the family. She feels anxious about telling her family members that she has an African American girlfriend. They have always been supportive of her in general, but she is

Table 10.1. A Continuum of Religious Attitudes toward LGBT

Position	Abomination	Change is expected	Celibacy is expected	Marginally acceptable	Equality	Liberation	Radical
Moral values	Profoundly immoral at all times	Individual can change sexual orientation with effort	Either change or be celibate	Committed relationships are tolerable	Morally neutral, seek equal rights	LGBT affirmative Biblical interpretations	Challenge patriarchy of organized religion
Typical comments	"An abomination, condemned to hell."	"Love the sinner, hate the sin."	"It's OK to be gay, but not to be sexually active."	"It's between the individual and God." "Judge not lest you be judged."	"Rights to housing and a job, like everyone else."	"Homophobia is the main evil."	"Create new expressions of spirituality, queer theology."

Adapted from Ontario Consultants on Religious Tolerance, available online at http://www.religioustolerance.org/hom7beli.htm
Source: Fukuyama, M. A. & Hernandez, C. (2006, February). *At the Intersection of Sexual Orientation and Religious/Spiritual Values: Perspectives in Therapy and Training.* Workshop presented at the 5th Annual Southeastern Conference on Cross-Cultural Issues in Counseling and Education, Savannah, GA.

aware that her mother would be concerned about "what the neighbors would think" if they knew the true situation. She also feels guilty for having left her faith tradition some years ago and wants her child to be raised in a religion.

Discuss the ways in which she feels disempowered by sexism, racism and heterosexism. How can religion be both a positive and negative for her? How can she maximize her strengths? What is the common ground between ethnicity, religion, and sexual orientation?

At times these worlds may feel dissonant and other times connecting. These social references groups (ethnicity, religion and sexual orientation) may overlap in various ways, as depicted in Figure 10.2.

It is important for Carolina to find support as a Latina in the context of coming out as a bisexual, including the dimensions of religion and ethnicity. Finding common ground where the circles intersect and overlap is an important step towards living an integrated life. Additional support can be found through resources on the Internet and through bibliotherapy (Espin, 1990).

Resolving conflicts over religious differences is another **hot topic** in the twenty-first century. Similar to the Venn-diagram in Figure 10.2, religious groups have distinctions which separate them and commonalities that overlap. Consider the following quote from Sandy Reimer (2006) on the topic of religious diversity and interfaith cooperation:

> So then for me the question of diversity becomes a question of finding the center circle, the place where we in our own circle at UCG can meet others in their own circles, be they African American, Muslim, Catholic, whatever other group. This is, I believe, one of the most important issues facing our country and our world. In every crisis we confront—locally, nationally and internationally—we have to respect the diverse grounds we stand upon and we equally have to seek that center place of inclusion—before we can go forward to solving our problems. If we are to survive as a planet, we need the vision of a new creation, a creation that both honors our diversity and also at the same time pulls us together, into the center, that place where we are all one. (Reimer, 2006)

From this perspective, there is *unity in diversity,* but that point of connection needs to be articulated and affirmed simultaneously while exploring cultural and religious differences.

Figure 10.2. The Intersection of Sexual Orientation, Religion and Ethnicity

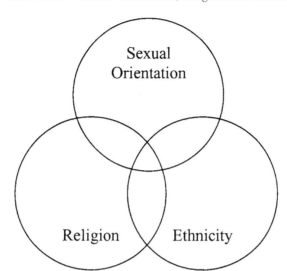

Multicultural Legacies

In this final section, we invite you to get in touch with your passion for MCC themes and decide what is most personally meaningful. In concluding this book, we are interested in inviting all to consider the following question, "What would you like your MCC legacy to be?"

We have drawn from various disciplines to inform the awareness, skills and knowledge base needed to become multiculturally competent, including arts and literature. As a closing ritual for teaching a multicultural counseling course, one of the authors (W.M.P.) has used favorite poems to illustrate key points, and invited students to share poems that they have written or favorite ones that they have found. Here we have selected a few favorite poems. First, from Sir Francis Bacon:

> *A little learning is a dangerous thing,*
> *drink deep or taste not the purian spring,*
> *thou shallow drought intoxicates the brain*
> *and learning largely sobers us again.*

To paraphrase the poet, "a little multicultural knowledge can be dangerous," especially if the learner believes that a single course coupled with readings and a seminar are sufficient to be accomplished in MCC.

It is our belief that no amount of knowledge about cultural diversity is sufficient to prepare counselors for the multiple cases they are likely to encounter. Yet, knowledge about different cultures is important especially in building rapport with culturally diverse clients. In addition, knowledge acquisition about cultural diversity is a lifelong process of learning through using a multifaceted approach.

As a case in point, a counseling student who was in the process of taking a multicultural counseling course had completed a project on the cultural values of Asians. Some of these values included being family oriented, showing restraint of emotions and respect for elders, and being sensitive to issues of saving face and avoiding shame. One afternoon she overheard a Japanese student asking her professor to explain why he had assigned her a "B" grade. The student politely explained to the professor all of the effort she had given to her assignments. When the professor disagreed with her assessment for a higher grade, she shouted, Bull*$#@ at the top of her voice and stomped out of the office. Needless to say, the counseling student was shocked that what she had learned about Asian cultures was different from what she experienced in real life.

Throughout this book we have emphasized the importance of learning MCC as a *process,* something to the effect that the *journey* is more important than the destination. The good news is that once learned, this process may be repeated over and over to adapt to new MCC challenges. Ultimately, this process of learning is intrinsically rewarding. We have changed and grown through this work over the years, it doesn't get boring; it keeps us fresh and engaged. On the other hand, the work is never done. But that can be construed as a positive message as well. Consider a poem by Berton Braley in Box 10.7.

Box 10.7

With doubt and dismay you are smitten
You think there's no chance for you, son [sic]?
Why, the best books haven't been written
The best race hasn't been run,
The best score hasn't been made yet,
The best song hasn't been sung,
The best tune hasn't been played yet,
Cheer up, for the world is young.

> *Don't worry and feel faint-hearted,*
> *The changes have just begun,*
> *The best jobs haven't been started,*
> *The best work hasn't been done.*
>
> Berton Braley

A great deal of progress has been made in the field of multicultural counseling, yet there remains much work to be done. The poet suggest, "The best jobs haven't been started, the best work hasn't been done." The poet is correct when we consider some of the following unmet needs in multicultural counselor training and research:

1. The need to train counselors and therapist to be multiculturally sensitive.
2. The need to recruit and retain graduate students of color in mental health professions.
3. The need to conduct research from a culturally sensitive perspective.
4. The need to meet the shifting societal needs and challenges with which counselors will be confronted.

In sum, you have an opportunity to contribute to the multicultural counseling field and larger society through designing action plans, engaging in debate, and developing culture-specific interventions through your practice.

One of the authors (M.A.F.) seeks to infuse MCC learning with inspiration. When the times get rough, she turns to spirituality, nature and the expressive arts. Here is a favorite poem.

Box 10.8

For You, Robert Frost
I lean toward writing, haphazard as a rail
fence, near-ends joined
before the fence turns in another
direction, and that's all
the time. This zigzag keeps nothing out
or in, ants go under, small
boys over—but marks where my property
ends, more or less, and how

> *I feel about ownership, which is all right*
> *if that's the best one can do.*
> *The fence says I believe in pattern*
> *so long as it doesn't take*
> *over and revise the one who started it;*
> *says there are some things*
> *I'm on the side of, like liacs and garden peas;*
> *and that life for all*
> *its order is a kind of balance*
> *between uneasy things.*
>
> (Poem by Betty M. Adkins Fukuyama)

To reiterate, we have emphasized that multicultural learning is a process of lifelong learning. Part of the process is to realize that "just when you think you know what's going on . . . things change!" However, lessons that are learned from the margins or edges of society inform consciousness raising for the middle or mainstream. Welcome to the frontier, and know that you are not alone; you are in good company!

Suggested Activity

We recommend that you find poetry and music or write poems that reflect your experiences in engaging in the ideas and activities provided through this book and share as a way of providing closure.

Recommended Films

The Way Home. Ethnically diverse women talk candidly about race, gender and class growing up in the United States. Available online at http://www.newday.com/films/TheWayHome.html

Daughter from Danang. The film maker accompanies an Amerasian (Vietnamese-white American) young adult adoptee as she flies back to Viet Nam to be reunited with her birth mother, from whom she was separated when she was 6 years old. The story illustrates many levels of cultural complexity and differences between American and Vietnamese family traditions. Available online at http://www.daughterfrom-danang.com/

Robot Stories directed by Greg Pak. An all-Asian American cast enacts four vignettes that span generations from youth to old age and provide a mix of futurist science fiction themes with human drama. Available online at http://www.robotstories.net/

REFERENCES

Boggs, G. L. (2005, Summer). Seven great ideas for movement builders, *YES! A Journal of Positive Futures*. Retrieved February 25, 2006 from http://www.yesmagazine.org/article.asp?id=1260.

Cross, T. L., Bazron, B. J., Dennis, K .W., & Isaacs, M. R. (1989). *Toward a culturally competence system of care*. Washington, DC: Child and Adolescent Service System Program Technical Assistance Center.

Espin, O. M. (1990). Third woman: The sexuality of Latinas. [Review of the book]. *Journal of Sex Research, 27* (1), 143–145.

Fukuyama, M. A. (2004). El otro lado. In G. S. Howard and E. A. Delgado-Romero (Eds.), *When things begin to go bad: Narrative explorations of difficult issues* (pp. 19–32). Lanham, MD: Hamilton Books.

Fukuyama, M. & Delgado-Romero, E. (2003). Against the odds: Successfully implementing multicultural competencies in a counseling center on a predominantly white campus. In G. Roysircar-Sodowsky, D. S. Sandhu, & V. E. Bibbins (Eds.), *Multicultural competencies: A guidebook of practices* (pp. 205–216). Alexandria, VA: American Counseling Association.

Fukuyama, M. A., & Ferguson, A. D. (1999). Lesbian, gay, and bisexual people of color: Understanding cultural complexity and managing multiple oppressions. In R. M. Perez, K. A. DeBord, & K. J. Bieschke (Eds.), *Handbook of counseling and psychotherapy with lesbian, gay, and bisexual clients* (pp. 81–105). Washington, DC: American Psychological Association.

Fukuyama, M., Miville, M., & Funderburk, J. (2004). The often unheard voices of counseling professionals: Stories told anonymously. In J. M. Croteau, J. S. Lark, M. A. Lidderdale, & Y. B. Chung (Eds), *Deconstructing Heterosexism in the Counseling Professions: Multicultural Narrative Voices*. (pp. 137–157). Thousand Oaks, CA.: Sage.

Funderburk, J. & Fukuyama, M. (2001). Feminism, multiculturalism, and spirituality: Convergent and divergent forces in psychotherapy. *Women & Therapy, 24* (3/4), 1–18.

Hage, S. M. (2005). Future considerations for fostering multicultural competence in mental health and educational settings: Social justice implications. In M. Constantine and D.W. Sue (Eds), *Strategies for building multicultural competence in mental health and educational settings* (pp. 285–302). Hoboken, NJ.: John Wiley & Sons.

Haldeman, D. C. (2004). When sexual and religious orientations collide: Considerations in working with conflicted same-sex attracted male clients. *The Counseling Psychologist, 32,* 691–715.

Hammer, M. (2003). *Intercultural Conflict Style Inventory Interpretive Guide*. Ocean Pines, MD.: Hammer Consulting. [Available on-line at http://www.hammerconsulting.org]

Howard-Hamilton, M., Ferguson, A., & Puleo, S. (1998). Multicultural counseling trends and issues: Implications and imperatives for the next millennium. In W.M. Parker, *Consciousness-raising: A primer for multicultural counseling* (2nd Ed) (pp. 257–275). Springfield, IL: Charles C Thomas.

Human Rights Campaign (2006, Winter). To boldly go. *Equality,* 15–17. Retrieved March 15, 2006 from http://www.hrc.org/comingout.

Israel, G. E., & Tarver II, D. E. (1997). *Transgender care: Recommended guidelines, practical information & personal accounts.* Philadelphia: Temple University Press.

Jandt, F. E. (2004). *An introduction to intercultural communication* (4th Edition). Thousand Oaks, CA: Sage.

Kennedy, A. (2006, January). Counselors without borders. *Counseling Today, 48* (7), 1, 30–32.

Pack-Brown, S. P. & Williams, C. B. (2003). *Ethics in a multicultural context.* Thousand Oaks, CA.: Sage.

Perez, R. M. (in press). The "boring" state of research and psychotherapy with lesbian, gay, bisexual, and transgender clients: Revisiting Barón (1991). In K. J. Bieschke, R. M. Perez, & K. A. DeBord (Eds.), *Handbook of counseling and psychotherapy with lesbian, gay, bisexual, and transgender clients* (2nd Ed). Washington, DC: American Psychological Association.

Perez, R. M., Fukuyama, M. A., & Coleman, N. C. (2005). Using the multicultural guidelines in college counseling center settings. In M. Constantine and D.W. Sue (Eds), *Strategies for building multicultural competence in mental health and educational settings* (pp. 160–179). Hoboken, NJ.: John Wiley & Sons.

Reimer, S. (2006, January 8). *Diversity's edge: Discovery and discomfort.* Sermon presented at the United Church of Gainesville.

Sager, J. B., Gustafson, L. M, & Byrd, C. E. (2006). The psychology of transgendered. In G. Teague (Ed.), *The new goddess: Transgendered women in the twenty-first century* (pp. 28–50). Waterbury, CT.: FineTooth Press.

Sheu, H. B. & Fukuyama, M. A. (in press). Counseling international students from East Asia. In H. D. Singaravelu and M. Pope (Eds.), *Handbook for counseling international students.* Alexandria, VA: American Counseling Association.

Soares, K. (2005). Cuban, Brazilian, Bisexual Me. *The apartment poets. A chapbook.* Gainesville, FL.: Creative Minds Advertising.

Sue, D. W., Carter, R. T., Casas, J. M., Fouad, N. A., Ivey, A. E., Jensen, M. et al. (1998). *Multicultural counseling competencies: Individual and organizational development.* Thousand Oaks, CA.: Sage.

Sue, D. W. & Sue, D. (2003). *Counseling the culturally diverse: Theory and practice* (4th Ed). New York: John Wiley & Sons.

Tateishi, J. (1984). *And justice for all: An oral history of the Japanese American detention camps.* New York: Random House.

Thumma, S. & Gray, E. R. (Eds.) (2005). *Gay religion.* New York. Altamira Press. Available online at http://hirr.hartsem.edu/gayreligion/resource.htm

Ting-Toomey, S. & Oetzel, J. G. (2001). *Managing intercultural conflict effectively.* Thousand Oaks, CA.: Sage.

Toporek, R.L., Gerstein, L., Fouad, N., Roysircar, G., Israel, T. (Eds.) (2005). *Handbook for social justice in counseling psychology: Leadership, vision, and action.* Thousand Oaks, CA.: Sage.

Appendix A

KEY CONCEPTS AND DEFINITIONS

Acculturation. Learning and adopting the norms, values, behaviors and customs of a new host culture. An additive model, not diminishing culture of origin, may lead one to becoming bicultural.

Assimilation. Giving up culture of origin and moving into full identification and participation in new host culture. May be accompanied by feelings of loss of cultural roots/identity with original culture.

Cultural relativism. Every culture is complete and equally developed with other cultures, and every culture has good and bad points. No one culture is superior to another.

Ethnicity. Identification with cultural heritage related to national/regional ancestry.

Ethnocentrism. Belief that one's culture is "central" to reality and that one's culture is better than other ways of construing reality.

High context culture. Much of the meanings in communication are determined by the context or environment of the communication. A nonlinear type of communication.

Low context culture. Much of the meanings in communication are determined by the words expressed, not context. A linear type of communication.

Marginality. On the edge of cultural groups.

 Constructive Marginality. Utilizes process of loose cultural identification to enter and experience different cultural groups. "Dynamic in-between-ness" (Bennett, 2005).

 Encapsulated Marginality. Isolated and disconnected from identification and participation in cultural groups, may feel stuck inbetween cultures, belonging to neither; feelings of alienation, anomie.

Multiculturalism. A set of values that accepts the existence of multiple world views and belief systems, encompasses social constructionism as ways of making meaning, and understands behaviors in a social context. As a social movement, multiculturalism includes principles of social justice (Sue et al., 1999).

Objective culture. Visible signs of culture include institutions, systems, artifacts, holidays, foods, kinship systems, knowledge.

"One drop rule" refers to early American beliefs that if a person had "one drop" of African blood through heritage that person was classified as black (and therefore denied privileges of the dominant white social class). This idea illustrates the purpose of racism as being to protect the dominant culture's power from those designated as 2nd class.

Other. To create a target for negative comparisons to elevate one's status at the expense of another group, creating artificial divisions through labeling language that emphasizes power relationships and domination (Jandt, 2004).

Post-ethnicity. The idea that group identification can be voluntary or individually constructed rather than determined by birth (Jandt, 2004).

Race. A construct historically established in the nineteenth century to differentiate groups of people based upon real or perceived biological distinctions (such as phenotype, physical characteristics, and genetic differences), but now recognized as a socially and culturally constructed way to create social divisions to perpetuate status differences wherein one group dominates another.

Racism. Systemic and institutionalized practices which advantage select groups of people over others based on race or skin color, constructed upon a hierarchical and competitive model of power and privilege.

Stereotype. The process of applying a fixed concept to all members of a cultural group; a pre-judging and categorizing of individuals that ignores or disregards uniqueness. Stereotypes may be positive or negative, but usually the combination of negative stereotypes and prejudice are perpetuated in a racist society.

Subjective culture. Sometimes visible and sometimes hidden communications styles, verbal linguistic competence, nonverbal cues, cultural values and behaviors.

Third culture. Mutual adaptation from contact of two cultures creating a third culture which embodies elements of both. "Third culture kids" refers to children of expatriates raised in foreign culture. When one is between Culture A and Culture B, there is a change in location of identity and a mutual adaptation implies emergence of third culture.

Value orientation. From a cultural anthropology perspective, values are expressions of "complex but definitely patterned principles . . . which give order and direction to the ever-flowing stream of human acts and thoughts" (Kluckhohn and Strodbeck, 1961 cited in Ting-Toomey, 1999, p. 57–58).

World view. A frame of reference consisting of assumptions, beliefs, and values that construct one's reality.

Xenophobia. The fear of the foreigner.

Appendix B

MULTICULTURAL MENTORING LAB (MML)

The course instructor can help prepare students for the MML experience, which will enhance the overall group experience. The MML which consists of small preassigned groups from the multicultural counseling course is held every two weeks for one hour at the end of the class meeting. MML sessions are conducted by student mentors who videotape each session for process recall and for supervision purposes.

Some of the following guidelines are suggested:

1. Discuss how some experiences or material in the course can be difficult to handle emotionally.
2. Explain how the mentoring lab will provide an avenue for free and open expression.
3. Explain that the role of the mentor is to create a safe climate for discussion and that mentors do not share what is discussed in lab with the instructors.
4. Inform students that the MML sessions may be taped for process recall and for supervision purposes only and that the course instructor will not view tapes.
5. Explore ways that students can participate more effectively by being respectful of others and by being more accepting of others regardless of where they are in their racial identity attitudes.

The delicate nature of the small group requires leaders who are culturally skilled and sensitive. Such leaders have qualities outlined by Helm's (1995) advanced statuses of racial identity, with these characteristics:

- well-grounded in their own racial identity;
- empathic with members of other racial/cultural groups;
- able to interact from a nonracist perspective;
- able to confront racist practices whether at the individual or at the institutional level.

229

The MML is a nonstructured group where members can feel free to discuss any feelings or thoughts from exposure to multicultural experiences, and other topics or issues that coincide with course content. More specifically, mentors in coordination with the instructor, prepare a list of possible discussion topics. Care is taken to insure that the group does not become a "gripe session" about the course. To maintain confidentiality, videos are not viewed by the instructor. Although students are not graded, they are strongly encouraged to participate and follow basic guidelines for effective member role and functions in a group.

Students are assigned to groups in a manner that gives them the best opportunity for personal growth and learning. Therefore, groups are assigned members based on diversity (race, gender, sexual orientation, age, religion, and cultural backgrounds). Otherwise, students tend to stay within their comfort zone by joining with others who are more similar to themselves. These social cliques reduce opportunities for developing culturally sensitive behaviors. Rooney et al. (1998) suggested that "students should never feel too comfortable in their multicultural development but should remain open and anticipate the experiences that push them just a little bit further" (p. 30).

Some basic group guidelines include:

- **Openness and acceptance.** The goals of the group are achieved when everybody's views are heard and respected.
- **Universalization.** It is useful to realize that you are not alone in your thoughts and feelings. People usually feel relieved and inspired to communicate and even take risks in deeper self-exploration. Through keen observation of multicultural discussions, common themes and issues can be linked together. Such linkages can also contribute to group cohesiveness.
- **Acknowledgement and support.** The group climate is created by the quality of the relations between group members. It is through group togetherness or cohesion that you are able to grow. When you feel appreciated, you not only experience growth yourself but are much more willing to help others grow and learn.
- **Engaging reluctant members.** You can help engage quieter members by creating a nonthreatening environment characterized by the consistent practice of interpersonal respect and a general sense of caring of other group members. Discussion topics on one's ancestry and world view and on family heritage are excellent topics for engaging reluctant members. As a group member you may invite silent members to speak their views as well.
- **Self-disclosure.** One way to let others know who you are is through self-disclosure. By sharing with others how you worked through incidences of guilt and shame, you model for others how to discuss their own feelings. It is

most valuable to hear how you worked through emotions of guilt and shame in your learning and growth process.

Mentor Supervision

Supervision is an important part of the learning process for mentors. After each MML experience, mentors spend a few days reviewing the videotape before reporting to the instructor for supervisory feedback. Individual confidentiality of group members is protected. The instructor uses the supervision hour to model good leadership strategies and techniques for mentors. The supervision meeting usually begins with the instructor using rounds like those outlined in Parker et al. (2004).

Round 1: How did you feel about your leadership?

Round 2: What aspects of your group leadership made you feel proud?

Round 3: What issues, if any, were raised with which you struggled?

Round 4: What, if anything, would you like to change about the way you led this session?

Round 5: What main issues were discussed and how did you respond?

Round 6: Having heard from other mentors, what questions would you like to ask or what comments would you like to make?

Round 7: What did you learn that you would like to share with your fellow mentors?

Round 8: What do you plan to do in the next MML session?

These questions have been used effectively to help mentors process their leadership experiences in such a manner that they identify both their strengths and weaknesses and are able to express and process their own feelings about their leadership and receive support while they learn.

REFERENCES

Helms, J. E. (1995). An update of white and people of color racial identity model. In J. G. Ponterotto, J. M. Casas, L. A., Suzuki, & C. M. Alexander (Eds.), *Handbook of Multicultural Counseling* (pp. 181–198). Thousand Oaks, CA: Sage.

Parker, W. M., Freytes, M., & Kaufman, C. J. (2004). The Mentoring Lab: A small group approach for managing emotions from multicultural counselor training. *The Journal of Specialists in Group Work, 29,* 361–375.

Rooney, S. C., Flores, L. Y., & Mercier, C. A. (1998). Making multicultural education effective for everyone. *The Counseling Psychologist, 26,* 22–32.

NAME INDEX

SUBJECT INDEX

239

Y

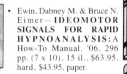

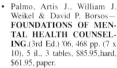
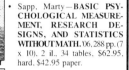
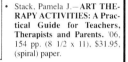

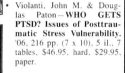
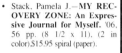

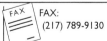